A Road Less Traveled

"If you want to understand the architecture of contemporary literacy studies, surveying Robert W. Blake's impressive body of work is a wise way to begin. Over the course of a decades-long career, Dr. Blake helped build a foundation that would support the 'language arts' growing into a professionalized field of study informed by a multi-dimensional theoretical framework. Dr. Blake, a creative educator and prolific writer, helped introduce and popularize a wide-range of innovations and ideas that radically changed classrooms across the country. Through his work we can trace how our profession came to embrace ideas from many corners of the academy—linguistics, socio-linguistics, psychology, composition studies, response theory, literary studies, general curriculum and pedagogy—but always with the student at the center of his concern. I will happily replace my 'course packet' of articles surveying literacy studies over the decades with this thoughtfully curated collection from one of our truly great educators."

—*Rob Linné, Professor and Director of English Education at Adelphi University*

A Road Less Traveled

Studies in Criticality

Shirley R. Steinberg
General Editor

Vol. 520

The Counterpoints series is part of the Peter Lang Education list.
Every volume is peer reviewed and meets
the highest quality standards for content and production.

PETER LANG
New York • Bern • Berlin
Brussels • Vienna • Oxford • Warsaw

ROBERT W. BLAKE
WITH BRETT ELIZABETH BLAKE

A Road Less Traveled

Critical Literacy and Language Learning in the Classroom, 1964–1996

PETER LANG
New York • Bern • Berlin
Brussels • Vienna • Oxford • Warsaw

Library of Congress Cataloging-in-Publication Control Number: 2017043222

Bibliographic information published by **Die Deutsche Nationalbibliothek.**
Die Deutsche Nationalbibliothek lists this publication in the "Deutsche
Nationalbibliografie"; detailed bibliographic data are available
on the Internet at http://dnb.d-nb.de/.

ISBN 978-1-4331-3263-6 (hardcover)
ISBN 978-1-4331-3262-9 (paperback)
ISBN 978-1-4331-4812-5 (ebook pdf)
ISBN 978-1-4331-4813-2 (epub)
ISBN 978-1-4331-4814-9 (mobi)
DOI 10.3726/b11661

The paper in this book meets the guidelines for permanence and durability
of the Committee on Production Guidelines for Book Longevity
of the Council of Library Resources.

© 2018 Peter Lang Publishing, Inc., New York
29 Broadway, 18th floor, New York, NY 10006
www.peterlang.com

To Dad, Dr. Robert W. Blake, Professor Emeritus of the State University of New York College at Brockport, father, mentor, co-author, fellow traveler, skier, sailor, and friend, who all my life never stopped teaching and believing in me.

Our final collaboration.

And,

To all my new (and old) friends in Paris, including the refugee adolescents I worked with during my 6-month research leave. You collectively gave me a new purpose and outlook on life during this difficult time, and reminded me what it's like to be truly human in this mysterious and beautiful world of ours. And, of course, to my friends in Scotland, Shirley Steinberg, Yasamin Yaghubzad, Jasmine Watson, and Ian, who gave me respite when being human didn't seem quite enough.

Our continued collaboration.

Brett Elizabeth Blake
St. John's University, Queens, NY
2017

CONTENTS

ACKNOWLEDGMENTS

This project would have never come to fruition without the insight of both Chris Myers and Shirley Steinberg who first believed in Robert's "pitch" to compile several of his most important articles into a book. In doing so, they afforded Robert the opportunity to make a long-held dream of his to come true. And, at the final stages of this project, Jackie Pavlovic, Production Manager, helped me, Brett Elizabeth, (often on a daily basis) to ensure that Robert's dream, indeed, would go from production to publication.

We would also like to thank the National Council of Teachers of English (NCTE) for the following permissions:

Blake, R.W. *I see you, I hear you, You're OK: Humanizing the English Classroom*. In the "English Journal." Copyright (1974) by the National Council of Teachers of English. Reprinted with permission.

Blake, R.W. The New English: *Hot Stuff, or Cool, Man, Cool*. In the "English Journal." Copyright (1971) by the National Council of Teachers of English. Reprinted with permission.

Blake, R.W. *Once upon a Morpheme: An NDEA Institute in Applied Linguistics for the Elementary School Teacher*. In "Elementary English."

INTRODUCTION

A Road Less Traveled: Critical Literacy and Language Learning in the Classroom, 1964–1996 has been a long time in the making. Indeed, 1964 *was* a long time ago—over 50 years—a time in U.S. history where the rebellious, turbulent, political and economic climate collided with the changing nature (and face of) schooling in 1960's America—an historical period in time when not only the Civil Rights Act (1964) was passed, but a "War on Poverty" was declared, and a crucial bill, the "Elementary and Secondary Education Act," was enacted, ensuring federal monies be given to poor schools. And yet, bringing this project to fruition has also been a long time in the making as I, Brett Elizabeth, have watched Robert W. Blake, my father, mentor, coauthor, and best friend extraordinaire, lose his wife (my mother) of 62 years, and then succumb to the debilitating effects of Alzheimer's disease within a year's time. Re-reading his journal articles, asking him to situate them in the educational context of the time, to recount his memories of being a teacher in the Armed Forces, a GED teacher, an English teacher and Vice Principal in a high school in upstate New York, to receiving his doctorate and becoming a professor of English Education, where he remained until his retirement, some 50 years later, has been both joyful, arduous, and ultimately painful. I now sit with a man who taught me so much about life and the field of education, who dedicated 60 years to the struggle of educating all our youth with respect and dignity, and could not now remember most of it.

And yet, there could not be a more propitious time for this collection to be published. Then, as now, the U.S. educational system finds itself once again mired deeply in the scourge of racism, poverty, segregation and the resultant inequities of schooling, as seen by accountability movements such as "No Child Left Behind," and the "Common Core State Standards" (CCSS)—a movement begun by a group of business leaders and the National Governors' Association (NGA), to direct not only what is taught in our schools, but also how it is taught, and then, how this so-called knowledge is measured. A return to a scripted "behavioral objectives" model is being touted, and basic skills (especially for those of immigrant and/or of-color backgrounds is being packaged.

But, like in 1964, there is a revolution brewing in education. Parents (albeit, at this writing, mostly in well-to-do suburbs) are opting-out of common core testing, teachers are once again closing their doors, and teaching what they know is considered worthwhile. Schools of education, although under pressure from both the federal and state governments to conduct studies using quantitative and statistical measures, are conducting observational and ethnographic research that captures the power and promise of reading good literature, of keeping poetry in the curriculum, and of pushing kids to use the writing process to help them become "real" and engaged writers. Like Robert explained to us in 1974, we are in the midst of trying to "re-humanize" our English and English Language Arts classes, once again, by asking the fundamental question, "how can a [English] teacher make a classroom more humane?"

Before his illness, Robert and I gathered together 24 of (what we agreed upon were) his most memorable, published journal articles, and since then, I organized them into general themes—genres, if you will, that seemed pretty commonplace in ELA/English, ELL, and literacy classrooms, including for example, "poetry in the classroom," and "drama in the classroom." The first and last sections, however, are a bit of an exception. In the first, Robert introduces "the New English," and the idea of "re-humanizing" the classroom, and in the last, Section VIII, he questions whether such ideas can really ever take hold. It is uncanny that these are many of the same conversations we, as educators in any field, are having today.

I introduce each section with a synopsis of each article, transitioning not only one section to another, but also one article to another, within each section. Many of these pieces begin with an historical and/or theoretical review, but all follow with real, classroom-tested ideas, activities, and strategies that Robert found worked in his classrooms and beyond. Section III is the longest section,

"Writing and the writing process in the classroom," because that is where Robert's true interest lay. Interestingly, again, today we see a renewed interest in teaching students to write better—to write at all, and organizations such as the Commission on Writing, and the Carnegie foundation have produced fact sheets and reviews on the topic. I should note there, that the states and federal government have gotten in on the act as well—for example, the Common Core State Standards heavily emphasizes writing across the curriculum in all content areas, with a firm push for teaching students how to write non-fiction, informational, and persuasive pieces to be "college and career ready."

In this era of accountability measures and common core state standards, a return to what works in our literacy classrooms is a refreshing addition to the mandates holding so many of our students back, and/or leaving them behind altogether. Indeed in Robert's and my own words from **Literacy and Learning** (2002) we describe the journey we hope more of us will embark upon as we move further into the 21st century; heads up; full of hope:

Literacy is a quest. As with all quests, we allowed the idea of literacy to lead us where it would [knowing that] literacy was no longer the special province of a privileged few but ... an activity available to all people. From our own explorations, we are confident that the notion of 'literacy for all' will survive in [our] society just as it has done for thousands of years. No one government, society, school system, university professor, middle school teacher, or neighbor should have the power to decide whose literacy is most desirable, or what one tried-and-true method will best teach literacy, or most importantly that someone's language (and hence literacy) is better than another's. We urge you here, the reader, as educator, parent, administrator, or even government official, to join us in our quest: to read, to write, to learn; to engage your students and children in literacy learning, but most of all to question and to challenge. That, perhaps, is the greatest legacy modern literacy has given us (Adapted from, Blake & Blake, 2002, xiii-xv).

SECTION I

THE ENGLISH/ENGLISH LANGUAGE ARTS CLASSROOM

In this first section, we have chosen what appear to be three quite disparate pieces—one on behavioral objectives, one on "humanizing" the classroom, and the last on what Robert termed, the "New English." However, we think you will find as you read them (as a genre, perhaps) you may find, as we did, that Robert was attempting to show in the early 70's how "rigid" our thinking about education had become.

In the first article, he reviews the notion that in part, behavioral objectives, should NOT be used for "problems of evaluation," but rather as a "means for improving instruction," by combining the cognitive and the affective as a "powerful way of looking at the learning process," ultimately searching for the "humanism" in our teaching and in students' learning.

The second article, "I see you, I hear you ... Humanizing the English Classroom," builds on this notion of humanism by suggesting that we *care* for our students—that we show our students that they are indeed, "worthy of love and respect," as they move through the journey of learning. By first defining "humanism" through the literature of Plato, Chaucer, Faulkner, and Vonnegut, among others, he shows us how he believes this can, and should, be done.

And finally, in the third piece of this section, written in 1970, he begs the question, "Why are kids so turned off to learning?" Robert makes the crucial point in this article that we must afford our students opportunities to use their language in the "widest variety of ways," eschewing the "excessive dogma" we see returning today in demonizing our students' dialects, cultural texts, and local literacies, Brian Street has written so eloquently about. Essentially Robert reminds us, we need to "enter the global village; the "world city" together if we are to move our language and literacy teaching and learning forward.

Imagine if you can anyplace on our planet in this moment in time where society and/or schools talk about a "global village," and a "world city." Today, we close our schools and our borders, allowing families and children, literally, to drown. The children who do make it out of their war-torn countries, find themselves, much like the 1970's in the U.S., laughed at, spat upon, and told by their very own teachers that their language and culture is inferior.

· 1 ·

BEHAVIORAL OBJECTIVES AND THE TEACHING OF ENGLISH

Robert W. Blake (1971)

Why Behavioral Objectives?

Very shortly after I had started teaching English in the secondary schools, I was asked by our department chairman to set up a course of study for college preparatory students in the ninth grade. My objectives for the year were as follows: 1. to establish and review basic tools of language; 2. to introduce students to fundamental techniques of expression, both oral and written; 3. to continue the study of basic forms of literature; and 4. to introduce students to fundamental approaches of critical appraisal of literature. At the time, I thought they were pretty fair statements of what I wanted to go on in my classes and, I suspect, I would not have been amenable to suggestions about revising my objectives so that they were in behavioral terms. I was fairly sure that what I was doing was academically sound; whether or not it was pedagogically appropriate didn't seem important.

Since that time, however, I've become less sure that what I had done could have been fully justified, and I've become more than vaguely dissatisfied with how I taught writing, literature, and language in the high school. As a result of my dissatisfaction, I've tried to think out better ways of having kids come to learn in the widest and deepest and in the most exciting fashion the basic facts, skills, and understandings of the discipline that I have come to have an allegiance to and affection for, the discipline which—for lack of a better term—we call English. I think I'm pretty typical of conscientious English teachers of average intelligence who wish to improve the teaching of their discipline. Furthermore, now that I'm concerned with the direct preparation of some fifty English teachers a year for the secondary schools—who themselves may come to be responsible for some six or so thousand high school students—I'm even more concerned with having them be prepared to encourage these kids to become as proficient as possible in reading and writing, to know a lot about the study of English, but, most of all, to come to have pleasure in doing the sorts of things those people who have been well educated in English characteristically do. I've devised some techniques which seem to work, but the one activity for increasing the success of English teaching in the schools, to my way of thinking, has been that of formulating behavioral objectives for the teaching of English.

Behavioral Objectives and Instruction

Although the idea of specifying behavioral objectives in terms of what students can actually do was originally discussed with problems of evaluation, I'm chiefly concerned with behavioral objectives as a means for improving instruction. All of my college students who are to become English teachers or graduate students who are working for advanced degrees in English Education must write behavioral objectives for each aspect of teaching English. As a result of having worked for several semesters on writing behavioral objectives, we have come up with a few suggestions for anyone who wishes to start the process. Setting up a behavioral objective in the right form is not too difficult; the setting down in written English fairly precise objectives for use in the teaching of a play like *Hamlet*, on the other hand, is something that tricks of format cannot prepare you for.

1. The behavioral objectives must be written in terms of the learner, not the teacher. I ask the college students to write down the kinds of activities they expect of their students after they have finished a lesson or unit, starting out with the phrase, "The student will be able to. ..."

2. The objectives should be written so as to describe in rather clear cut terms what the student will actually be doing at the end of instruction. The statement "The student will be able to understand the elements

of poetry" is not specific enough. "The student will be able to identify in writing the elements of poetry such as tropes, rhythm, rhyme, mood, and voice" is more specific.

3. A statement of a behavior that is capable of being met and is valuable should be devised. Such a behavior as the following for ninth graders is difficult to meet: "The student will be able to write a five-thousand word short story." On the other hand, such an objective as this one is capable of being met, but how valuable is it? "The student will be able to match the names of American poets of the nineteenth century with their most famous poems."

4. Sometimes, especially when a specific evaluation is sought, the conditions under which the behaviors are to be performed should be explicitly stated. These are the "givens" or restrictions which govern the behaviors, the rules by which the learning game is played. For instance, the following objective might be appropriate: "Given a new poem which the student has not seen before, in one hour the student will ask the appropriate questions about meaning, mood, structure, and value, and answer them satisfactorily in a written essay."

5. Finally, objectives covering a wide range of learning experiences— not just those reflecting the knowledge of facts and places—should be devised. All appropriate areas of the cognitive domain—knowledge, comprehension, application, analysis, synthesis, and evaluation—as well as the areas of the affective domain—receiving, responding, valuing, and organizing—should at least be considered.

Robert W. Mager states that if you have specified well your behavioral objectives and "if the learner has a copy of the objectives, you may not have to do much more."[1] I'm not quite as optimistic as Mager, but I do think that as a result of carefully prepared, appropriate objectives, both teacher and students know where they're headed, how they're going to get there, and how they will be able to find out whether or not the trip was successful—or even necessary.

Behavioral Objectives and the Teaching of Poetry

Now let us turn to some sample behavioral objectives that I have been working on for the teaching of poetry and the teaching of writing in the secondary school English classroom. With the teaching of poetry, I think it is vitally important to proceed from a liking of a poem to an understanding of its components. Therefore, the first objectives to be considered, to my way of thinking, should be those related to the affective domain.

Affective Domain

After varied experiences in the classroom, the student will be able to

1. listen to poetry read in the classroom.
2. respond to questions about poetry when the teacher asks such questions.
3. voluntarily bring poems to class and express satisfaction when they are read and discussed.
4. justify the value of poetry as a significant aspect of figurative communication.
5. give reasons for valuing meritorious poetry and attempt to convince others of his position.
6. display by his behavior that he has internalized an ordered view of the poetic experience and its importance for a full, humane existence.

Cognitive Domain

Knowledge: As a result of instruction in poetry, the student will be able to

1. identify orally or in writing the components of poetry such as images, metaphor, rhythm, rhyme, mood, and voice.
2. describe the various forms of poetry such as the lyric, sonnet, and ballad.
3. outline trends in the development of poetry, such as British nineteenth-century romantic poetry or early twentieth-century American poetry.
4. define some of the approaches to the criticism of poetry such as formalistic, socio-cultural, or mythic.

Comprehension: As a result of the study of poetry, the student will be able to

1. relate or paraphrase the plain-sense meaning of a poem.
2. explain in his own words the explicit meaning of a poem.

Application: As a result of reading, writing, discussion and instruction in poetry, given a new poem which he has never seen before, the student will be able to ask the appropriate questions about poetry such as these and answer such questions satisfactorily, either orally or in writing:

1. What is the meaning of the individual words and the patterns or words in context? What is the "plain-sense" meaning of the poem?
2. What is the mood of the poem? By what specific words and patterns of words has the poet created the mood?
3. What is the structure of the poem? How do rhythm and rhyme contribute to the total effect?
4. What is the value of the poem? Is it worthwhile or a shoddy, superficial poem? By what criteria?
5. How does this poem fit into my idea of what the valid poetic experience is?

Analysis: After instruction in poetry, the student will be able to

1. identify the elements of poetry, such as images, tropes, rhythm, rhyme, mood, and voice.
2. explain the relationships of such elements to the total effect of a single poem.
3. illustrate what the different patterns of poetry are.

Synthesis: After reading, discussion, and instruction in poetry, the students will be able to

1. write more striking images and metaphors.
2. compose original poems, starting with couplets, quatrains, or haikus and then moving on to more sophisticated verse.
3. derive a generalization from data and express it explicitly or implicitly as part of a poem, *e.g.* Robert Frost's generalizations from "Mending Wall": "Good fences make good neighbors" or "Something there is that doesn't love a wall."

Evaluation: After varied experiences in the classroom with poetry, the student will be able to judge meritorious poetry by the following kinds of internal criteria developed jointly by the teacher and students:

1. fresh, accurate images.
2. details directly related to concrete referents.

3. rhythms and rhymes appropriate to the total poem.
4. value system implicit or explicit in the poem which is both profound and basic and ultimately humanistic, inasmuch as the essential worth of the individual is upheld.

These are some of the behavioral objectives for the teaching of poetry that I hold appropriate. Of course, all objectives cannot be met with every lesson or even with every unit at a particular grade level. The objectives having to do with the affective domain may only be evaluated fully after many years of formal instruction and personal experiences. Because, however, the objectives for the acquisition of knowlege are more easily and unequivocally met, this does not mean that they are the only ones to be considered in the classroom. Primarily, I hope that the student will come to possess the necessary feelings, facts, skills, and understandings about the nature of language, the elements of the patterning of words and phrases, and the effect of patterned sounds in English so that he can grow in his power to enjoy initially and to read a variety of increasingly subtle and sophisticated poetry by himself.

Behavioral Objectives and the Teaching of Writing

In helping students to learn to write, it seems to me, we must proceed first from the basic assumption that writing is indeed not some mysterious gift given only to rare men like Dostoevsky and Melville and second that the act of writing is a skill, a skill that can be developed by all men to some degree. If men are capable of writing—of manipulating written symbols— and if the act of writing is a skill, then the conclusion must follow that it can be taught and learned. And if it can be taught, it is then necessary to determine what behaviors the learner is performing when he is "writing successfully"—which leads us directly to behavioral objectives for the teaching of writing.

A word of explanation is due about my objectives for writing. The affective objectives and the cognitive objectives for synthesis and evaluation are at the heart of the writing process. The knowledge aspect of the cognitive domain is the least important. If there is any danger that teachers were to regard these objectives as all-important, then they should be omitted entirely. The ability to define terms such as "unity," "coherence," or "adequate development" are almost totally unrelated to an ability to produce writing.

Affective Domain

As a result of varied and essentially pleasant experiences with writing, the student will be able to

1. attend to samples of writing read in class.
2. respond to samples of writing when the teacher asks questions.
3. voluntarily write and express satisfaction in writing and in reading his writing out loud in class.
4. defend a belief in the value of knowing how to express one's self in writing.
5. express reasons for writing well and attempt to persuade others to write well.
6. justify an ordered viewpoint for expressing one's self accurately and forcefully in writing.
7. act consistently in all of his writing, proceeding from the assumptions that he holds about accurate and forceful writing.

Cognitive Domain

Knowledge: As a result of instruction about writing, the student will be able to

1. define terminology related to the process of writing, such as "topic sentence," "controlling thesis," "unity," "coherence," and "adequate development."
2. describe the arbitrary labels for various kinds of writing, *e.g.* exposition, persuasion, narration, and description.
3. outline trends in writing such as romanticism and realism.
4. define some of the major approaches to the criticism of prose, such as formalistic, socio-cultural, and mythic.
5. relate the characteristics of various kinds of writing such as short fiction, long fiction, the essay, drama, and poetry.
6. describe the components of Aristotelian rhetoric and subsequent modifications of this theory of rhetoric.

Comprehension: As the result of instruction about writing the students will be able to

1. paraphrase a paragraph, changing the words of the original.
2. write a precis of a paragraph.

Analysis: After instruction about writing, the student will be able to

1. identify the elements of fiction such as character, plot, setting, mood, and theme.
2. detail the components of expository prose such as the use of details, development by example, definition, and comparison and contrast.
3. explain how the components of fiction and non-fiction are related to produce an overall effect.
4. differentiate among such organizational structures as the short story, novel, and essay.

Synthesis: As a result of instruction and practice in writing, the learner will be able to

1. follow through the process of writing, including some of these several steps:
   a. develop an idea.
   b. make an assertion about the idea.
   c. find examples, quotes, and information supporting the idea from introspection, reading, research, discussion, and observation.
   d. construct a rough, personal outline.
   e. write a zero draft, in which ideas are put down as fast as possible without regard to conventional mechanics.
   f. be able to revise critically the zero draft, asking the following sorts of questions:
      (1) Are my ideas intelligible?
      (2) Are my examples concrete, pertinent, and accurate?
      (3) Do my assumptions (assertions) proceed from convincing evidence?
      (4) Are my sentences varied?
      (5) Is my mood sustained?
      (6) Are my words precise and interesting?
      (7) Is my writing smooth, *i.e.* can the reader move from idea to idea without being interrupted? Are my transitions smooth?
      (8) Is my command of mechanics (spelling, capitalization, punctuation, conventional formal English usage, and format) perfect?
      (9) Have I said something worthwhile?

Evaluation: As a result of wide and varied reading, discussion of writing, and of writing itself, the student will be able to

1. judge his own writing and the writing of others by internal criteria developed by both the teacher and other students, such as logical consistency, accuracy of detail, and expression of generalizations both basic and profound.
2. judge his and the writing of others by external criteria, by a comparison to models of professional and non-professional writing.

Behavioral Objectives and a Stance Toward Teaching

Such then is my tentative position on the use of behavioral objectives for the teaching of English, tentative not because I'm unconvinced that attempting to formulate in specific terms behaviors for learners in the field of English is desirable, but tentative because I'm in the process—as are many other men of good will in English Education—of attempting to work out those behavioral objectives that will assist me to help beginning teachers encourage others to perform the complex intellectual skills and to develop the appropriate attitudes associated with the discipline of English.

What is most valuable to me about the process of formulating behavioral objectives is the fact that it forces a certain powerful—if sometimes painful—kind of stance, a way of looking at the learning process. From this stance, the teacher is forced to ask disconcerting yet crucial questions. Why am I teaching what I am teaching? Of what value is it—besides its intrinsic intellectual excitement—for the student? Of what use can this learning actually be? What can an individual *do* with it? Even more importantly, will the particular learning that I have set up influence the student to continue to learn what is worthwhile, or will the learning be so distasteful that he will have an aversion to this area of knowledge after he leaves the formal classroom? If these questions are attended to conscientiously, then much of the learning situation follows quite naturally. Once the behavioral objectives are established, the particular content, the appropriate learning experiences, and the means of evaluating how well the objectives have been met are naturally determined. If we want a student to be able to write a logical, detailed paragraph, free from mechanical errors, we don't select content having to do with essays *on* writing, give him lots of practice in correcting incorrect sentences from canned textbook exercises and in writing out spelling demons from dictation, and then evaluate him on the objective to be able to write an essay by giving him a test with usage questions, sentence structure items, and spelling words. At least, I hope we don't.

Behavioral Objectives and Humanistic Values

There *are* criticisms of behavioral objectives, of course, some of which are quite valid. First, don't behavioral objectives tend to fragment knowledge? There is a danger in the over-zealous teacher developing objectives so specific that only very discrete learning experiences will be met. It is therefore important to keep the expression of objectives on such a level of generality that fragmentation has less chance to occur. Furthermore, it must be emphasized that no one should expect every objective on every level to be met with every lesson. Some objectives lend themselves to the beginning of a unit, some to the acquisition of facts, some to the application of principles, and some to generalizing. What Bloom has to say about this danger of such a system of taxonomy tending to fragment or stultify the educational process is appropriate here.

> Although there are dangers in devising a classification scheme which might tend to rigidify our thinking about education, the relatively chaotic nature of our field at present and the great emphasis on persuasive skills rather than on research findings for claims in the field of education justify some procedure such as this for ordering the phenomena with which we deal.[2]

Another criticism which is more deep-seated than the one aimed at fragmentation has to do with the humanist's virtually innate distrust of the technician. For most teachers of English—who would if you asked them probably classify themselves as humanists—behavioral objectives smack of a mechanistic, unnatural technique applied to a discipline which does not lend itself to scientific analysis. Essentially, if I may speak for the mass of English teachers, the important question becomes: Aren't behavioral objectives essentially anti-humanistic? Such an attitude of distrust for the "merely technical" has time-honored origins in Western culture. Discussing the characteristics of classical humanism in his book, *A History of Education in Antiquity*, H. I. Marrou points out that the ancient proponents for a humanistic education were chiefly interested in the man himself, not in a technician for a specialized job.[3] This belief in the supremacy of an education chiefly through the study of a body of traditional works of literature over a preparation in technology has persisted to this day. Marrou sums up this position well.

> There is a terrible tyranny at the heart of technology. Any particular technique tends by its own inner logic to develop exclusively along its own line, in and for itself, and thus ends by enslaving the man whom it serves. It is only too clear today that science can make scientists inhuman, biology can make doctors forget that it is their duty to

cure people, and political science can turn doctrinaire politicians into tyrants. The classics tell us again and again that no form of government, no branch of knowledge, no technique should ever become an end in itself: since they were created by man, and supposed to serve man, they should always, no matter what the results, be subordinated in the way they are used to one supreme value: humanity.[4]

But one of the hallmarks of the humanistic viewpoint is to "Know thyself." And any technique that helps man learn more about himself, that helps him learn more economically, and that helps him to learn that which is based upon careful study and scrupulous observation rather than upon unsubstantiated opinion is valuable. As we know only too well in the twentieth century, science can be used for anti-humanistic ends, but we are also aware that science—broadly conceived—can help man to understand his intrinsic nature and thus help him become more human. What more humane study could there be than how man perceives and uses that most marvelous invention of his—his language? The constant attention to identifying precise education objectives—and the consequent stance toward the whole learning process it forces—seems to me a most humanistic activity.

Notes

1. Robert F. Mager. *Preparing Instructional Objectives*. Fearon Publishers, Palo Alto, Cailf., 1962, p. 52.
2. Benjamin S. Bloom, ed., *et al. Taxonomy of Educational Objectives: Handbook 1: Cognitive Domain*. David McKay Company, Inc., New York, 1956, p. 24.
3. H. I. Marrou. *A History of Education in Antiquity*. A Mentor Book, The New American Library, New York, 1956.
4. *Ibid.*, p. 306.

· 2 ·

I SEE YOU, I HEAR YOU, YOU'RE OK

Humanizing the English Classroom

Robert W. Blake (1974)

"Everybody knows what humanism is, but nobody ever does anything about it." "Humanism is a marvelous thing in the classroom, except that no one has ever tried it."

These phrases—meant half jokingly—suggest my feelings about terms like "humanism" and "humanistic teaching." I can see that the study of *Oedipus Rex, Hamlet, Our Town*, the music of Beethoven, and the paintings of Cezanne and Picasso is the study of humanism. But I also hear that the study of humanism includes attention to the works of Cleaver, Baldwin, the Beatles, Anne Sexton, Robert Bly, Richard Brautigan, Kurt Vonnegut, and Andrew Wyeth. I am told that the study of values clarification, confluent education, transactional psychology, and humanistic psychology will make one a "humanities" (or "humanistic"?) teacher. And there are those who tell me that if I meet with students and other teachers in informal groups—touching, feeling, and expressing my longings, desires, and fears in a completely honest way—that I'll be immersed in humanistic education.

I'm sure that all of these definitions of the humanities are right for the people who live and teach by them, but I'm not convinced that such an array of plays, novels, poems, paintings, music, psychological theories, and value clarification techniques can all come under the heading of humanities.

What I'd like are some satisfying answers to these questions:

What is humanism? Is it made up of bodies of literature, art, and music to be studied? Is it primarily content, I wonder? Or is it a process, a way of relating to other human beings? Or is it both—a way of relating to other persons while studying a general body of artistic products?

What is humanistic teaching? And if humanistic education is a way of relating as teacher to student and student to student, what are some general guidelines that I can follow if I want to be a humanistic teacher? How do I act? What do I say? How do I react? In other words, what kinds of noises does a humanistic teacher make? How do you tell a humanistic teacher when you see one?

What is it to be human? I know that a human is an animal belonging to the genus and species of *Homo sapiens*. But what makes him tick? Is he the weapon-toting, aggressive, gregarious, talkative, sexy, naked ape that the anthropologists make him out to be? Is he "in action how like an angel! in apprehension how like a god! *the beauty of the world! the paragon of animals!*" and "the quintessence of dust" as Hamlet describes him? Or, is he the creature that produced the gas for the chambers at Auschwitz, stoked the fires of the crematoria at Treblinka, interrogated men in cellars in Algiers, and defoliated the village of My Lai? This last question is the hardest. *No wonder we despair at the task.*

First, what is humanism? I had always thought that humanism was an intellectual movement during the Renaissance in Europe in which men turned away from the religious dogma of the Middle Ages to promote the literature of the *ancient Greeks and Romans.* But now I find I must re-define my old notions of humanism. There's a new breed of humanist, and I don't know him very well.

In his book *The Real World of the Public Schools*, Harry Broudy makes the distinction between the "old-line standard humanists" and the "new or existential humanists" and states that the real battle in education is not, as C. P. Snow believes, between science and humanism, but between the old and new humanists.[1] Although Broudy warns us that his descriptions of the two factions will oversimplify the issue; nevertheless he outlines them. For Broudy, the standard humanist believes in controling his emotions by reason in order to comply with the laws of the universe. From Plato on, according to Broudy, the standard humanist found the explanation of moral laws in the masterworks of literature, and the young were inducted into humanism by studying expressions of man's recognition of these laws.

Maybe I'm quoting out of context, but Broudy presents the classical humanist as an ineffectual pedant: "The scholarly humanist, confronted by evil, goes back to his study to study some more (or he appoints a committee to study), while the poor become more wretched, the environment is ruined, and men wreak violence on each other and ultimately upon themselves."[2]

I'm not happy with this definition of the classical humanist—simplistic as Broudy acknowledges it to be. It certainly does no justice to the tradition of humanism—classical, Christian, or modern existential. For the classical humanist, rational thought was not a means to itself but a necessary basis for responsible action. Doing, feeling, and thinking were all part of one's character. For Aristotle, tragedy is the "imitation of an *action*," of some deed done by a man and of its consequences. The ancient Greeks knew only too well the result of unbridled emotion and hubris—arrogant pride—and they learned to value reason, moral law, and restraints as antidotes to man's tyrannical nature.

And lest we believe that the first humanists, when confronted by evil, turned their backs on it and went back to their studies to study some more, we should remember that Aeschylus fought the Persians in the battles of Marathon and Salamis, that Sophocles was for forty-five years a general in the Greek army and later served as a civic leader in Athens under Pericles, that Socrates took the hemlock rather than cop a plea to escape the trumped up charge that he was a corruptor of youth, that Plato, who *did* spend much of his life within the shelter of his Academy, traveled widely throughout the Mediterranean and worked at practical politics while trying to turn the tyrant Dion of Syracuse into a philosopher king, and that for the Athenian Greeks of the fifth century A.D., the word *idiot* meant a "peculiar, private person" who had nothing to do with the day-to-day running of the good state. How far removed from the idea of the scholarly humanist, turning his back on evil and returning to his study to study some more.

And many later writers, whose works we value as expressions of the humanist tradition, balanced doing and feeling with thinking. Cervantes was a fierce soldier. Chaucer was an active public servant. Shakespeare was a practical—and enormously successful—playwright. John Milton maintained such a vital relationship to his time—chiefly as servant to the Puritan Commonwealth—that he was called "the organ voice of England." Melville sailed the oceans of the world as a merchant seaman, sailor in the United States Navy, and whaler. Faulkner—a gentleman farmer—talked, hunted, ate, and drank with all kinds of people around Oxford, Mississippi. And Kurt Vonnegut, as a soldier in World War II, was a participant in the fire-bombing of Dresden.

It would be unfair to suggest that all men who have called themselves humanists were vigorous men of action as well as artists and writers. Many were not. But the ideal of humanism, as I understand it, requires me to base all of my actions upon the assumption that man is a worthy creature, capable of becoming something noble.

During the Renaissance in Europe—when the term humanism was created—scholars repudiated the dogma of medieval theology. Such men as Petrarch, Erasmus, Castiglione, and Sir Thomas More turned to the writings of the ancient Greeks and Romans because they found in them such ideas as these: Man has dignity and is capable of becoming a better creature. We should live and love in the world here and now, rather than concentrating upon eternal bliss or damnation in the hereafter. We should value reason and rational discourse over mystical emotionalism and religious revelation. We should educate men as well as women to become well-balanced individuals with all of their capabilities, mental and physical, fully developed. A Latin poet in the second century A.D. first wrote what was to become the unofficial motto of humanism: "We should pray for a sound mind in a sound body." And we should teach through reason and gentleness rather than by authority and brutality. Strange ideas for bloodless scholars who turned their backs on their communities to study some more in their studies.

By way of contrast, who are the modern humanists? Again, let me quote Broudy, "... the existential humanists do not want to wait for the cosmos to carry out its design, or for the second coming, or for whatever distant millennium. They do not regard Platonic self-mastery through ordered thought and feeling as the glory of the species; they prefer freedom from all preconceived restraints. This freedom creates a compelling need to commit oneself to a significant deed-one that will authenticate the self. One must change the evil situation now and not stop with the understanding of it."[3] Many classical humanists did commit themselves to significant deeds and, on the basis of their understanding of what was evil, went on to change inhumane situations. If the militant humanists were not so uninterested in classical humanism, they might be buoyed up in their struggle against inhumanity by learning how other men throughout the ages met the same kinds of problems and responded to them.

In a way, the existential humanists, although they turn away from the traditional values of the past, reflect the essence of humanism. They wish to be free men, free from restraints, and free to act against evil whenever they encounter it. The classical humanist was also distrustful of all artificial restraints and believed that any philosophy, any branch of science, any religious doctrine, and any brand of social engineering—no matter how well intentioned—if carried to its extreme, would end up not by serving man but by enslaving him.

So what is humanism? Humanism is a set of attitudes, a complex of values, what psychologists call "internalized" ideas and feelings about what human beings are like and what they are capable of becoming. Initially we find a clear expression of these ideas and attitudes in the writings of ancient Greeks and Romans, and later, in the works of men during the sixteenth and seventeenth centuries in Europe. But humanism does not stop there, and this is what makes it such a vital concept. Any book, any poem, any painting, any piece of music that says that the proper study of mankind is *man* is true to the spirit of humanism.

In one sense, humanism is the study of ideas about man's nature and the way these ideas affect his actions. But in another sense, humanism is the study of the condition or quality of being human. Such a notion leads directly to the question of humanistic education. How does an English teacher make a classroom humane?

The person who has helped me the most in this search for guidelines to humanistic teaching has been Carl Rogers. For a beginning, I refer you to his collection of essays, *On Becoming a Person*.[4] You might then wish to move on to his later books, *Freedom To Learn*[5] and *Carl Rogers on Encounter Groups*.[6]

"The Characteristics of a Helping Relationship," from Rogers' book, *Becoming a Person*, can be used as the basis for an exploration of what a humanistic teacher might be.[7] I first read the article shortly after it was published in 1958, and I tried to use his counseling techniques with my high school English students. I found out right away that there was one dramatic difference between the counselor's situation and mine. A counselor talks with one client at a time, usually an articulate, mature person who has voluntarily come for help. As an English teacher, I interact with groups of from twenty to thirty-five adolescents who are required to be there. Furthermore, Rogers makes it a rule never to judge his client's behavior. But I am required to give grades for quizzes, tests, essays, and end-of-year examinations.

Over the years, then, I have asked myself, do these techniques work with large groups of people? with children or adolescents who have difficulty verbalizing their feelings? with people who come from a cultural background different from mine? On the whole, I have found that his guidelines do work, even when they are modified for classroom situations. I have learned to ask myself almost continually, is this action consistent with what I believe? Am I being humane? Many times I found myself in painful situations because, while I was trying to have students learn about themselves, I was learning about myself. And always, as a result of trying to apply the principles of client-centered counseling to my *relations with my students*, I experienced a heightened sense of well-being as a person and as a teacher.

In his consideration of the "helping relationship," Rogers describes the qualities that a successful psychologist or counselor should have. Let me offer you my interpretation of these characteristics applied to the humanistic English teacher.

I am a humanistic teacher if I am a consistent, dependable person. Of course I plan by the week, day, and year. I meet my classes on time regularly. I keep track of my students. I am conscious, in other words, of the outward consistency of my profession. But, more importantly, I am inwardly consistent. This is not to say that I am always pleasant and smiling even when the students are particularly raucous or uncooperative. Rogers describes this inner consistency: "I have come to recognize that being trustworthy does not demand that I be rigidly consistent but that I be dependably real."[8] "I'm a person, too," I say in many ways to my students. "This is what I like and what I don't like, what I value and what I won't stand for. And I believe that you can understand and accept me as a real person."

I am a humanistic teacher if I am able to communicate unambiguously to my students what I think and feel. I actually talk to my students about the why and how as well as the what of learning. I don't try to trick them. I don't try to make myself feel superior by making them look stupid. But most of all I am able to communicate my feelings to my students. I am able to say, "I'm tired. I've been up all night with a cold, and I don't feel well." If I feel annoyance at my students, but attempt to conceal it-revealing it through extraverbal clues—they will detect my annoyance and be confused.

I am a humanistic teacher if I allow myself to have positive attitudes toward my students. I hesitate to use the word because it has been over-used and misunderstood, but I *care* for my students. Some teachers show they care by planning extensively, by getting compositions and tests back as soon as possible, and by never missing a day of school. (Such caring, though, makes me think of Harlow's experiment with the baby monkeys and surrogate mothers. Harlow prepared two substitute mothers for the monkeys, one made of wire and another of soft terrycloth. Both contained a bottle with a nipple, and both gave milk. It was not surprising to find the monkeys preferring the soft mother over the wire mother.) I like my students and I let them know it, but the liking is dangerous, for when I like somebody, then I am responsible for him. He can make demands on me. He wants a piece of me. And the most precious gift I can make is my time. (The taxi dancers in "Sweet Charity Brown" express this well: "Big spender, spend a little time with me.")

I am a humanistic teacher if I keep myself a separate human being and allow my students to retain their separate identities as well. One of the great temptations facing beginning teachers is to enter completely into the lives of their students. One inexperienced highly sympathetic teacher took on all of the personal problems of her students. She met them after school, on weekends, and at home. She let them call her at any time of the day or night. Eventually, her students took so many pieces of her that she had nothing left of herself. She was frustrated and despairing because she could not solve all the problems unloaded on her. She had to learn that she could not be depressed because one of her students lost a boyfriend, that she could not become angry because one of her students had a fight with his father, or that she could not become defeated because one of her students failed a test.

As a humanistic teacher I also allow my students to be separate persons. In the initial stages of our relationship, I may encourage students to imitate my actions, but very soon I want them to strike out on their own, to try new ways of doing things, to become original, separate persons. I suggest different ways of solving problems, of writing essays, and of seeing characters and themes in literature. I ask questions like these: "What do *you* think?" "How do *you* see it?" "Is that how you'd like to try it?" "What would happen if you assumed this point of view in your essay?"

I am a humanistic teacher if I am able to put myself in the shoes of my student. I learn my student's language, find out how he sees his world, learn what myths he lives by. I can only do that if I ask questions and then listen to what he says when he responds. I make it a point to read the books he is reading, see the movies he is seeing, and listen to the music he is playing.

I am a humanistic teacher if I accept each student as he is, a human being capable of being respected and loved. I may find it difficult to like an aggressive, belligerent kid who is different from me in many ways, but I remember that he is a human being and worthy of respect. We all know how well the self-fulfilling prophecy works with kids who are told they are worthless. They live up—or down—to our expectations. In Robert Frost's narrative poem, "The Death of the Hired Hand," Warren defines home as "the place where, when you have to go there,/they have to take you in." But his wife Mary, with quiet wisdom, muses, "I should have called it/Something you somehow haven't to deserve." If I can paraphrase Frost, school is a place you shouldn't have to deserve.

I am a humanistic teacher if I gradually free my student from all external evaluation, from relying on others to tell him what is good or bad for him. In schools we mark and test and judge continually. We say "You're good," "You're bad," "That's a good paper," "That a bad test," "You've failed," "That's a 97," "That's a 64," "You're not college preparatory," and "You're valedictorian."

The counselor, working with only one person, makes it a point never to evaluate his client. But isn't the English teacher, who must teach *many* students how to discuss, to read and write, and to master certain skills, obligated to evaluate the performance of his students?

Not necessarily. For the Rogerian counselor, the aim of a helping relationship is to help the client become an autonomous, fully functioning person, who accepts blame and praise from others but who, as a mature and responsible person, realizes that ultimately he is the only one who can say whether an experience is good or bad for him.

And likewise the English teacher. My job is aimed at making myself unnecessary. I glory in the day when my student can discuss in a group, setting forth rational arguments, listening to the positions of others, and advancing his own opinions based upon reasoned judgments. I glory when my student can read fiction, poetry, or essays, and understand how the writer has used words to move and inform, when he can see significance for his life in the fictional characters of a story. I glory when my student can move through the process of writing, testing ideas, using examples, seeking variety in sentences, and emerge confident in his ability to inform, persuade, or move through his use of words.

I offer my students standards of excellence, but they are standards which they themselves see as possible for them. I would no more expect a junior high school kid to be able to ski like Jean Claude Killy, sail like Paul Elvstrom, or play baseball like Reggie Jackson than I would imagine that he could write a poem like James Dickey, an essay like James Baldwin, or a short story like John Updike. When he has become something more than a beginner at skiing, though, I would let him see how he stacks up against somebody like Penny Corcoran. And when my student realizes that there is more to writing than correct spelling I would let him see how Salinger uses dialogue, how Vonnegut handles plot, and how Oates builds character.

One final point about evaluation. As Rogers does not blame his clients, he does not praise them either. He reasons, if I can say "That's a good job," it implies that I have the right to say, "That's a bad job." I have tried his approach, but have halfway abandoned it. I try never to say "That's a bad paper" and, in fact, I do not give a numerical or letter grade for writing. Instead, I read the papers carefully, suggest sentence revisions, and ask questions aimed at thematic concerns. I never say or write negative things about student writing but rather attempt to describe my honest reactions to the thoughts the student has expressed.

Contrary to Rogers' position on positive evaluation, however, I do praise—in realistic terms—whenever I can. This is especially important with writing. I like to say or write things like these: "What an opener! There was immediate tension," "Good choice of words," "Good description. I can taste and feel the scene," or "You felt deeply about that person, and your feelings came through in your writing."

And finally I'm a humanistic teacher if I accept my students as persons in the process of what Rogers calls "becoming." All humanistic counselors that I know of—Rogers, Maslow, Berne, and Harris—operate on the principle that not only *can* most people become autonomous, reliable, self-reliant persons who respect themselves and who see themselves as capable of being respected, but that they *want* to become such persons. Rogers calls this process "becoming." Maslow calls it "self actualization," becoming, in reality, what you have the potential to become. Harris, the transactional psychologist, calls this not "growing up" but "growing." And Martin Buber, the existential philosopher of the University of Jerusalem, uses the phrase, "confirming the other." Rogers quotes Buber's explanation of this concept. "Confirming means ... accepting the whole potentiality of the other. ... I can recognize in him, know in him, the person he has been ... *created* to become. ..."[9]

How does this help me as a teacher, as a human being? First, it repudiates the Freudian doctrine that we are captive to our past, shackled by infant and childhood upbringing. Freud said to me that if I was immature, belligerent, neurotic, and psychologically paralyzed as a child and adolescent, I would remain that way throughout my later life. But the humanistic counselor says a person can grow, can become, and can change. Not only can I free myself from childhood immaturities and excesses, but, more importantly, I want to.

So what does the humanistic English teacher do with five classes of twenty-five students? Students who argue constantly? Students who are belligerent? Students who are obnoxious? Students who are immature, uncertain, confused, unsure, but who desperately want to grow, to become?

I try to teach humanistically. If I sometimes forget the tenets of humanistic teaching—and I know how easy that is—then I think of these three simple phrases.

I see you. I acknowledge you. I'm aware you exist. You're something, a real person.

I hear you. This is especially hard for English teachers who are so notoriously verbal. I hear what you're saying. I listen, and I try to understand what your words mean to me and what they mean to you. I also show that I'm listening by extraverbal means. I look at you and pay attention to what you say. I don't tap my fingers or glance at my watch or jump up out of my seat. And I respect that whatever you are saying—whether or not I like it or disagree with it—is true for you.

And you're OK. This is only half of the jazzy phrase that Harris uses to express the mature relationship between two people, "I'm OK—You're OK." What the full phrase means is that I like myself as a person, and I think you're worthy of respect and love, too. I'm secure. I like myself pretty well. And you're OK, too. The burden of responsibility rests with me to make sure I keep on saying, in all kinds of ways, that you're OK. That you can read and write. That you have ideas and feelings that are right—if not for other people— certainly for you.

So if humanism is a touchstone by which we test our qualities as human beings, and humanistic teaching is a set of generalized approaches by which we encourage others to become fully human, then how can we separate the two? And, I submit, that if we teach humanistically what humanism is all about, then we just might come up with *human* beings.

Notes

1. Harry Broudy, *The Real World of the Public Schools* (New York: Harcourt, Brace, Jovanovich, 1972), p. 50.
2. Ibid., p. 52.
3. Ibid.
4. Carl R. Rogers, *On Becoming a Person* (Boston: Houghton Mifflin Company, 1961).
5. Carl R. Rogers, *Freedom to Learn* (Columbus, Ohio: Charles E. Merrill Publishing Company, 1969).

6. Carl R. Rogers, *Carl Rogers on Encounter Groups* (New York: Harper and Row Publishers, 1970).

7. Carl R. Rogers, "The Characteristics of a Helping Relationship," *On Becoming a Person*, pp. 39–58.

8. Ibid., p. 50.

9. Ibid., p. 55.

· 3 ·

THE NEW ENGLISH

Hot Stuff or Cool, Man, Cool?

Robert W. Blake (1970)

What the new English is or will be in the future is of great concern to me. The more I read about the preparation of teachers of English, about majors and minors, about the differences in merit between a background in English versus American literature, about the need for understandings from educational psychology and skills in empirical research, the less certain I am about how an English teacher should be prepared. Although such official statements as the 1965 CEEB's Commission on English's *Freedom and Discipline in English*, the reports from the Anglo-American Conference at Dartmouth in 1966, the 1967 Viall English Teacher Preparation Study, and the 1968 Squire and Applebee report on *High School English Instruction Today* have revised considerably my notion of what the preparation of an English teacher should involve, they still seem unable to suggest solutions to the major problems produced by the instruction going on in the English classrooms in our schools. I'm beginning to suspect that we'll find little help from the usual English texts, curriculums, and programs, because the seemingly novel approaches almost always proceed from such traditional assumptions about the teaching of English. At this point, I am personally distressed because all of the bodies of content and traditional methods of teaching English which I learned in an arduous and humbling apprenticeship now seem virtually worthless—or, at best, innocuous remnants of a bygone era. Many of the kids in the schools that I have observed are turned off by what's happening—or not happening—in the English classroom; they are not sharing in the excitement and joy that comes from being deeply involved intellectually and emotionally in the study that we have an allegiance to and deep affection for, the discipline we call English.

There is considerable distress voiced by English teachers of good faith that the term "traditional" is used solely as a derogatory term and that such a person as a "traditional" English teacher as commonly described is a caricature, a strawman erected by the radicals and ultra-progressives in English teaching who wish to see anything from sensitivity training to Quaker meetings—in which students contribute when the spirit moves them—take the place of legitimate English teaching. The point is well taken.

Perhaps I should define my notion of what a "traditional"—in a derogatory sense—English teacher is. First, the traditional English teacher teaches what he calls grammar as the identification of parts of speech, phrases, and clauses; the types of sentences according to meaning and structure; and a number of shibboleths of usage like the proper use of *who* and *whom* and *I* and *me*, although in many cases, such a practice has almost no relation to the legitimate study of English grammar, except from an historical point of view. The text in the hands of the students is some handbook like Warriner's, and the method is recitation-drill, with the kids working in canned textbook exercises and the teachers correcting their mistakes.

The traditional English teacher teaches writing as a set of rhetorical principles, originating with Aristotle and subsequently modified through the centuries, to be memorized by the students and applied—after extensive reading of essay samples by professional writers—to teacher-devised or textbook-devised, narrowly conceived topics which fail to recognize the fact that worthwhile writing begins with the writer himself having a deeply felt idea that he wishes to express. The teacher proofreads these first—or, at the best, second-draft compositions—marking for the most part on spelling, punctuation, and "grammar." The approach involves essentially principles of rhetoric, extensive reading of essays by outstanding professionals, the writing of first-draft papers on canned topics, and proofreading with a red pencil of the essays by the teacher.

The traditional English teacher teaches literature as everything *but* the piece of literature ostensibly being read. We are told that whatever the traditional English teacher does, he has been well-trained in the close analysis of a novel or an essay or a poem, and he *does* know how to teach literature.

Unfortunately, the evidence just does not seem to bear this out. But do not take my word for it. Listen to what James Squire had to say about the teaching of literature in superior high school classrooms in *College English*, May 1966:

> Our real quarrel is with the incessant superficiality of much classroom study of litera-
> ture—with, if you will, the evasion of literature represented in too many classrooms.
> Despite a decade of recommendations to the contrary, many teachers continue to
> teach the dates and places as if these and not the literary works were the essence of
> our subject: an over-reliance on history and geography, a preoccupation with the lives
> of the poets, a fascination with the Elizabethan stage, a concern with definition and
> memory work (the Petrarchian sonnet, the heroic couplet, the accepted definitions of
> figures of speech)—these clutter the minds of too many teachers and students alike.[1]

This, then, is my rough sketch of what I mean by a traditional English teacher. I wish he *were* a strawman that I had invented so that I could demol-ish him, but I am sad to say that I have seen him for too long in too many school and college classrooms.

However we move away from the traditional English classroom taught by a traditional English teacher and do move toward a new English, I feel certain that it will eventually be an almost totally different way of using all aspects of language to view reality, in which the learner is led to an ever-increasing aware-ness of an ability to use his language in the widest variety of ways. No single discipline has the terms to describe the new English, and this perhaps is one of its identifying characteristics: the new English transcends formerly discrete disciplines. Possibly one of the best means of describing this new English is by using Marshall McLuhan's terminology for "understanding media."

The new English is cool and, as such, will be at the core of what McLuhan calls the retribalization process, in which modern, print-oriented man is being wrenched away from his one-thousand-year-old love affair with the printed word. This reverence for the "book," for the printed word, epito-mized by the civilized detachment of literate man, contrasts drastically with the total group involvement of nonliterate man who relied upon instantaneous oral communication. The new English is cool because it eschews the exces-sive dogma of the printed word and involves men in oral interaction as well as allowing them to continue to use printed matter. "Basically," states McLuhan, "a hot medium *excludes* and a cool medium *includes*; hot media are low in participation, or completion, by the audience and cool media are high in participation. ... A lecture by the same token, is hot, but a seminar is cool. ... In a cool medium, the audience is an active constituent of the viewing or listening experience" (p. 61).[2]

The provocative concepts of "hot" and "cool" as defined by McLuhan are tough ones to assimilate for many people, especially traditional English teachers. At least one English teacher remarked that McLuhan's metaphor was perplexing, that one usually associated the word "hot" with vital, stimulating experiences and the word "cool" with uninspiring, dull activities. At first glance, we might think this would be so, but such an inability to attend to new meanings for old words represents—in the clearest fashion—what McLuhan terms the "institutional biases of literate man." Since what McLuhan says seems so lucid—once we attempt to free ourselves from traditional ways of thinking—we should let him explain his meaning for hot and cool media in his own words.

> A hot medium is one that extends a single sense with high definition. High definition means a complete filling in of data by the medium without intense audience participation. A photograph, for example, is high definition or hot; whereas a cartoon is low definition or cool, because the rough outline drawing provides very little visual data and requires the viewer to fill in or complete the image himself ... In any case, the overwhelming majority of our technologies and entertainments since the introduction of print technology have been hot, fragmented and exclusive, but in the age of television we see a return to cool values and in-depth involvement and participation they engender (p. 61).

That the medium of television provides men opportunities for instantaneous depth involvement among men is viewed as nonsense by some critics of McLuhan's ideas. Much of the material on television *is* inferior, shoddy, passive, and mind dulling, especially the situation shows and soap operas which attempt to tell a story by essentially literate means. But much of what we have access to on television is direct, intimate, and literally "touching." The world has never been the same since the coverage on television of the assassination and funeral of President Kennedy. The sense of communal grief and interaction was felt throughout the world. This sort of communication among men—the last Democratic convention at Chicago was another good example—can occur only through television.

With the advent of different kinds of media—like television, with its instant indepth involvement with other men throughout the world—the new, cool, media-oriented generation, accustomed to experiences of total participating communication, are being turned off in the classrooms, where instruction is almost exclusively in terms of the hot medium of the printed page. In fact, the conflict between the old and new generations is seen most graphically in the schools. McLuhan's evaluation of much of our present educational system is disturbingly accurate:

Question: Why do you think they [the students] aren't finding it [personal identity] within the educational system?

McLuhan: Because education, which should be helping youth to understand and adapt to their revolutionary new environments, is instead being used merely as an instrument of cultural aggression, imposing upon retribalized youth the obsolescent visual values of the dying literate age. Our entire education system is reactionary, oriented to past values and past technologies and will likely continue so until the old generation relinquishes power. The generation gap is actually a chasm, separating not two age groups but two vastly divergent cultures. I can understand the ferment in our schools, because our educational system is totally rearview mirror. It's a dying and outdated system founded on literate values and fragmented and classified data totally unsuited to the needs of the first television generation. ... The challenge of the new era is simply the total process of *growing up*—and mere teaching and repetition of facts are as irrelevant to this process as a dowser to a nuclear power plant (p. 62).

Although the new English essential for lighting the fires of the first television generation is far from being defined exactly, I am confident that, if anything, it must be cool. The new English is cool, first, because the learners will be actively involved in the process of learning. The lecture, a method used by professors in the medieval European universities to provide students with a copy of their notes—before the era of printing, required college textbooks, and university bookstores—is a useless remnant in the media era when many kinds of factual information can be transmitted so much more effectively by means other than the lecture. On the other hand, concepts, generalizations, attitudes, and values are best sharpened and assimilated through discussion and interaction. The new English classroom should be a seminar or a guided bull session where students are given practice in discussing, questioning, ana-lyzing, and testing values with other students and the teacher.

But, questions the critic, isn't such a recommendation to be found in any standard English methods textbook? That's just the point. With few excep-tions, such an idea has remained in the textbooks. I still see too much "talking to" students by teachers, too much recitation-drill under the guise of "dis-cussion" as the dominant mode of instruction, too much drill on vocabulary words, too many tests evaluating low-level learning activities, too many unin-spired and distasteful writing experiences, and too much superficial teaching of literature.

The learning psychologist, Jerome S. Bruner, describes this essential aspect of student involvement in education in his *Toward a Theory of Instruc-tion* (Norton, 1966). Here are some of Bruner's assumptions about learning: "Instruction should approximate the give and take of a seminar in which discussion is the vehicle of instruction." "The principal deficit in the lack of learning is the lack of opportunity to share in a dialogue." "Intellectual development depends upon a systematic and contingent interaction between a tutor and learner." and "Since the instructional process is essentially social— particularly in its early stages when it involves at least a teacher and student— it is clear that the child, especially if he is to cope with the school, must have minimal mastery of the social skills necessary for engaging in the instructional process." Education, especially in the new English, must then cease to be represented solely by an artificial division between the teacher and the student or between a student and a book. What results is a new tutorial, a pedagogical happening, in which the teacher and students work and learn together. Since language is the medium by which human beings interact and realize their humanity, then it follows that language is the key to functioning as a human being. Speaking, writing, and reading—and all facets of verbal and extraverbal communication—are simply different manifestations of the same medium. We're coming to realize, furthermore, the importance of *how* something is communicated rather than *what* the content is. To use McLuhan's figure, the *message* of "A-bomb" stencilled on an atomic bomb is infinitely less important than the bomb itself—the *medium*. The medium of a message is, in the most accurate sense, many times more powerful than the message itself.

The new English is cool, moreover, because the learner will be involved in the "total creative process of *growing up*." Such a statement implies that the teacher will tell less and encourage the student more to learn how to create by himself and to cope with his environment independently. A historical survey of American poets, for instance, which results in an activity of matching poets' names with the titles of their poems is virtually inconsequential to this new English. The assimilation of pre-digested facts will be replaced by the inductive process. If the student is to learn how to write—rather than to repeat theoretical aspects of classical rhetoric—he will go through the actual steps of writing and will produce varied pieces of communication for selected audiences. He will "read" and react to all kinds of communication, including newspapers, radio, movies, and television, comprehending how they affect man, so he can use them for his own purposes and not be tyrannized by them in his ignorance. Bruner, in *Toward a Theory of Instruction,* describes the classroom environment which fosters individual maturity this way: "Instruction is a provisional state that has as its object to make the learner or problem-solver self-sufficient. Any regimen of correction carries the danger that the learner may become permanently dependent upon the tutor's correction."

The cool English teacher becomes not a watchdog of his learner's mistakes but someone who helps the learner come to have confidence in his ability to evaluate his own performance. It should be axiomatic that no person will ever become a competent writer until he is able to evaluate his writing and revise it with respect to clarity and the audience to which it is directed. The study of language becomes not a list of mythological do's and don'ts about usage but the actual practice of using media in all sorts of situations. And the study of literature is no longer the exclusive concern with *belles lettres,* written by a literate elite and constantly revered by later generations, but a consideration of the written record of how man has used language to amuse, to inform, and to enlighten other men. The object of the new English is not to initiate a learner into an arcane and highly selective society but to make the learner—through the conscious mastery of language—independent, mature, and, essentially, humane.

The new English is cool, finally, because it will help the learner enter into what McLuhan calls the "global village" and what R. Freeman Butts terms the "ecumenopolis," the world city. "Building the ecumenopolis is the overriding task before the world's educators. This is what the educational innovation and technology are for, this is the goal of the social sciences in education, and this is the purpose of comparative study and international education."[3] But, McLuhan says, a new English is needed to cope with the "totally new society ... coming into being, one that rejects all our old values, conditioned responses, attitudes, and institutions" (p. 72). At the heart of the new English is the study and awareness of language as it is represented in forms other than the printed page, especially in television. Without communication sophistication, no man can become a citizen of the ecumenopolis. Such topics as the nature of human communication; the general characteristics of all languages; extraverbal systems of communication and how they affect men's behavior; and regional, social, and functional differences in language have already been studied to varying degrees of intensity by anthropologists, comparative ethologists, and linguists, but much more research and analysis are obviously needed. But are not such subjects the proper domain of linguistic study and has not such an emphasis in the English classroom been advocated for decades? Isn't the study of language a vital part of the teaching of English at all levels? Again, what is made available from research in bona fide language study and what is practiced in the classroom are two entirely different matters. Much more could be said about the great credibility and knowledge gap between what researchers and scholars say should be a part of language study in the schools and what is actually going on in the classrooms; but some observation would bear out the fact that for the most part what has been made accessible in the areas of phonology, modern grammars, paralanguage, kinesics and proxemics, generative semantics, and social and regional dialectology is virtually unknown in most English classrooms throughout the country.

In this exciting search for the meaning of media, the first step is basically to understand how the cool English works. "The first and most vital step of all … is simply to understand media and its revolutionary effects on all psychic and social values and institutions. Understanding is half the battle. The central purpose of all my work is to convey this message, that by understanding media as they extend man, we gain a measure of control over them" (p. 74). If we simply translate the word "media" as "language"—to include all the communication extensions devised by man such as the telegraph, telephone, radio, phonograph, movies, television, as well as the use of print and all other means of visual communication—then the scope and immensity—and the excitement—of the task before man of acquiring full citizenship in the global village can be appreciated. After the understanding of language and how man uses it to communicate and interact with other men comes a willingness to continue to learn and to profit from the learning—which is, after all, the abiding task of all men.

When asked what made him change his bias for the printed word to a search for the understanding of media, Marshall McLuhan answered "Experience. … I ceased being a moralist and became a student" (p. 74). What McLuhan ceased moralizing about was the supposedly pernicious influence of media. McLuhan himself had the traditional training in literature, like most of us English teachers, and enjoyed the traditionally hostile attitude toward all means of communication except for the printed word found in the "great books." McLuhan acknowledges this original prejudice.

As someone committed to literature and the traditions of literacy, I began to study the new environment that imperiled literary values, and I soon realized that they could not be dismissed by moral outrage or pious indignation. Study showed that a totally new approach was required, both to save what deserved saving in our Western heritage and to help man adopt a new survival strategy (p. 74).

The new English, the cool English, requires that teachers and students alike become learners together in this quest for the understanding of language. Rather than spouting nonsense, McLuhan speaks directly to all English teachers, and by providing insights into the crucial changes in communication that are now going on, he helps to show us the way to a new English. If we fail to listen to him—or to any other thinker who helps us to understand how man communicates—we do so at our own peril.

Notes

1. James Squire, "The National Study of High School English Programs," *College English*, 27 (May 1966) 619.
2. Marshall McLuhan, "Playboy Interview," *Playboy*, 16 (March 1969). All subsequent references to McLuhan are from this interview. Reprinted by permission of Marshall McLuhan and *Playboy*.
3. R. Freeman Butts, "Charting Our Position on the Way To—," *The Record*, 70 (March 1969) 493.

SECTION II

LINGUISTICS IN THE CLASSROOM

Here, through some of Robert's earliest articles in this collection, we learn about the role of linguistics in literacy teaching and learning. In the first piece, Robert asks the fundamental questions, "What is linguistics," and "Why use it in the classroom?" Reviewing the research in the field at the time (1965), he concludes that through a study of basic linguistics, students will gain an "increased awareness of range of thought available in language."

The next article, published in "Elementary English" when Robert himself was the Editor of the prominent New York State journal, "The English Record," reviews a program he and others conducted for elementary English language arts teachers to afford them the opportunity to gain a better "awareness of linguistics and language." What he found, however, was that this Institute moved teachers to *understand* that those students who "speak English differently are not ... immoral and stupid." Further, the teachers saw ways in which they, then, could help their students to not only be more linguistically "sophisticated," but also more linguistically "tolerant."

To situate the crucial nature of this piece—especially through Robert's findings—was an incredible leap in 1965. Remember, this was a turbulent time in our history—and in our schools. We as a society had only just given African Americans the right to vote, and had only begun to understand the inextricable connections between poverty and inferior and inequitable schooling. Jump forward to 2017—to today—and many, many of these same issues have reared their ugly heads—as politicians and parents alike demand English only classrooms, no tolerance for other languages nor other cultures—meaning all things taught in schools, too, must be white and middle class.

And finally, in the last piece of Section II, Robert takes us through the beautiful (and often frightening) nature of extra-verbal communication—how we "speak" through our gestures and our eyes. Explaining that making use of extra-verbal communication in the classroom allows for, "a richer interaction with our environment and other humans" as we perceive our environment "more richly," he ends with beautiful excerpts from "The confessions of Nat Turner," as we are, once again, taken on a journey through our linguistic "extra-verbal systems"—tone of voice, physical touch, we are reminded after-all, of the beauty of language, linguistics, love, and life.

· 4 ·

LINGUISTICS AND THE TEACHER

Robert W. Blake (1965)

What does linguistics have to say to the secondary-school English teacher? Unfortunately, at the present, very little. There are a few excellent textbooks for high-school use,[1] some fine pamphlets of an introductory nature designed for public-school teachers,[2] and one textbook, that I know of, that is aimed directly at the junior high school.[3] That, unfortunately, is all.

What is linguistics? It is simply the scientific study of language, especially the study of the language about which we're most interested, English. Actually, the general study of linguistics covers many aspects of language—some areas more thoroughly than others—and is represented by a considerable body of scholarship. One specific area is the history of language; another is comparative linguistics. A third specific area is descriptive linguistics, which includes semantics, the meaning of meaning, and phonology, the study of the characteristic sounds of a language. Morphology, a third division of descriptive linguistics, is of especial interest for English teachers because it is involved with the various descriptions, or grammars, of language.

I must stress that the information from the original research done in these fields cannot be grasped easily or quickly because the approaches and attitudes are new and differently oriented from the traditional approaches to describing the English language that we have held dear for years. An excellent start has been made with the few available secondary-school textbooks which accurately reflect linguistic principles, but much more work needs to be done.

Furthermore, even if we do make use of our language methods and ideas, we won't find all of our language problems solved. Nor do I wish to imply that traditional English grammar is incorrect in every respect. Not at all. Many techniques used by English teachers to present traditional grammar are valid and effective. For many years, I taught English grammar by the traditional approach, and I think that I achieved some fairly effective results. I came to the study of linguistics reluctantly, as many other converts have, but after I had done some reading and had actually worked with some of the materials in the public schools, I came to the inescapable conclusion that linguistics was a valuable study. It seemed to describe the English language more accurately than did the traditional approach. It seemed far more logically defensible. And, I found it eminently more interesting than the old process of memorizing and picking out the eight parts of speech, learning the four kinds of sentences according to meaning and structure, and conjugating regular and irregular verbs.

We have been told that traditional grammar is obsolete and inaccurate largely because it is based upon Latin grammar; it is, like the Ptolemaic astronomy which postulated the earth as the center of the universe, falsely oriented. This criticism makes sense. For instance, I can remember the Latin teacher in one high school collaring me in the hall to ask why I didn't teach my students grammar. She had to teach her students English grammar, she said, before she could teach them Latin grammar Later, I realized what the problem was. She wanted me to teach traditional English grammar, which, in reality, was modeled directly after Latin grammar.

Why doesn't the traditional, Latinate grammar accurately describe the English language? In explaining the language, for example, we usually start with a definition of the sentence as *a group of words expressing a complete thought*, but as Charles C. Fries states, this is actually only one of two hundred definitions of a sentence.[4] This particular one has been dated before 500 A.D., by the way, and still does not give the student a workable method for recognizing the sentence. Another definition of a sentence may be that *a sentence has subject and predicate and that the subject performs an action*. "The dog is barking" is a sentence, we might say. The word *dog* represents an animal, *barking* represents an action, and action is attributed to *dog*. But the group of words, "the barking dog," meets the same criteria and expresses the same situation. An animal, *dog* is named; an action, *barking*, is named; and the dog is the performer. The same is true of such statements as these: "the red book," "a beautiful white dress with a wide lace hem," "who the man is," and "why he will come." The traditional definition of a sentence just doesn't allow the student to identify a sentence *unless he already knows what people call a sentence.* In other words, only those students who can sense unconsciously what a sentence is can profit by such a definition. It is the student who writes fragments and run-on sentences, and who doesn't know he is doing so, who needs help. The traditional definition of sentence simply doesn't fill his need.

How well does the traditional method of identifying parts of speech in English work? All traditional grammar books deal with parts of speech and usually list eight. As Fries points out, however, the number has ranged from three to ten, and the current conventional classification of English words into eight parts of speech seems to have been made official by Joseph Priestley and to have been generally accepted in grammar books since 1850.[5] How well do these terms describe words in English? A noun is commonly defined as the "name of a person, place, or thing." Blue, red, and yellow are the names of colors; yet in expressions such as blue tie, a red coat, and a yellow flower, we don't call blue, red, and yellow nouns. Run is the "name" of an action, as are jump and arrive. Up, across, and down are the "names" of directions, but we don't call them nouns. We can only help a student by saying, "See how the words work in the sentence. You can tell what they are by their position." This is one of the approaches that linguist uses to identify parts of speech.

To continue with the parts of speech, an adjective is traditionally defined *as a word that modifies a noun or pronoun*, but what are the words *boy's* and *his* in the phrases *the boy's hat* and *his hat*? Are they adjectives or possessive pronouns or even possessive adjectives? Very few teachers would agree that they are adjectives, yet the words fit the definition. We have all been in this spot in the classroom. What do we say? We tell the students, "These words do the work of adjectives in the sentence because of their position." Again, this is the same approach which the linguist uses.

The definition of a pronoun—*a word that takes the place of a noun*—presents even more difficulty. In such a sentence as "Wednesday is the time to see him," as Fries points out, which of the following words that can take the place of *Wednesday* are pronouns?

> Wednesday
> Tomorrow
> Today
> Next week
> Later
> Now
> When
> This
> That
> It
>
>   is the time to see him.[6]

The definitions of the remaining parts of speech cause the same sort of problems. How can we identify the parts of speech in the English language more effectively and more accurately? The answer is by structural means. This process can most easily be shown by analyzing a nonsense sentence such as

A stuny rang spickled the linnest blurbs tetly.

We don't know the lexical—or dictionary—meaning of the individual words because there are only two words, *a* and *the*, that we recognize. Yet the grammatical meaning of the sentence is clear. The article *a* identifies *rang* as a noun, which can be made plural—*rangs*. *Blurbs* has the plural inflection of a noun and occupies the position which nouns frequently do in English, after an adjective. *Stuny* is an adjective because of the suffix *y* as well as its position between an article and a noun. The word *linnest* is also an adjective because it is located between an article and noun, and it is further distinguished as an adjective by the inflection *-est* (*lin, linner, linnest*). *Spickled* is a verb because it has the past tense inflection *ed*, and it also has the derivational suffix *le* of such common verbs as *rattle, crackle,* and *battle*. *Tetly* must be an adverb because it ends in *ly* and because it occurs at the end of the sentence where adverbs frequently appear. All of this grammatical meaning is apparent because of structural clues and word order rather than because of meanings applied to individual words.

The total linguistic meaning of any sentence, then, consists of the lexical, or dictionary, meaning plus structural meanings. For the linguist, grammar consists of the devices that signal structural meanings. The traditional procedure seeks to ask what names should be applied to the various words in a sentence. The traditional, if you will, is a deductive approach; it assigns terms to elements of the sentence and then formally proves their existence. The linguistic, on the other hand, is an inductive approach; it analyzes actual spoken and written sentences and then describes the process whereby words within these sentences achieve their meaning.

If the traditional definitions of parts of speech don't seem to describe English words in sentences accurately, then what description, or grammar, of English have the linguists substituted? First of all, the linguists state that since there are more English grammars than one, we should speak of grammars in the plural, not in the singular.

What are the different grammars identified by linguists? Traditional grammar, the grammar which is based upon Latin syntax and with which we are all most familiar, may be designated as grammar "A." This grammar, agree all serious students of language, fails to describe English accurately. Historical grammar, which follows the elements of change in English from Old English through Middle English to Modern English, may be called grammar "B." Structural grammar, which analyzes English according to its "immediate constituents," or its distinctive components, may be termed grammar "C." Generative grammar, which attempts to describe the process whereby an individual can create an infinite number of basic or kernel sentences, can be designated as grammar "D." Because all English teachers are acquainted with grammar "A" and because most teachers have some knowledge of grammar "B," let us examine in the briefest fashion the theoretical bases of grammars "C" and "D" and consider some possible uses for them in the public school classrooms.

A valuable book for an understanding of structural grammar, or grammar "C," is *The Structure of English* by Charles Carpenter Fries. Fries took fifty hours of tape-recorded conversations amounting to 250,000 words spoken by people using standard English and analyzed the utterances according to their use in the sentences. He found that four groups of words—or *form class words*, as he designated them—accounted for 93% of the samples of the language. Although Fries states that these form class words are not nouns, verbs, adjectives, and adverbs, they correspond closely enough to these parts of speech so that we might retain the traditional nomenclature. For Fries, the form class words are words that can appear in the following positions in grammatical sentences.

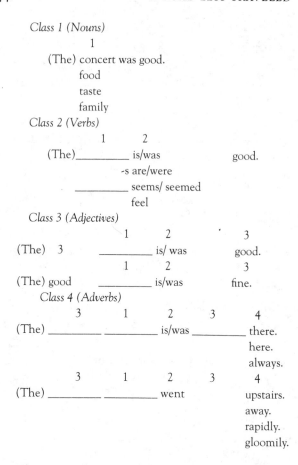

Class 1 (Nouns)

         1

(The) concert was good.
       food
       taste
       family

Class 2 (Verbs)

      1   2

(The)_____ is/was   good.
         -s are/were
    _____ seems/ seemed
        feel

Class 3 (Adjectives)

        1   2   3

(The) 3   _____ is/ was   good.
        1   2   3

(The) good   _____ is/was   fine.

Class 4 (Adverbs)

      3   1   2   3   4

(The) _____ _____ is/was _____ there.
                              here.
                              always.

      3   1   2   3   4

(The) _____ _____ went   upstairs.
                                away.
                              rapidly.
                              gloomily.

The remaining 7% of the words are called *function words* and include such words as *the, may, not, very, and, at, do, why, after, well, yes,* and *no*. There are other structural signals that help us to identify form class words, but word order, or position in the sentence, is one important means of recognizing the various classes.

Using symbols for the form class and structure words, as Paul Roberts does in his high-school textbook, *Patterns of English*, we can easily indicate sentence patterns and create new sentences from designated patterns.

Form Class Words

    1—any noun or pronoun
    2—any verb
    2L—linking verb
    3—adjective
    4—adverb

Structure Words
   D—determiner (the, a, an, every, this, each)
   A—auxiliary (can, do, does, may, could)
   V—intensifiers (very, somewhat, rather)

Sentence Pattern
D   V   3   1   A   4   2   D   1

The very frightened woman had quickly seen the snake.

How can such an approach aid the student? First, it helps him to understand from actual English sentences, spoken and written, how the language is constructed. He is not attempting to apply a Latin structure, or any other language description, to English. Furthermore, as the student goes on to analyze how more complex sentences in English are built by compounding, by adding qualifying adjectives and adverbs, and as he begins to understand how modifying phrases, clauses, and verbals are used in more complex sentences, he should begin to have an increased awareness of the range of thought available in our language.

The newest explanation of English grammar—and the one that has probably caused the most discussion among linguists—is called generative or transformational grammar, which we shall designate grammar "D." If you want a first-hand, but extremely difficult, description of this grammar straight from one of its most important proponents, you should probably start with *Syntactic Structures* by Noam Chomsky.[7] However, if you don't feel ready to begin your study of generative grammar with such an abstruse, theoretical statement of English grammar in which symbolic logic is utilized throughout, then you'd better wait before you try Chomsky. Fortunately, you can get an accurate and clear interpretation of this grammar in Roberts' second high-school textbook, *English Sentences*. His third high-school book is *English Syntax*, a programed text, and I rather doubt that any high-school students except the most adept at handling verbal symbols would be able to profit from it. Again, high-school teachers and students would have to use the book before any conclusions about its effectiveness could be made.

Generative grammar is built upon the assumption that there are a finite number of basic or kernel sentences in English from which all other sentences are formed. A person learns these basic sentence patterns, usually by the time he is four or five years old, and he then learns how to transform these kernel sentences into an infinite variety of new sentences. In a recent study to support this theory of language, Brown and Bellugi observed the development of speech in children between the ages of eighteen and thirty-six months.[8] The authors found that imitation by the children of words and phrases spoken by the mother was one method of learning the language. Another method was by expanding those speech patterns of the mother. The third and most difficult process observed by Brown and Bellugi was that of the child trying out new patterns of speech. These patterns were completely new for the child— he was *not* imitating words spoken by the mother—and, of course, the new patterns were frequently not acceptable English sentences. The following are some examples of the new but incorrect speech patterns made by the children.

Saw it ball.
Miss it garage.
I miss it cowboy boot.
I Adam drive that.
I Adam drive.
I Adam don't.[9]

Transformational or generative grammar attempts to describe the process whereby a native speaker of English creates—or generates—an infinite number of gramatically correct sentences from a few kernel structures. For instance, the sentence "John saw Bill" is a kernel sentence. From this kernel we can create such transformations as the following:

Kernel Sentence.
    John saw Bill.
Transformations
    Did John see Bill?
    John didn't see Bill.
    John did see Bill.
    Who saw Bill?
    Bill was seen by John?
    that John saw Bill

In the middle of the night, *John,* who had been looking through the fields, suddenly *saw Bill,* lying with his face down in the mud and with his arms outstretched, as if he had been drawn taut on some ancient rack.

It does not matter what auxiliaries, negatives, relatives, interrogatives, or modifying devices we add, all of these patterns are transformations of the kernel sentence, "John saw Bill."

By observing actual speech, we find other kernel sentences which can be represented by symbols.

Kernel Sentences.

	(D)	N	V	(Adv.)		
1.	The birds sing sweetly.

	(D)	N	V	Adj.
2.	The pie tastes good.

	(D)	N	V-t	(D)	N
3.	The man shot the wolf.

	(D)	N	be	Adj.
4.	The lions were hungry.

	(D)	N	be	(D)	N
5.	That boy is my brother.

The symbols tell us the following facts about the sentences. The determiner (D) in parenthesis may or may not occur, but the noun and verb *must* occur in sentences one and two. The verb in sentence three is a transitive one because it takes an object. Although we have traditionally called *to be* a verb, most linguists maintain that the word should be in a class by itself and should simply be designated as the "word *be*." In any event, either an adjective or adverb may follow the word *be* in sentences four and five.

How may generative grammar work in the classroom? By creating a variety of sentences from the basic kernels, students should have a better understanding of the structure of English. More importantly, however, as students learn how modifying structures such as words, phrases, subordinate clauses, and verbal phrases can be added to kernel sentences to create new, complex, and subtle thought patterns, they should become more proficient in the actual writing of varied, interesting, and grammatically acceptable English sentences.

Many studies have been made which attempted to show a relationship between a student's knowledge of English grammar and his ability to write well, by whatever criteria. The results consistently have failed to show any such significant relationship, but all studies have been conducted with the elements of traditional grammar or with the ability of the students *to recognize* grammatical relationships. No one has yet made a study to find out if students who have a great deal of practice in writing complex and varied sentences, using a generative grammar approach, will write more mature prose. I feel confident that they will. In fact, I am now conducting such an exploratory study with seventh and eighth-graders to find out if such an approach will produce significant improvement in writing ability.

That the findings of modern linguistics will be incorporated in public-school English teaching is inevitable. The College Entrance Examination Board's special Commission on English has designated Language—as well as Reading and Composition—as one of the major areas of preparation for English teachers. At summer and yearly institutes for secondary-school English teachers sponsored by the Commission on English, a graduate course in modern linguistic study is required. The National Council of Teachers of English, as well as the Commission, also stipulates that one area of competency for teachers should be that of English language study, including the history of English and modern linguistic analysis. James B. Conant in his *The Education of American Teachers*[10] has even gone so far as to recommend that all teachers in public schools, elementary and secondary, should have six semester hours of academic preparation in the study of the English language.

I am strongly of the view that a general education hardly deserves the name unless it insures a reasonable familiarity with the nature of the language we use. A year's work devoted to an understanding of its structure, its history, its relations to other languages, and its use seems little enough ... the serious study of the English language should be an essential component of any collegiate program and particularly of a teacher's education.

Linguistic study for the public schools is definitely here to stay. There are powerful forces at work which will help to ensure that all public-school teachers, and secondary-school English teachers in particular, will have some sort of preparation in linguistic analysis. As soon as the English teacher finds out that linguistic science is not an unassailable, unintelligible subject and that, furthermore, it holds much promise for better English language instruction, I am confident he will. He must do this because he is an English teacher and because teaching an understanding of the English language in the most interesting and accurate way possible lies at the heart of his job.

Notes

1. Paul Roberts, *Patterns of English, English Sentences, English Syntax* (Harcourt, Brace, 1956, 1962, 1964); David A. Conlin and George R. Herman, *Modern Grammar and Composition* (American Book Co., 1965).
2. For instance, the NYSEC monograph announced in this issue.
3. Neil Postman, et al., *Discovering Your Language* (Holt, 1963).

4. *The Structure of English* (Harcourt, Brace, 1952), 9.

5. Ibid., 66.

6. Ibid., 69.

7. Mouton and Co.'s—Gravenhage, The Hague, Netherlands, 1957.

8. Roger Brown and Ursula Bellugi, "Three Processes in the Child's Acquisition of Syntax," *Harvard Educational Review*, 34 (Spring, 1964), 2:133–151.

9. Ibid., 150.

10. McGraw Hill, 1963. The quotation below is from p. 95.

· 5 ·

ONCE UPON A MORPHEME

An NDEA Institute in Applied Linguistics for the Elementary School Teacher

Robert W. Blake (1967)

Introduction

No one should be more directly concerned with encouraging the development of language skills and linguistic awareness in children than the elementary school teacher. A majority of the school day is spent in language work or in linguistically related matters. He teaches reading, an incredibly complex skill involving the instantaneous recognition of printed symbols and the understanding of the meaning of individual words and of words in patterns. He teaches spelling, a process which includes a perception of sound-symbol correspondence as well as a knowledge of historical reasons for sound-symbol discrepancies in English. He teaches language structure, or the study of how meaning in language is achieved by the manipulation of linguistic patterns—the grammar of a language. He teaches the sounds and oral rhythms of language, the phonology of a language. He encourages children to use for varied audiences different styles—or functional varieties—of oral and written language. He teaches the use of the dictionary, which involves many disparate linguistic matters such as spelling, syllabication, pronunciation, etymology, and semantics. He helps children to learn that people in different areas of our country and throughout the world speak English with a difference which is known as regional dialectology. He helps children, furthermore, to become aware that people use English in different ways that sometime prevent them from enjoying the full social and economic benefits of our culture, the study of which is known as social dialectology. In a real sense, he helps children to become *linguistically sophisticated*—to begin to acquire a full understanding and ability to use in all its complexity and variety, man's wonderful invention, his language. He also helps children—and this may be even more crucial— to become *linguistically tolerant*—to become deeply aware that other children may use different forms of English, not because of any lack of innate intelligence but because of differing environmental and social backgrounds.

Most elementary school teachers carry on much of such a language program intuitively and unconsciously, but they are often unaware of the reasons for the solid foundations of their language instruction. Though they sometimes may not realize it, accurate and important information about our language as well as tested techniques for gathering new information about language are being produced by linguistic scholars at an impressive rate. This information is appearing in new elementary school language arts textbooks and in Project English experimental curricula as well as in college and university courses and inservice workshops in applied linguistics. Valuable as these sources are, they are not enough. There is an urgent need for teachers in the elementary schools to be aware of the most recent research in the fields of linguistics, to possess the minimum skills of linguistic analysis, and to be able to apply such understandings and skills in the elementary school classroom. In order to meet this need in an introductory but fairly comprehensive fashion, I helped to develop and conducted at the State University College at Brockport, New York, the first part-time NDEA Institute in English: Applied Linguistics for elementary school teachers and supervisors, grades 1–6. This report is a record of the initial aspirations, the births and deaths of ideas, the academic travail that only truly professional teachers can understand, and the tentative but potentially productive insights that the participants and members of the staff experienced during the 1967–68 academic year.

The Program

What should be the objectives of such an institute? What several areas of linguistic study should be included? What experiences should be provided for the participants? What special texts, reference books, experimental curricula, video tapes, movies, and recordings should be available? These were the kinds of questions that needed to be answered if the institute was to be successful.

The most important objective of the institute, it was felt, was to introduce and constantly reinforce appropriate attitudes about language, for example, that language changes constantly and that such change is normal, that spoken and written forms of language have distinctly different characteristics, that so-called correct usage is determined not by English rhetoric textbook writers but by the ways in which educated, native speakers of English use the language, and that people use different forms of English not because of hereditary reasons, but because of social and geographical factors.

The second major objective was to provide the participants with an understanding of five major areas of linguistic study: the history of the English language, American English, modern English grammars, lexicography, and linguistics and rhetoric. Since the institute was to be held in the State University College Campus Demonstration School during the school day and since the school was involved in a special program for the urban disadvantaged—in which seventy-five black children were bused from the city of Rochester to the Campus School—further major objectives were to give the participants opportunities to observe from one-way glass observation rooms children using non-standard English and to listen to and analyze their dialects as well as to watch trained Campus School Teachers use linguistically-oriented materials in the elementary grades during the institute. Final objections were to provide a wide range of textbooks, articles, pamphlets, and special curriculum materials for participants and to provide workshop opportunities so that participants could study selected materials, discuss their implications, and develop curriculum materials for actual use in their schools.

Such was the proposed general plan for the institute, but we found out rather quickly that some special problems would arise that would prevent the carrying out of the original proposal. First, the teacher from the Campus School—who had worked in special curriculum projects in applied linguistics with me, who had taken nine hours of graduate work in linguistics at our college, and who was to have used linguistically-oriented materials with her fifth grade class—left the school and area. Another teacher from the Campus School volunteered, but her interests and abilities did not, unfortunately, prove to coincide with those of the institute. She dropped out during the middle of the fall semester. No suitable replacement was found.

The second problem encountered—which affected the program most adversely—was the fact that some school superintendents would not provide released time for their teachers to attend the afternoon sessions of the institute, originally proposed to be held from 1:00 to 4:00 p.m. so that participants could observe classes using linguistic materials in the Campus Demonstration School. One of the *Criteria for Admission* printed in the Brochure was that each participant "must be given by his district released time for one afternoon per week without penalty and with no extracurricular duties from September 1967 through May 1968." I am afraid we were terribly naive. Some administrators would provide released time, but many would not. The ones who would not, all stated—by phone or in letters—that such an institute would have been all right after school or on Saturdays. This, of course, was exactly what we did *not* want. One superintendent from a large city school district refused to let his teachers apply; another allowed one teacher to attend but required her to pay her own substitute teacher for the one afternoon per week when she was absent. One board of education allowed its teacher to attend but would give him no in-service credit for his work. The result of such a lack of cooperation on the part of some school administrators was that the time of the afternoon sessions had to be moved to 3:30 p.m., with alternate Tuesday evening sessions from 7:00 to 9:30 p.m. No Campus School classes, therefore, could be observed by the participants, and one very important feature of the institute was destroyed. The valuable lesson that I learned was that many school systems still only pay lip service to helping their teachers continue their professional preparation.

In spite of these roadblocks, the twenty-seven participants, three professors of English, one professor of education, and two administrative assistants met September 19, 1967, to commence the institute. The fairly formal program of study involved, as has been noted, instruction in five major strands of linguistic study to be handled by the four professors. The history of the English language included an examination of Anglo-Saxon through Middle English to Early Modern English with regard to changes in grammar, vocabulary, and pronunciation. The major text for this segment was Baugh's *A History of the English Language*. The second strand was a consideration of the historical, regional, social, and functional aspects of American English, with Malmstrom and Ashley's *Dialects—U.S.A.*, Marckwardt's *American English*, and Shuy's *Social Dialects and Language Learning* as the required texts. The study of modern English grammars was restricted to structural and generative-transformational descriptions; the texts were Finder's *A Structural View of English*, Fries' *The Structure of English*, Jacobs and Rosenbaum's *Grammars 1 and 2*, and Thomas' *Transformational Grammar and the Teacher of English*. The study of lexicography included historical backgrounds of English lexicography and modern developments in dictionary making with Lodwig and Barrett's *The Dictionary and the Language* as the main source. The final strand, linguistics and rhetoric, had modern theories and practice in language and rhetoric. The texts were Bailey's *Essays on Rhetoric* and Christensen's *Notes Toward A New Rhetoric*.

The guest lecturers who met with the participants were chosen because of their unique and outstanding knowledge of a particular area of linguistics or of rhetoric. Henry Lee Smith, Jr. spoke on General Linguistics and Reading; Raven I. McDavid, Jr., on Social Dialectology; Dean Obrecht, on Regional Dialectology; Roderick Jacobs on Generative-Transformational Grammar; Philip B. Gove, on Lexicography; and William Owens, on Language and Writing.

Special materials—other than the required textbooks—were chosen so as to give the participants a general survey of other texts, records, and films available in the field of applied linguistics. Project English Curriculum Center Materials such as those from Georgia, Northern Illinois, and Oregon were available; copies of the University of Nebraska *Language Explorations for the Elementary Grades* were given to each participant and were used extensively throughout the Institute. Further resource materials were ordered from the Modern Language Association Materials Center, The College Entrance Examination Board and the National Council of Teachers of English. Recordings on "Our Changing Language" from the EMC Corporation and "Americans Speaking" from the NCTE were part of the Institute program. Several Henry Lee Smith, Jr. films from Indiana University on "Language and Linguistics" were shown as well as films from the Encyclopaedia Britannica Educational Corporation; a number of the Commission on English kinescopes on language and rhetoric were also available. Finally, complete sets of linguistically-oriented elementary school textbook series were ordered for use by participants.

The most popular special material, it is important to note, was the overhead transparency; it was, without a doubt, the single most frequently employed instructional tool during the Institute. Such transparencies were either professionally prepared by members of the Instructional Resources staff of the College or were personally prepared by the individual staff member. One faculty member—a professor of English—had attended a Special Media Institute in Los Angeles in the spring of 1967; he became a distinguished proponent of the overhead transparency. Another English professor—whose special interest was medieval linguistics and who, like Miniver Cheevy, had always prided himself that he was far removed in spirit from the technological age—remarked, "I had always thought that AV was a dirty word," as he proceeded to use transparencies extensively with his presentations on the history of the English language.

Post Mortem

A *Participant Questionnaire* was given to all members of the Institute so we could get some idea of their attitudes toward the over-all program. Questionnaires at best are rather unsatisfactory, but such instruments are better than nothing, and, besides, some general conclusions can be inferred from the responses.

What were the major weaknesses of the Institute? The major limitation, as we all knew only too well, was the lack of observation of classes with children using a non-standard dialect and the lack of observation of Campus School teachers using linguistically oriented materials with elementary school children. "Not getting into the classroom to see the linguistic materials at work," "Less theory and more application," and "Lack of application and implementation of these new ideas on the elementary level" were the kinds of comments made by participants. Some noted personal problems such as "The time of year and duration," "Much difficulty with travel during winter months," and "Grave pressures with job and classroom." Some criticized aspects of the academic program and the administration of the program itself. There were, finally, some miscellaneous complaints like these: "Too many coffee breaks," "Too much give and take among professors," "The films were boring at times," and "More films could have been used." Such complaints were normal enough, but the sometimes contradictory nature of them only underscored the old saw that "You can't please all of the people" even some of the time.

What were the major strengths of the Institute? Many participants commented on special areas of linguistic study: "History of language was most interesting," "Social dialects," "Structural and generative grammar," and "Writing and rhetoric." Others appreciated the general knowledge of the faculty; most participants commented on the excellence of the guest lecturers; and a few found the organization of the Institute commendable. Most importantly, the majority of the participants were pleased that all four faculty members were present at all sessions and that a friendly yet professional atmosphere was established and maintained throughout the Institute. Here are a few representative reactions: "The give and take among the four was exciting and interesting and enlightening," "All professors made me feel very much at home," "Humor and attitudes of participants and professors," and "Freedom of discussion and expression was appreciated."

What satisfied me most, I suppose, was that a majority of the participants felt that an atmosphere of cooperation and mutual respect during an ambitious and sustained academic undertaking had been fairly well maintained throughout a long, hard year. The following comment seems to sum up what was most valuable about the Institute: "The Institute has been a very worthwhile personal experience for me. The awakening it has stirred will go on in many areas long after the immediacy has passed."

Had the Institute provided the participants with any knowledge of several areas of linguistic study? And, probably most importantly, had the Institute affected the attitudes of the participants toward the learning and teaching of language? As anyone knows who has ever been intimately concerned with teaching, the evaluation of what of real importance has been learned seems a hopelessly slippery task. The knowledge of facts is fairly easy to gauge, but the measurement of understandings and attitudes seems impossible to assess. The evaluation of what had happened to the participants—or of what they thought had happened to them—was no exception.

Two objectives of the Institute had been to "reinforce appropriate attitudes about the nature of English study" and to "provide the participants with an understanding of the five major areas of linguistic study." The responses to the question, "What do you think was the most significant thing that happened to you during the Institute?" gave us some assurance that these objectives might have been at least partially met. The following comments reflect the general opinion of the participants.

I gained a great admiration for and delight in my own language. My reading and writing on a personal level have been tremendously enhanced.

I have a better understanding of linguistics and thus do not feel quite so fearful or inadequate in this area. I should be able to encourage others along these lines.

More than anything, this Institute gave me a confident attitude towards the teaching of English in the classroom.

A completely new and dynamic awareness of our English language. Never again shall I be able to teach English in the same old way.

Some of the best remarks are naturally quoted here—some didn't respond to this item at all or wrote, "none"—but these reactions are typical. If such statements are true for only a few participants, then the Institute was a success beyond our most sanguine expectations.

Linguistics in the Elementary School: Where Do We Go From Here?—The EDPA

The NDEA Institutes belong to the past; the Education Professions Development Act now takes over. But the Institutes in English, I think, served their purpose well. They were designed to strengthen the capabilities of in-service teachers, and, in many instances, an unintended by-product was that college professors from varied academic disciplines came to develop an interest in the education of teachers and to catch some of the excitement of public education. The NDEA Institutes also provided colleges and universities with financial support so that they could set up experimental instructional programs without the usual local institution's bureaucratic red tape. Such institutes were valuable, but they weren't enough to do the required job. Our Institute, for instance, served only twenty-seven elementary school teachers. What further steps should be taken to strengthen the knowledge of present teachers and to ensure the preparation of future teachers in applied linguistics?

First of all, in-service work for teachers presently teaching is needed. The federal government may be able to support future programs in applied linguistics for teachers under its new Education Professions Development Act, but the local systems must begin to assume more responsibility for assisting their teachers to keep abreast of new developments. In conjunction with nearby colleges and universities, school systems can set up part-time institutes during the school year or workshops and local institutes during the summer. Public and private schools should also encourage teachers to attend important professional meetings, and, what is more, they should pay the expenses of teachers at such meetings.

Secondly, the colleges and universities must ensure that all teachers—elementary teachers as well as high school English teachers—have training in selected aspects of linguistic study. Ideally, when teachers achieve the position of true professionals in our country, one of their obligations will be to develop their own curriculum materials in language such as regional dialectology, modern English grammars, or functional varieties of English. This they cannot do, however, if they have not had basic instruction in these fields of study, have not acquired fundamental tools of linguistic analysis, or don't know what the important books and periodicals in linguistics are. Teachers, as a start, should be able to prepare comprehensive English curricula for the elementary schools or for the high schools and then for complete school systems, kindergarten through the twelfth grade. This they cannot do well, either, until they are relieved of non-professional duties in their schools and until they can spend time during the school year and in the summer preparing fully integrated and rationally based curricula which reflect the best thinking of both academic scholars and pedagogues.

How do we know, though, which skills and understandings from the discipline of linguistics—from any organized body of knowledge, for that matter—are necessary for school children to know? What good is linguistics in the elementary school classroom? might be another way of phrasing the question. And a very important question it is, too, one that should be attended to at the beginning of any considerations about the elementary school language arts program. First of all, it seems to me that we should teach in the schools that information and those attitudes which are available to us from our most respectable scholars and theoreticians. We shouldn't continue to teach something simply because it is there and we are familiar with it. We no longer teach the Ptolemaic view of the universe, except as an historical oddity. We no longer teach—with a straight face, anyway—alchemy or astrology, even though they may be interesting and familier. We do, however—without tongue in cheek, I'm afraid—still teach that educated native speakers bother about the distinctions between "who" and "whom," that English grammar is a replica of Latin grammar, that the formal, written language is the initial and most important form of language, and that people who speak English differently from us are probably dirty, immoral, and stupid. The study of alchemy is no more erroneous than such beliefs, and it is certainly a whole lot less harmful. Linguistics has been called the most scientific of the social sciences—this may or may not be—but it is evident that some of the finest minds in our country are engaged in discovering how man's most humane invention—his language—works. It seems only reasonable that if reports of such findings are available to the elementary school teacher that he should attempt to assess their value and to possibly use them in his classroom. The discoveries in historical linguistics, psychological language development, regional and social dialectology, and grammatical descriptions—to name a few—have been at least as important as the invention of the polaroid camera, the development of machines to place a man on the moon, or of the process of xerography.

The ultimate consideration, however, of what to include in the classroom has to do with the future value of it for the individual. Can a person make use of this skill or understanding tomorrow, in ten years, or in twenty years? Will it help him learn, ultimately, how to become more human? Despite the ferocious advance of technology—or possibly because of it—there is an even more desperate need for people to acquire a profound understanding of their language. What questions are more important then these for human beings to ask?—What is language? How did human beings come to invent it? How does language differ from animal communication? Where did English come from? Where is it going? Why is it that native speakers of English sometimes seem to talk funny? Even more importantly, why do we attach such enormous significance to these differences? How do we describe in written symbols the sounds of speech? How do we describe how words are put into patterns to express meaning? How can we come to the widest and deepest and most profound knowledge of language and be able to use this knowledge in our dealings with other human beings? The study of linguistics can contribute in no small way to the answers to such questions, and our NDEA Institute in English: Applied Linguistics made at least a start toward helping teachers learn how to frame these questions in the elementary school classroom.

· 6 ·

I SEE WHAT YOU MEAN—
BUT NOT BY WORDS

Extraverbal Communication

Robert W. Blake (1973)

In 1872, Charles Darwin, at the end of a detailed study of the origins of basic gestures made by men, entitled *The Expression of Emotions in Man and Animals*, wrote of the importance for human beings to understand their modes of extraverbal communication:

> The movements of expression in the face and body, whatever their origin may have been, are in themselves of much importance for our welfare. They serve as the first means of communication between the mother and her infant; she smiles approval, and thus encourages her child on the right path, or frowns disapproval. We readily perceive suffering in others by their expression; our sufferings are thus mitigated and our pleasures increased; and mutual good feeling is thus strengthened. The movements of expression give vividness and energy to our spoken words. They reveal the thoughts and intentions of others more truly than do words, which may be falsified [p. 364].[2]

It is ironic that one hundred years after Darwin's book was published modern man is finally coming to realize that extraverbal communication is indeed "of much importance for our welfare." A great deal of study in Western culture has been expended upon man's use of language, especially his written language. The origins and description of the Indo-European family of languages and the historical development of English have been thoroughly explained.

In the last several decades, the intricacies of oral language have been partially described, and only recently a tentative description of man's ability to create and comprehend an infinite number of novel grammatical sentences has been explored under the heading of generative grammar. Finally, as if to substantiate the axiom that man studies last that which is closest and most intimately his, scholars from many disciplines are picking up where Darwin left off to ask questions like these: Where did man's extraverbal system come from? What elements of it are basic to all men? What features of it are culturally determined? How does man's extraverbal communication system work? How can we describe consistently by written symbols a non-verbal system? If we do come to a fairly extensive knowledge of man's extraverbal system, how will this help us to understand his attempts to communicate with his fellow man?

What are needed are more direct ways of helping people become aware of modes of extraverbal communication so that they can apply this understanding to their interactions with others. Although scholars and researchers in anthropology, biology, zoology, psychiatry, ethology, and linguistics have made amazing advances in describing man's extraverbal systems of communication, they have provided, in most cases, only preliminary descriptions. Skimpy though these statements are, they at least provide a basis for further study. Konrad Lorenz, the comparative ethologist, whose studies of the behavioral patterns of higher animals and human beings have led to significant insights into extraverbal systems—especially in relation to aggressive behavior—maintains that the best scientific knowledge about human behavior other than language must be made available if people are to become enlightened, increasingly humane creatures.[6] There is considerable evidence available that after many centuries of reverence for the printed word and insistence upon equating all progress with rational, linguistic communication, mankind is now coming to acknowledge the basic nature of his extraverbal communication systems. According to the psychologist Herbert A. Otto, the chairman of the National Center for the Explanation of Human Potential in Lajolla, California, a full explanation of the dimensions of human potential is largely a mystery, but from "the depths of the mystery there are numerous indicators of the human potential," especially the capacity for communication via the senses.[7]

In modern urban society, unfortunately, people have allowed the foundations for their extraverbal systems to become unused and dulled, but it is possible for them to regain the use of their senses and to enter into a richer interaction with their environment and with other human beings. One price mankind may pay for his technologies is the dulling of sensual abilities, including kinesic, tactile, and proxemic capacities. Because we don't perceive well, we shut ourselves off from our environment, from other creatures, and ultimately from other human beings. But there are already signs of modern man's unwillingness to live partially aware of the signals that other creatures send out, in a world where sensual awareness is dulled and stunted. There are inarticulated gropings for nonrational communication, for "love-in's," "sit-in's," and "happenings." The statement "I feel" is coming to be as important as the assertion "I think." More people are turning to sports that stimulate the kinesthetic aspects of men's existence: motor boating, waterskiing, surfing, skin-diving, sailing, skiing, and sno-mobiling. It's as if they were determined to regain their ability to perceive their environment more richly!

How do we describe extraverbal systems, and what are their discernible components? How can we become more expert in using extraverbal communication? Although we could consider the topics of kinesics—the use of expressive gestures to communicate, and paralanguage—popularly known as "tone of voice," a subtle system of extraverbal communication used simultaneously with language to convey meaning—we shall at this time attend only to the subject of proxemics—how people use space in their interactions with others.

The Dimensions of Proxemics: The Anthropology of Space

Proxemics is the study of how human beings (mostly outside of awareness) structure microspace, the distance between people during their daily interaction, the arrangement of space in their houses and other buildings, and finally space arranged for utilitarian and aesthetic purposes in towns and cities. The anthropologist Edward T. Hall categorizes most of the types of spatial relations as *fixed features, semi-fixed features, and informal features.*[4]

1. *Fixed feature space* refers to how fairly permanent houses, schools, churches, office buildings, airplane terminals, department stores, restaurants, villages, towns, and cities are designed with or without conscious attention to how the space is to be used.
2. Humphrey Osmond, a physician who directed a health and research center in Saskatchewan, distinguishes between two basically different kinds of *semi-fixed spaces.*[4] *Sociofugal* spaces are those proxemic patterns that tend to drive people apart. *Sociopetal* spaces are those that

encourage people to stay close together, such patterning of spaces literally pushing people together.

3. The patterning of *informal space* involves how individuals maneuver
proxemic patterns while they are relating to one another. Individuals
use informal space within the categories of *intimate, personal, social,*
and *public* distances.

We use the *intimate-close* for love-making, wrestling, comforting, groom-
ing, and protecting. At this distance we perceive the greatest amount of sensory output. We feel body heat, smell personal odors and breath, and touch all
parts of the body. While the senses of smell, taste, and touch are greatest at
this distance, the importance of the sense of sight is diminished. Vocalizations
at this distance play a minor role, except in a paralinguistic fashion, and tone
of voice is more important than the semantics of any rational communication
in this proxemic sphere.

When we move to the *intimate-far* space of from six to eighteen inches, we
begin to use sight. Pores of the skin are enlarged, all blemishes are mercilessly
seen, and features like nose, lips, and ears are distorted. Unless the individuals
are extremely familiar, any extended communication in our culture at this
distance is extremely uncomfortable. Common expressions associated with
this distance reflect our uneasiness:

"You're so close to me I'm cross-eyed."

"He shook his fist right in my eye."

"Don't poke your nose into my business."

Within the *personal distance*, from one-and-one-half to four feet between
communicating persons, we can hold, grasp, hug, and touch each other. Close
friends of both sexes, husbands and wives, lovers, and relatives operate within
this sphere of contact.

We use *social distance*, from four to twelve feet, for business meetings and
impersonal social affairs. Receptionists in offices, people meeting around a
table to conduct fairly serious discussions, students and teachers in semi-
nar-fashion at a table or seated in a circle, and people at semi-personal gatherings all make use of the social distance. Usually we do not touch at this
distance, although people may shake hands or touch shoulders and elbows
before and at the end of the formal meeting. Social distance is a perfectly
appropriate spatial pattern for people conducting business or impersonal
social affairs with a maximum of effectiveness and a minimum of emotional
involvement.

Public distance, from seven to twenty-five feet or more, is reserved almost solely for one-way communication from a speaker or entertainer to an audience, the message being obviously more important than the opportunity to interact with another person. Certainly people in an audience can ask questions, heckle, applaud or react by sighing, moaning, or laughing, and this in turn can affect the speaker, but the interaction is different from that enjoyed within the intimate distance. Once the physical limits of the public distance were reached, however, the extensions of the ability to communicate—with the loudspeaker, the radio, and now television—made the public distance literally an infinite distance. Ironically, television has re-transformed the public distance of a speaker back into an intimate distance. A person on television can unconsciously elicit liking and trust from his viewers, and the viewers may, in turn, feel that they and the speaker are on intimate terms.

A Notation System for Proxemics

Before we can describe how people unconsciously pattern their living spaces, we need a simple but fairly accurate set of symbols for recording behavior. Anthropologists assume that the systems of any culture have a discernible structure which can be learned by its members. Obviously proxemic patternings—along with language, kinesics, and paralanguage—are picked up by all members of that culture. If proxemic patterns can be learned, then they must have a coherent organization and permit analysis and description. Hall has established eight classes for identifying the main categories of space relationships and for describing how man determines when and under what circumstances these relationships are to be employed.[5]

1. *Postural-Sexual Identifiers*. The sex and posture of individuals communicating make up the first category. The persons may be either male or female, and they may assume one of three positions: lying down or prone, sitting or squatting, and standing. Using a simple code, the numbers for a male prone, sitting or squatting, and standing are respectively 1, 3, and 5. The numbers 2, 4, and 6 are used for a female in the same positions. Thus a woman standing and exhorting her husband to take out the garbage, while he is sitting in his easy chair reading the evening paper, is 6, 3. For a boy and a girl lying on a beach, with the girl doing the talking, we use the numbers 2, 1.

2. *The Sociofugal-Sociopetal Axis*. As we have noted, the term sociofugal describes space arrangements that push people apart while the word sociopetal

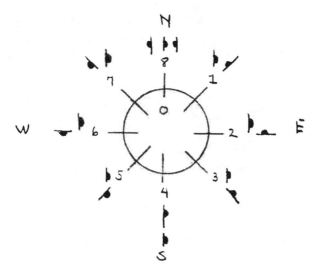

Sociofugal-Sociopetal Axis (SFP Axis)

identifies patterns that pull people together. We note the various positions that people may assume on an eight-point compass scale.

Both 0 and 8 are at the north position with 2 at the east, 4 at the south, and 6 at the west, with the intermediary points 1, 3, 5, and 7 intersecting these angles. Thus 0 represents two individuals face to face with maximum sociopetality, while 8 shows a sociofugal situation, with two people back to back. The number 2 symbolizes two individuals at right angles to each other. The number 4 stands for people side by side, watching something like a football or basketball game. The number 6 represents the position for disengaging oneself.

3. *The Kinesthetic Factors.* The notation system for showing the kinesthetic factors in human communication is based upon four ways of relating with the body. First, there may be touching with the head or trunk, symbolized by the number 1. Second, there may be touching with forearms, elbows, or knees, number 2. Third, there may be touching with the arms fully extended, number 3, and fourth, there may be touching with the arms and legs extended and the body leaning, number 4.

4. *Touching.* Once we note the kinesthetic factors, we can describe the amount and kind of touch that occur. The number 0 stands for caressing and holding; 1, for feeling or caressing; 2, for extended or prolonged holding; 3, for holding; 4, for spot touching; 5, for accidental touching; and 6, for no contact whatever.

5. *Visual Combinations*. We know very little about the part that eyes play during communication. For Hall, the structure of the retina serves as a model for a simple retinal code. *Foveal* vision provides a visual angle of only one degree, but what we see within that one degree is in incredibly sharp detail. The number 2 represents *macular*, or clear vision, with a vertical visual angle of about three degrees and a horizontal visual angle of approximately twelve degrees. The number 3 stands for *peripheral* vision of 180 degrees, and 8 is used for *no visual contact* at all. If a boy were being scolded by his father with the father staring at the boy, whose eyes are directed at the floor, the notation would be 2, 8.

6. *The Thermal Factors*. Although we have scant information about the effect of body heat upon human interaction, we are all aware that there are thermal differences in others and react accordingly. We note our awareness of changes in body heat by expressions like these:

"You turn me on."

"She kisses like a cold fish."

"She finally warmed up to me."

Such comments are more than casual remarks; they represent verbal expressions of basic physiological reactions to emotional situations and may be thought of as "behavioral fossils," which, in turn, represent the most primitive of communication systems. In any case, the number 1 represents conducted heat detected; 2, radiant heat detected; 3, heat probably detected; and 8, heat not detected.

7. *Olfaction*. Although Americans, because we frequently insist upon inordinate cleanliness, may have neglected our powers of olfaction, the chemical basis for smell is fundamental to interaction among many creatures. Male dogs seem to be able to smell a bitch in heat from miles away. Dogs also seem to sense fear in humans, possibly from body odors, when other signs may not be clear, and some psychoanalysts report that they can smell the distinctive odor of anger in patients at a distance of up to six feet. We report the relation of olfaction to communication by this notation system. Number 1 stands for differentiated body odor detectable; 2, undifferentiated body odor detectable; 3, breath detectable; 4, olfaction probably present; and 8, olfaction not present.

8. *Voice Loudness*. Voice loudness is the final factor in the proxemic notation system. For the most part we adjust voice loudness according to cultural norms. The number 0 represents silence; 1, for very soft; 2, for soft; 3, for normal; 4, for normal plus; 5, for loud; and 6, for very loud.

Now that we have described a system for noting proxemic behavior, let's examine a transaction between two women at a tea who are sitting at right angles to each other on a chair and on a couch. They are close enough to touch each other on the shoulders, arms or elbows, but they don't. They are viewing each other only peripherally since they are much too busy watching what is going on around them. They are not close enough to smell the other's breath, but their perfumes are detectable. Since there is a good deal of noise from unrestrained conversation, the speaker must raise her voice to an above the normal level.

Proxemic Notation

Sample Recorded Transaction: Two Women at a Tea

Category	Description	Code
1. *Postural-Sex Identifier*	Two women sitting;	4,4
2. *Orientation of Bodies*	able to see each other at right angles;	2
3. *Kinesthetic Factors*	close enough so that hands can reach shoulders and elbows;	202
4. *Touch Code*	touch does not play any part;	6
5. *Retinal Combinations*	woman speaking, looking peripherally at partner; partner also viewing speaker peripherally;	3,3
6. *Thermal Code*	not close enough for radiant heat to be detected;	8
7. *Olfaction Code*	breath is not detectable, but perfume is;	4
8. *Voice Loudness Scale*	voice normal plus.	4

If I Don't See What You Mean, I'm in Trouble

Scholars from many fields continue to study extraverbal systems. Though the researchers use different terms and techniques for collecting this data, they all appear to draw the same general conclusions: mankind must come to be aware of his extraverbal systems. In one shuts himself off from his own senses, if he disregards what we call proxemics, he does so at his own peril. Literally, he must see and taste and feel and smell what his fellow man means. If he doesn't, he's in trouble, both physically and psychologically, for the chief distinguishing characteristic of a mentally ill person is his inability to communicate with other creatures by words or by extraverbal means.

Tactile communication for instance, one of the most elemental of man's communication systems, plays an important part in personality development. Lawrence K. Frank hypothesizes that if human infants do not enjoy wide and varied tactile experiences, they will lack a reservoir of events upon which to develop the ability to communicate with others.[3] Rather than being able to draw upon a reserve of touch experiences, which will allow them to construct an accurate picture of the world, they will have to rely on what others— their parents and later their teachers and other authority figures—tell them is the accepted meaning of what they perceive. Such children either submit to authority figures or react in an opposite fashion and rebel against all rules.

A team of ethologists under the direction of Michael Chance in Birmingham, England, studied the relationships of proxemics to communication with large groups of nursery school children between three and five years of age.[1] The researchers found that the children formed small groups, fought with other children, and played games, largely on the basis of extraverbal signals; words played only a small part in their activities. Brannigan and Humphries, who reported the studies, concluded that we can use a knowledge of extraverbal communication to help people whose verbal communication systems are inadequate or have broken down completely, as in serious mental illness.

Mental disease is intimately associated with disturbances in sign behavior, language, and overall communication according to the psychiatrist Jurgen Ruesch.[5] Ruesch found patients with disturbances of a milder nature unable to talk easily but those patients who couldn't use nonverbal means of communication exhibited the most severe and long-lasting mental illnesses. People who cannot function in society—who find that their communication systems have broken down—lack the ability to use nonverbal signals, to use verbal signals, or to use both kinds of signals simultaneously in natural interaction. In extreme mental illness, such as psychosis, the most successful kinds of therapy are those aimed at providing for nonverbal expression—music therapy, psycho-drama, dancing, play, occupational therapy, and activities directly related to the senses such as wet packs, baths, and massage.

Although scientists have described many of the aspects of extraverbal communication and have provided us with techniques for analyzing what we see in a consistent fashion, novelists and poets—some more extensively and profoundly than others—have frequently made us aware of extraverbal systems and how they affect interactions. One such account is found in William Styron's *The Confessions of Nat Turner*.[9] Nat Turner, a young, well-educated black slave in Virginia in 1831, is taking his young mistress, Miss Margaret

Whitehead, by buggy to her friend's house down country. Nat and Margaret have grown up together, and although Nat is a slave he can read and write and appears intelligent and sensitive. Margaret and he have frequently talked at length. During the ride, Nat noted her hand close to him and "sensed her eyes again, the saucy tilt of the dimpled chin, her face turned, poised, waiting." When Margaret told Nat of an argument she had had with a girlfriend over the question of freeing the slaves in Virginia, her voice was "grave, pensive, filled with a kind of ample, questing, hurtful sorrow." Nat answered in a "tone of humility." When Margaret talked about the plight of the blacks, her voice "changed abruptly, the quality of lament still there but now edged with indignation."

As they rode along, Nat sensed her physical proximity. "Her closeness, her presence stifled me, even now as the summer air flowed past my face, wafting toward me an odor—a disturbing smell of young-girl-sweat mingled with its fine sting of lavender. I tried to inch myself away from her but was unable to, found instead that I could not avoid touching her nor she me, elbow lightly kissing elbow. With a longing that made me wet beneath the arms, I ached for the ride to be finished ... Again I smelled the warm-girl-sweat, sensed her presence, soap, skin, hair, lavender."

They stopped the buggy and walked across a dry field and through a patch of woods to a brook for a drink. Nat smelled the "ferny coolness" and the "sharp bittersweet odor of rosin" and "felt the pine needles underfoot." For Nat, "the closeness, the stillness, the seclusion here created once more a voluptuous stirring in my blood. I turned now to guide her by my glance, and for an instant her eyes met mine unflinchingly, not so much coquettish as insistent—inviting, daring, almost *expecting* my gaze to repose in her own eyes while she prattled blissfully on. Although as brief and fleeting as the space of a blink, it was the longest encounter I could remember ever having with a white person's eyes."

As Margaret moved from the side of the stream, she tripped and fell against Nat, "clasping" his arms, "with her still-wet hands." He grabbed her shoulders, smelled "her skin and her closeness," and felt "the electric passage across" his cheeks of "strands of chestnut colored hair. During that moment I heard her breathing and our eyes met in a wayward glint of light—that seemed to last much longer than any mere glance exchanged between two strangers journeying of a summer afternoon to some drowsy dwelling far off in the country."

Although the messages of prohibited longing and attraction for each other could not be expressed in words, they were unmistakably conveyed through the extraverbal systems—by the tone of voice, by physical contact, and by scent. The message was made unequivocably apparent through the basic and primitive modes of nonverbal communication. Both the profundity and limitations of extraverbal communication are beautifully expressed here.

References

1. Brannigan, Christopher & Humphries, David. I See What You Mean ... *New Scientist*. May 22, 1969, 406–408.
2. Darwin, Charles. *The Expression of Emotions in Man and Animals*. Chicago: The University of Chicago Press, 1965.
3. Frank, Lawrence K. Tactile Communication. *Communication and Culture*, ed. Alfred G. Smith. New York: Holt, Rinehart & Winston, 1966, 199–209.
4. Hall, Edward T. *The Hidden Dimension*. Garden City: Doubleday & Company, 1969.
5. Hall, Edward T. A System for the Notation of Proxemic Behavior. *American Anthropologist*, 1963, LXV, 1003–1026.
6. Lorenz, Konrad. *On Aggression*. New York: Bantam Books, 1967.
7. Otto, Herbert A. New Light on the Human Potential. *Saturday Review*. December 20, 1967, 14.
8. Ruesch, Jurgen. Nonverbal Language and Therapy. *Communication and Culture*, ed. Alfred G. Smith. New York: Holt, Rinehart & Winston, 1966, 323–330.
9. Styron, William. *The Confessions of Nat Turner*. New York: Random House, 1966.

SECTION III

WRITING AND THE WRITING PROCESS IN THE CLASSROOM

As I've said previously, this section on writing is Robert's longest. Beginning with a piece written relatively late in his career, he makes another strong pitch for using the "writing process" or what was often called then, "the composing process" in the classroom if one wants students to become real and engaged writers.

Beginning with a review of the composing process from such important researchers of the time, including Peter Elbow, Janet Emig, and William Moffet, Robert synthesizes how "complex," the "discovery of writing is—like a juggler", Emig reminds us, students using the composing process *juggle* key elements all at once: message, audience, and tone in producing knowledge. Knowledge *follows* writing, Robert reminds us, not the other way around.

The second article, in reviewing teaching "fundamentals in teaching writing," Robert makes the very crucial point that, "we probably teach too much; talk too much about writing," rather than giving prompts and showing good models. These are the true "fundamentals" of teaching writing—modeling and giving good prompts.

In the next piece, Robert reviews the then-relied-upon brain/cognitive research in writing that espoused the notion of left/right hemispheres and speech/language, he makes a case for tapping into student's left brain, as it were, to tap into the creative, non-logical expression that writing creates.

In the "Albion writing project," an upstate New York school district in which Robert and several of his colleagues designed and delivered a model for a "longitudinal inservice" on writing, he found that the content that took the longest for the teachers participating in this in-service found to internalize were: how long the composing process really takes, and how beneficial the notion of sharing and peer conferencing really were on one's writing.

Following this in-service, Robert applies this knowledge in writing, "Setting up an effective writing program in the schools." Here, he first debunks myths about writing and the teaching of writing, then lays out the "essentials" of setting up a program, and ends, finally with a section called, "How to Get It Done."

And finally, in this section on writing, Robert talks about assessing attitudes towards writing, using an attitude scale he designed. Used widely after this publication in 1976, measuring "attitudes" around various content area tasks throughout the curriculum has become much more commonplace.

In sum, these 6 articles review essentially that which we are seeing today as a resurgence—in considering what we believe is important in teaching both teachers and students to write, and to write well. Bucking up against the so-called traditional models of writing as espoused by the accountability models that ask kids to deliver "quick fixes" in their writing, we are reminded that good writing takes time; it takes students to see that their own teachers are writing, and that the composing process is a complex process that produces knowledge, not the other way around.

· 7 ·

THE COMPOSING PROCESS AND ITS RELATIONSHIP TO THE TEACHING OF WRITING

Robert W. Blake (1980)

The composing process is not only related to writing. It *is* writing. I'll go even further. To paraphrase a competitor admire a great deal, the composing process isn't *everything* to do with writing; it's the *only* thing.

If you want to teach writing, then you need to do a lot of writing yourself, different kinds of writing in different modes for different audiences. You need to analyze what you do as you compose; then you need to arrange what you do in the writing classroom to reflect this internalized knowledge about how people compose with words. If you don't follow some sort of process like this, you will be needlessly frustrated as you set out to discover how to teach others to write well.

Understanding Composing in Writing

Why do you need to understand the composing process? Most importantly, if you know about the stages in composing, this knowledge will help to dispel myths about writing.

Many textbooks on writing state or imply that to write, you must first make a detailed outline, find out exactly and completely what you want to say, and simply write out what you now know. But experienced writers tell you this isn't at all what they do. E. M. Forster, the novelist, made this now classic statement about how with him knowledge didn't precede writing but followed it. "How do I know what I think until I see what I say?" John Updike, the novelist and poet, put it this way: "Writing and re-writing are a constant search for what one is saying." And William Stafford, the poet, describes how his writing is discovery, not simply writing out what he already knows. "I don't see writing as communication of something already discovered, as 'truths' already known. Rather, I see writing as a job of experiment. It's like a discovery job; you don't know what's going to happen until you try it!" (cited in Murray, 1978, p. 103).

I'm aware that the writers I've marshalled to support my point write chiefly poetry and fiction, what we traditionally call "creative writing". Isn't that quite different from the types of writing we teach in the school classrooms, those being chiefly expository and persuasive? It surely is, but the fact remains that writers of exposition and writers of fiction and poetry describe composing in a similar way. Here, for instance, is a college writing teacher, Peter Elbow, in his provocative and useful little book, *Writing without Teachers*, explaining the composing process in writing. Says Elbow:

> The commonsense, conventional understanding is as follows: Writing is a two-step process. First you figure out your meaning, then you put it into language. ... This idea of writing is backwards. That's what causes so much trouble. ... Only at the end (of writing) will you know what you want to say or the words you want to say it with. You should expect yourself to end up somewhere different from where you started. *Meaning is not what you start out with but what you end up with.* (Italics mine) (pp. 14–15)

That statement is the exact opposite of the traditional notion of writing. But what Elbow and the others say about writing is true. People—students included—do write to discover meaning.

What, then, is the composing process in writing? How do we use it as the basis for a writing program in the schools?

In general terms, composing in writing—like composing in drawing, painting, or music—is a complex process in which thinking, feeling, and performing a physical act, like handwriting or typing, are all interrelated. Janet Emig makes a convincing case for the crucial connection among the hand, eye, and brain (1978). During the composing process, while the writer's hand, eyes and brain interact to produce a piece of writing, the writer, like someone playing three-dimensional chess, needs to keep in mind virtually simultaneously the key elements of message, audience, writer's role, focus, and structure, while, at the same time, she or he moves forward as well as backwards, sometimes circling with words, sentences, and larger structures, in which the unconscious mind may be as influential as the conscious intellect, acts leading to a piece which the writer many times may not be able to explain until she or he has worked completely through a draft. Indeed, the composing process is so complex and mysterious and yet, in many apparent ways, such a natural human process, that some individuals hold simply that writing is thought made visual by written symbols. Supporting this notion, James Moffett defines writing as the revision of an individual's inner speech and quite flatly states that writing "is nothing less than thinking" (1979, p. 278).

Stages in the Composing Process

There are many schemes for describing the composing process. In her seminal study of how senior high school students write, *The Composing Processes of Twelfth Graders*, Janet Emig describes these stages: 1. Context of Composing, 2. Nature of Stimulus, 3. Prewriting, 4. Planning, 5. Starting, 6. Composing Aloud (a special stage related to her study), 7. Reformulation, 8. Stopping and 9. Contemplation of Product (1971). Donald Murray identifies Prevision, Vision, and Revision (1978). James Britton labels these stages in the process: Conception, Incubation and Production (1975). There are other descriptions, of course, but I have found for the purposes of school instruction the following scheme to be simple, fairly accurate, and readily understood by both students and teachers. My categories are Prewriting, Drafting, Revising, and Editing.

Even though we label stages in the composing process and know something about what they are like, it doesn't mean we fully understand what goes on during these stages. For instance, the subconscious mind may have a far greater role to play during writing than most people—other than professional poets and novelists–realize. Let me explain what I mean.

If we review the work done by neurosurgeons, psychiatrists, and psychologists, as reported in the general literature dealing with what is commonly called "right-left brain research," we find information about the workings of the human brain, which, in turn, teaches us how people create in writing. Robert Ornstein, one of the interpreters of this research, presents in his book, *The Psychology of Consciousness*, a review of the findings of right and left brain hemisphere operation (1972).

According to Ornstein, our brains are divided into two parts. The left hemisphere controls the right side of the body, the right hand, so to speak, and it deals with those mental activities we might label as *intellectual*. The operations include analyzing and thinking logically, especially with words and mathematical symbols, and handling information sequentially. States Ornstein: "This mode of operation of necessity must underly logical thought, since logic depends upon sequence and order. Language and mathematics, both left-hemisphere activities, also depend predominantly on linear time" (p. 67).

The right hemisphere, on the other hand, controls the left side of the body, the left hand, to continue the metaphor, and is responsible for activities we might label as *intuitive*. This right hemisphere handles information, not in a sequence, but appears to grasp reality all at once, as a whole. Ornstein describes the activities of the right hemisphere as learning with the "left hand": "If the left hemisphere can be termed predominantly analytical and sequential in its operation, then the right hemisphere is more holistic and relational, and more simultaneous in its mode of operation" (p. 68).

That's what men of science say about two general functions of parts of the brain dealing with language. Such an observation is amazing enough, but what is more uncanny is that experienced writers report that when they write, they go through mental stages which are strikingly like the two modes of consciousness pictured by the scientists. Too many writers to be discounted talk about at least two distinctly different stages in the composing process. The first, they report, is unconscious, personal, irrational, intuitive, the stage of thinking, meditating, recreating dreams, of producing a first draft without concern for mechanics, of relying on their individual muse or daemon or personal inner voice to lead them in writing where it will. After this initial, subconscious stage when the "left hand" is in control, the "right hand" takes over. Once they have produced the first draft, the writers then become conscious, impersonal, rational, and intellectual, as they revise the words which originally seemed to pour out of them.

Experienced writers describe what they do after they have moved through the prewriting stages and have a draft before them. F. Scott Fitzgerald, in notes made when he was writing *The Great Gatsby*, reported that he wrote out by hand the entire first draft of the novel and then set out to revise it, line by line, word by word. In a recent advertisement for International Paper Company on "How to Write with Style," Kurt Vonnegut says this about revising: "*Have the guts to cut. ...* Your rule might be this: Be merciless on yourself. If a sentence, no matter how excellent, does not illuminate your subject in some new and useful way, scratch it out" (1980).

We know, then, what experienced writers do as they follow through the stages of the composing process. If you write a lot yourself, and, after you have written, analyze what you do as you move from an idea or image to a finished piece of writing, I'm confident you'll discover you're following the same sort of process.

What do you do to help your students use the process as they write? First, you need to make them aware of the stages. The first stage of writing, you might tell them, is a period of "incubation" or "gestation," quite literally a time before birth, a time for seeing an image in a dream, a time for developing seemingly unrelated ideas and feelings into a plan, however tentative, for first draft writing. Throughout this stage, writers draw upon their knowledge, past experience, and relations with human beings and with other creatures as the raw material for a draft.

During this stage, encourage your students to rely on their personal, creative powers, trusting that one word will lead to another. To help them comprehend this step, make available to them quotes like this one by William Stafford:

> To get started I will accept anything that occurs to me ... If I put down something, that thing will help the next thing come, and I'm off. If I let the process go on, things will occur to me that were not in my mind when I started. These things, odd or trivial as they may be, are somehow connected. And if I let them string out, surprising things will happen. (p. 44).

Go on to point out that experienced writers spend as much as forty to fifty percent of their time for pieces with the prewriting stage and that they should not expect things to go much differently for them.

Once they have an idea of this stage, you need to supply them with situations for prewriting in the classroom. The following are some activities I've found useful at different times.

Activities for the Prewriting Stage

1. *Free Writing*. Use free writing with your students to get them started with the physical act of writing, which in turn tends to trigger more writing. For Peter Elbow, the "most effective way ... to improve your writing is to do free writing exercises regularly. At least three times a week" (p. 3). With free writing, your students take pencil to paper and start writing anything that comes to mind for a specific period of time, from ten to fifteen minutes. Don't let

them stop for anything during the period, not even to think about a partic-ular word. If they can't think of the right one, then they may leave a blank. Certainly they are not to check correct spellings or bother with punctuation. And, of course, make it clear you're not going to grade this free writing.

The idea of free writing is simply to get the student moving the pencil across the paper until an image, idea, or even a pattern of ideas appears; the image, idea, or pattern then becomes something for the student to continue writing about.

Free writing is not all there is to writing instruction. It's only a specialized technique for getting people started.

2. *Remembering.* Encourage your students to cultivate their memories, to rely upon their past experiences as the single richest and most important storehouse of raw material from which to draw for writing. They need to be trained, as experienced writers have trained themselves, to extract this raw material from their minds, like a miner digging gold nuggets from deep in the earth. Or a better simile might be that the memory is like a subterranean lake of clear fresh, life-giving water, an almost limitless pool from which ideas and feelings continue to flow.

Here are questions for them to ask themselves.

What was my earliest memory?

What was my first house like? What's my chief image of my house?

What do I remember most about my mother, my father?

What did I fear the most as a child, love the most?

3. *Asking and Answering Questions.* Try to get your students used to listen-ing to what they have to say to themselves, to have them make their inner voices external through words. Have them learn literally to talk to themselves, probing their memories and minds with questions about their ideas or feelings.

Is this what I mean?

What else should I include?

Is this logical? Does this make sense? What else should I know about this?

4. *Noticing How Things Change.* A fundamental technique for learning about the world is noting how things change.

How did my friend that I want to write about change over the last few months when her parents were being divorced?

How has my family changed? My town or city?

How has the treatment of women changed in the last ten years?

5. *Contrasting.* We learn about one thing by contrasting it with something else.

In what specific ways is this different from that?

How is junior high different from senior high?

Soccer from football?

How do the roles of men and women differ in our society?

6. *Reading and Taking Notes.* Reading and reacting to what you read by jotting down notes on the reading is a time-honored means of interacting with another mind, with getting your ideas to bounce off the words of another. Students should get used to reading newspapers, magazines, pamphlets, and books for new positions dealing with topics they want to write about. It's useful for them to outline and summarize the ideas they find, chiefly so they'll understand them, but sometimes they need to make personal and critical comments as well on their reading.

That doesn't sound right to me.

I wonder where she got that idea.

Boy, is this writer biased.

7. *Writing Dialogue.* Have your students write dialogue. Dialogue is, of course, necessary for fiction, but dialogue can also be used to articulate varied points of view on a controversial issue, to help students become sensitive to differing points of view, and to assist them in learning how to turn formal, academic prose into lively and immediate speech.

8. *Role Playing and Recording What Happens.* An extension of writing dialogue. People assume roles—usually conflicting—and spectators record what they say.

9. *Playing with Sentence Frames and Other Language Structures.* Such formal frames help students to gather and order details. Here is one kind of useful frame, employed successfully by Kenneth Koch for teaching school children to write poetry (1970).

I used to be _____, but now I am _____.

10. *Brainstorming.* With brainstorming, individuals say words related to a given topic—or to the words said—as fast as they can, while someone writes down what is reported. After the list of details is recorded, students may find a direction to the brainstormed words.

Remind your students that during this prewriting stage they may want to write just to find out the ideas and images which appear on paper. They will probably plan in some way before a first draft by making a scratch outline or by jotting down a short list of points. Whatever they do, they don't need a full-blown outline with heads and subheads. All experienced writers—sometimes before they start a draft and sometimes after they have written freely in order to find directions for a draft—do gather images, explore feelings, and order ideas; your students need to accept this preparation.

Writing the First Draft. Whatever has happened during the prewriting stage, the writing of the first draft is an often frightening and intimidating time for the inexperienced writer. You should let your students know you accept this. Your major aim at this level is to provide an atmosphere supportive enough so the students will have removed for them as many roadblocks as possible, so they can get some words down on paper, even though they know in the backs of their minds that what they have written—ideas, openings, endings, or even entire pages–may change dramatically before the piece is completed. In a practical sense, you need to be there, like a long distance running coach or swimming coach, cheering your runners and swimmers on simply to finish the course.

No matter how experienced at writing they become, your students—like all other writers—will always feel the stark terror of a blank page. If they are to become effective writers though, they must get used to that sense of dread, and, rather than being paralyzed by it, go beyond the feeling to finish a draft.

Janet Emig advances three substantial reasons why writing out by hand a first draft is so crucial to the composing process (1977). First, the physical act of writing appears to trigger ideas and images—the raw material of language— from the brain. Second, the crafting of words on paper—like painting or draw- ing—gives some writers aesthetic pleasure. And third, we need to write out a first draft because that's the only way a part of our brain works, by stringing out words one after another on a page. We write out a first draft simply because that is how, as human beings, we must do it.

The decision to start writing a first draft may be likened to that moment when a well-trained athlete makes the decision to start competition. Have you ever watched a high jumper or pole vaulter as he or she decides to commit himself to action? Much like a finely tuned athlete, the writer must meditate, psyche himself or herself up, gather all his or her internal forces, and then make the decision to go for it, to start writing.

Phillip Lopate says that teaching our students this feeling of inner readi- ness, of knowing how to listen to one's own "energy voice," of recognizing this "absolute moment to write," of feeling ready to begin writing, may very well be the most important thing about writing we can teach them (1978). In fact, for Lopate, once we know inside that we are at that moment to start writing, we have probably solved two-thirds of the technical problems—focus, struc- ture, beginning, ending—with a piece.

How can you help beginning writers prepare themselves for starting and completing the first draft? Essentially, based upon the experiences they have had with the drafting stages, they need to be able literally to talk themselves through this stage, giving themselves pep talks and compelling themselves to keep on writing in spite of the quite normal gut feeling that what they're hacking away at is, without a doubt, the lousiest thing ever put down on paper. They must know, however, that they must pass through the first draft stage of lousy writing if they are ever going to produce anything worthwhile.

Here is advice they might give themselves during the frustration of the first draft.

Advice for Writers To Give Themselves During the First Draft

1. *Having Words Bounce Off Each Other.* Elbow calls the process of playing off ideas against summing up what the ideas seem to mean "cooking" (p. 73). If your students appear to have trouble with the balance between writing out words and thinking about what they mean, have them alternate the two activities. They can write for ten minutes and then sit back and see how what they wrote adds up. They might talk to themselves like this.

> Now that I've written that, let's see if I can find out
> what it means.
> What was I trying to say here?
> What's the main idea, focus, center of gravity here?

2. *Getting Started with Words on Paper.* Here are some suggestions, mostly from Elbow, for getting words down on paper.

> I'm going to write without stopping for exactly ten minutes and find out what happens.

> I'm stuck with this beginning. I've tried three different versions and none of them are right. Never mind, I'll write it through by brute force. If nothing else works, I'll start out with "What I'd like to write about is this _____." Whatever I start with will probably be cut out or revised anyway, so I'll just start in and then go back and fool around with the beginning after I've done the complete draft.

> I'm really stuck with this piece. I'm going to pretend that I have a half hour to write out what I'm trying to say to a friend. Here I go.

I'm still stuck. Nothing seems to work. My mind feels like mush, like hot oatmeal. I'd better do something else and then come back fresh. I've had enough experience with this stage to know I'm going nowhere. I'd better leave it and come back to it when I feel better.

3. *Other Advice for Writers During the Drafting Stage.* Don't worry about handwriting, punctuation, spelling, capitalization, format, or paragraphing right now. Just keep on moving. You can always go back. Trust yourself to find out what you want to say. Let your pencil do the talking.

Don't worry about how good it is now. It *will* be good. Trust yourself. What you're writing is important for you.

What you want your students to learn to say to themselves at this frustration stage is something like this:

"I've done a lot of work before the first draft. I've gotten together facts, dates, and specifics, read, talked to some people, made notes, thought about what I want to write about, and have made some kind of scratch outline.

"No more stalling. It's time to begin."

Revising. "Rewriting," says Mario Puzo, as one of his Godfatherly Rules for Writing a Bestselling Novel, "is the whole secret to writing."

Your students must not continue to believe, like all inexperienced writers, that after they finished a first draft and made some minor corrections, that the composing process is over, that they can now "copy it over in ink." But the more they write, the more they know a new kind of work, far different from the spontaneous, intuitive activities of prewriting and drafting, remains. During these first two stages of writing, he or she listened only to self as the writer. Now the writer must think about what the audience will make of the writing and rely on his or her conscious, rational self, and with ruthless calculation, revise the writing so another can read it without obstruction, so there will be no barrier to communication. Donald Hall sums up well the stance a writer must assume at this stage: "The attitude to cultivate from the start is that revision is a way of life." Revision, your students must come to accept, goes with the writer's turf.

Just what is revision? How do we talk about it? Donald Murray describes two kinds of revision. *External revision*—what I call editing—has to do with all matters related to proofreading, such as spelling, punctuation, capitalization, and usage. *Internal revision* for Murray, on the other hand, has to do with major changes in a draft, including changes in content—mostly adding specific details or examples—changes in form and structure, changes in language, and even changes in point of view or voice (1978).

Your students need to learn that when they revise, they make more or less conscious decisions about altering significantly what they have written in the first draft. They tinker and reformulate. They rearrange words, trying one word in place of another, possibly replacing it with the original. They tighten up by cutting out unnecessary phrases and clauses. They can change the design of an entire piece by throwing away an extensive opening, moving complete sections around, or substantially revising an ending because the original structure had changed during the writing. They might rewrite the entire piece, changing the tenses of all verbs, switching the point of view, or altering the overall tone of the composition. Or they may even, in some cases, abandon the first draft altogether, at least for the time being, to turn to something else which flows more easily.

After they have produced a first draft, it's necessary that the students get feedback about the piece from somebody who can be viewed as being honest and knowledgeable—what I call a "trusted reader." This can best be done by having the student writers read aloud their drafts in pairs or in small groups of from four to five students. The groups need to be small enough so the writers won't be inhibited by listening to feedback about their writing. The feedback is crucial because it lets the students have an audience, allows them to realize how others perceive their writing. The subject of workshopping and of providing guidelines for the students to follow is a matter of enormous importance. You might, as a start, pursue these writings: Beaven (1956), Blake (1976), Elbow (1973), Macrorie (1980), and Rogers (1961).

Here are some specific activities for you to have your students engage in as they listen to each others' drafts as they read them out aloud in small workshop groups.

Activities for the Revising Stage

1. *Finding Striking Parts*. Elbow calls this "pointing" (pp. 85–86). Have students "point out" words or phrases which struck them as beautiful, true, or somehow unusual. Pointing also means noting words or phrases which are especially tried or worn out. Rather than use the pejorative terms "cliche" or "trite"—which is what they are—I call them "easy shots."

What word or phrase stood out most clearly in my mind?

What word or phrase have I heard many times before? "nice guy," "tall, dark, and handsome," "in the nick of time," etc. How can I rephrase it so it's new and fresh?

2. *Finding the Focus.* This is what Elbow calls the "center of gravity." What's the focus?

What dominant impression do I get of this piece? What is the main feeling or most important idea the writer is trying to convey to me?

What one sentence sums up the piece for me?

What one word from the piece summarizes the main idea?

What one word not in the piece summarizes the piece for me?

3. *Determining Structure.* Within this category students ask and answer questions designed to help both readers and writer to see how the piece is put together.

What's the plan of the piece?

How does it fit together?

Can I see the parts clearly?

Do the opening and ending relate to the whole piece? To the focus?

Is there a cyclical or rhythmic pattern to the parts?

4. *Perceiving Unity.* Essentially, here the students want to relate whether or not the parts relate to the whole.

Have I left out unnecessary or irrelevant stuff? From the whole piece?

From paragraphs or even from sentences?

5. *Achieving Coherence.* With these questions the students try to find whether or not parts lead smoothly one to another.

Have I used devices like repetition of key words or technical devices like transitional words (first, second, therefore, and nevertheless) or have I used key pronouns? Does the writing—sentences as well as paragraphs—proceed smoothly?

6. *Choosing Exact Words.* The traditional term for this category is *diction*. Have I used general words like "nice" and "big" where specific ones are needed?

Have I used big, "schoolish" words where simpler words would be more in keeping with what I'm trying to say?

Have I sometimes used synonyms for a key word?

Or, have I used the same word over again when repetition is called for?

Am I unsure about what words I want to use, or do I know exactly which words go where?

7. *Varied Sentences.* A sign of a mature writer is the ability to use a variety of sentences in his or her writing.

Have I written sentences that are easy and even fun to read?

Have I sometimes combined short, choppy sentences into longer but still readable ones?

Have I, at other times, balanced long, complicated sentences against short and direct sentences?

Have I used my own judgment in revising sentences so they are interesting and occasionally surprising?

8. *Finding the Best Balance Between Specifics and Generalizations.* Effective writers use details and examples to support statements but frame generalizations to give shape to a mass of details. Both specifics and generalizations are important for effective writing.

Have I found enough details to support my thesis?

Does my thesis—implied or stated—support the details I have gathered?

9. *Using Words Related to the Senses.* Words related to the senses give a rich sense of immediate experience.

Have I used words which make the reader experience the senses of smell, touch, taste, and hearing as well as that of sight?

10. *Showing. Not Telling.* Rather than *telling* that the person is happy, the experienced writers knows he or she makes a situation dramatic by *showing* a specific girl as she laughs, claps her hands with delight, and exclaims, "Wow! I feel great!" Have I used details related to the senses, anecdotes, and examples to make my writing vivid, colorful, dramatic, and immediate?

11. *Effective Openers and Satisfying Endings.* Openings and endings are often the most difficult parts of compositions to get just right, and students need to realize these parts never come easily; they must be worked on and worked over before they do the job.

How does the piece open? Does it grab the attention of the reader with an anecdote, a dramatic quotation, or a provocative example?

Does the ending satisfy? Not merely by summarizing what was written before but by leaving the reader with a sense of completeness, with the satisfaction of feeling, "Yes, that's the way this should end."

Editing. Perhaps for experienced writers, there are only three stages to composing in writing: prewriting, drafting, and rewriting and rewriting until one stops. Some writers report they never stop revising until the piece is in print. As one writer commented, "I never stop rewriting. I just let the piece go."

From time to time, your students need to learn how to edit a piece, to prepare it for print. This means that, however distasteful for them, they must observe conventional editing procedures, bringing a paper to as nearly a perfect state as possible. They should learn to be satisfied with nothing less than what editors call "good, clean copy."

The common elements in editing—at least at the simplest level—are these conventional manuscript format, correct capitalization, spelling, punctuation, and what is traditionally known as acceptable "grammar and usage."

During this editing state—as with all but the drafting stage—students can help each other. One student can read his or her paper aloud to another, with both of them pointing out errors. Or one student can read to himself or herself a revised manuscript and mark with a pencil all mechanical errors. Several students may take turns editing each others' papers. Or you, as the teacher, can make a quick reading of a students' paper, catching as many mechanical errors as you can. Remember, the more errors you pick up before the last draft, the fewer superficial mistakes you'll be bothered by when you read the final manuscript. As a teacher of writing, your job is not to proofread; that task belongs to the writer.

Here are some simple activities related to the editing stage.

Activities for Editing

1. *Conventional Format.* Have I followed conventional manuscript format? This means I must write on one side only, on 8½ x 11" paper with a pen that does not smudge or blur, or type double-spaced with wide margins all around, on paper which takes writing or typing well (not erasable bond). Have I identified my paper by writing my name, date, title, and the course name—if my teacher wants it—on the first page?

The students should realize that the originality of their papers lies not in the format, mechanics, or in the paper's appearance, but in its content.

2. *Mechanical Errors.* Have I corrected all errors in spelling, punctuation, capitalization, and standard usage?

3. *Proofreading.* Have I made one last reading of my paper to pick up careless errors in handwriting or typing in the final draft?

Teach students to listen to their inner speech and to put down what they hear on paper. Teach them to follow the composing process, for composing *is* the curriculum. It is a model for seeing, thinking, perceiving, writing, and interacting with other human beings. Writing through composing is a model which actually defines us as human beings.

THE INSTRUCTIONAL COMPOSING PROCESS

Model for Creating Writing Lessons
Type of Writing _____
Title of Writing Activity _____

Grade Level _____ Teacher _____

The Instructional Composing Process Format

General Approach	Specific Application
1. Stimulus	– an idea to which students may react; may be in the form of a film, picture, reading, discussion, or experience.

PREWRITING

2. Prewriting	– opportunity for students to explore the stimulus; may be discussion, research, study guide. Should focus on specific areas (e.g. conflict, character, setting, etc.) preparatory to writing.

DRAFTING

3. First (rough) draft	– concerned with getting thoughts on paper, not with revising or editing.
4. Skills Instruction (optional)	– work on one or two specific skills, e.g., workshopping, end marks, agreement, commas. Use students' own works as much as possible. Allows students to apply skills instruction immediately.

REVISING

5. Revising/ Workshopping	– opportunity for students to examine their writing and share ideas with others before writing the final draft. Often works best moving from pairs to small groups to whole class. Concentration should be on total discourse and specific skills to be developed.

EDITING

6. Second (Final)	– incorporate suggestions from workshopping and concepts from skills instruction.
7. Submission	– for reaction, not grade. Unless the student has not revised or incorporated skills instruction in this draft, the student should not rewrite it.

Bibliography

Beaven, Mary. "Individualized Goal Setting. Self Evaluation, and Peer Evaluation," *Evaluating Writing*. Urbana, Illinois: NCTE, 1977, pp. 135–156.

Blake, Robert W. and Frederick B. Tuttle, Jr. *Composing As The Curriculum: A Guide for Instruction in Written Composition, Grades K-12*. Albion, NY: Albion Public Schools, 1978.

———— "Writing for the Left Hand: Writing Activities for the Intermediate Grades." *Facilitating Language Development*. Buffalo, NY: State University of New York at Buffalo, 1978.

———— "How to Talk to a Writer, or Forward to Fundamentals in Teaching Writing," *English Journal*, Vol. 65 (November, 1976), No. 8: 49–55.

Bradbury, Ray. "How to Keep and Feed a Muse." *On Writing. By Writers*, ed. William West. Boston: Ginn and Company, 1966.

Didion, Joan. "Why I Write," *The New York Times Book Review*, December 5, 1976, p. 98.

Elbow, Peter. *Writing Without Teachers*. New York: Oxford University Press, 1973.

Emig, Janet. "Hand, Eye, Brain: Some 'Basics' in Writing Processs," *Research on Composing*, ed. Charles R. Cooper and Lee Odell. Urbana. IL: NCTE, 1978.

———— "Writing as a Mode of Learning," *College Composition and Communication*, May, 1977.

———— *The Composing Processes of Twelfth Graders*. Urbana, IL: NCTE, 1978.

———— "The Uses of the Unconscious in Composing," *College Composition and Communication*, XV (February, 1964), 1.

Koch, Kenneth. *Wishes, Lies, and Dreams: Teaching Children to Write Poetry*. New York: Vintage Books, 1970.

Lopate, Phillip. "Helping Young Children Start to Write," *Research on Composing*. Urbana, IL: NCTE, 1978, pp. 135–149.

Macrorie, Ken. "The Helping Circle," *Telling Writing*. Rochelle Park, NJ: Hayden Book Company, Inc., 1980.

Mills, Hilary, "Creators on Creating: William Styron," *Saturday Review*, (September 1980), pp. 46–50.

Moffett, James. "Integrity in the Teaching of Writing," *Phi Delta Kappan*, Vol. 61 (December, 1979), No. 4: 276–279.

Murray, Donald M. "Internal Revision: A Process of Discovery," *Research on Composing*, ed. Charles R. Cooper and Lee Odell. Urbana, IL: NCTE, 1978.

Ornstein, Robert E. *The Psychology of Consciousness*. New York: Penguin Books, Inc., 1972.

Rogers, Carl. "The Characteristics of a Helping Relationship," *On Becoming a Person*. Boston: Houghton Mifflin Company, 1961.

Stafford, William. "A Way of Writing," *Responding: Three*, ed. Robert Weinberger and Nathan S. Blount. Lexington, MA: Ginn and Company, 1973, pp. 44–46.

Vonnegut, Kurt. "How to Write with Style," Advertisement for International Paper Company, Elmsford, NY, 1980.

Welty, Eudora. "Review of Selected Letters of William Faulkner, *The New York Times Book Review*. February 6, 1977, p. 30.

· 8 ·

TEACHING IDEAS

Back-to-basics: How To Talk to a Writer, or Forward to Fundamentals in Teaching Writing

Robert W. Blake (1976)

What's basic in teaching writing? That—and I can't resist using the word again—is the basic question here. I've never believed spelling, capitalization, and naming parts of speech were the basics in writing anyway. Rather than going back to those so-called "basics," I'd rather move forward to what I'll call the *fundamentals* of writing.

How do I know what's fundamental in teaching writing? When I see a piece a kid has produced, I believe I know whether or not the teacher was concerned with the fundamentals. For example, it seems clear from the following composition that the student's writing teacher was interested mainly in the superficial elements of writing—the traditional "basics"—and the result, although mechanically correct, is a sterile and lifeless paper:

> *The first snowflake launches the sportsman into a flurry of cleaning, waxing, and readying his equipment for the joys ahead. The long hours of preparation pass quickly as he anticipates the first heavy snow. While he works, the skier sees himself conquering Nose Dive and hot dogging the North American. Perhaps this year he will ski Aspen. The tobagganer imagines happy shouts of his friends dragging the wooden moster toward the aroma of hot chocolate. The intent bobsledder checks and rechecks his equipment, knowing that carelessness could result in disaster.*

The next two pieces show what I think is *fundamental* to good writing. In the first piece, a ninth grade girl is not afraid to tell of her inability to communicate with others. And in the second piece, an eleventh grade girl writes a particularly personal letter—to accompany work she had written during the summer out of school—to an English teacher who has evidently earned the girl's affection and trust.

EXPRESS MYSELF
I try to talk, but no-one listens.
I give my opinions, but it's not worth it.

I listen, but no-one talks.
I try to be happy—but no-one's there.
I try to live—but no-one cares.

I don't really want to insult you by explaining any of it [her writing], but I do want to say something about the piece entitled "for her." It is, as you may have well guessed, an autobiography of my fears. It took a lot to write because, in doing so, I am in a way standing mentally naked in front of you. For me it is a personal contradiction. I am trying to break ties with people and trying to rely on my own inner strengths for support. In short, become more independent and keep my personal life and feelings inside me. By showing you this piece I am opening up myself so that you can see me. In some ways that makes me feel uneasy. I know that you will be gentle with it, with me. I don't feel that in the literary sense that any of these are triumphs. But then I don't know if that is what I'm striving for in writing.

So what's fundamental in teaching writing? Because we find writing a complex mental, social, psychological, and physical act, probably one of the most complex acts humans can perform, we may despair of identifying its fundamental properties. Some point to the mechanics of writing as the basics. Others beg the question with, "All writing is self taught." I don't agree with either position. I believe we can help almost everyone learn how to write if we pay attention to these five categories.

The Composing Process

Both the teacher and the student must go through the composing process and become intimate with it. What is composing in writing? It is at once logic and rationality and mystery and magic. When we compose in writing, we order what we see and think, the ordering affected by our intuition and unconscious.

On a simple level, when we compose, we gather our thoughts, write them in sentences, and then fool around with the sentences until they sound right. All writers—experienced or inexperienced—follow this general process.

Although composing in writing is an occult activity to those who haven't tried it, writers agree about its major characteristics.

Composing As Seeing Ourselves. Writers report that composing helps them to understand themselves. When we compose, we use written symbols to find out about ourselves, often in a fragmentary and unsatisfactory way, but the composing itself often helps us to see what events and people helped to make us what we are.

In this first draft composition, a young adult reveals forces that shaped his life, influences that he possibly wasn't aware of until he wrote them out.

A Childhood Experience

When I was little, I used to be sent to my grandmother's house for the summer. I hated it there. My brothers and sisters, who remained home, envied me for this visit I took annually, but I hated it. They envied the fact that I got to eat a lot of food, Italian food, while they ate only what was provided on the farm. You see, when I was young, my family lived with my mother's people, in Vermont. My mother is an Iroquois Indian and her family was poor. My grandmother, whom I visited, and who lived in Albany, was an Italian woman who I guess, would be considered middle class economically but who we thought was an extremely wealthy person.

I hated my summers with her. She would take me to stores and buy me little outfits to wear—with short pants and beany hat. She would show me off in front of her friends, make me do little tricks for them. She would make me bow, and do the alphabet, and the times table, and the capitols of the states.

She always gave me more than I could eat when she fed me and then hollered at me when I didn't finish—mentioning poor people in China who would give their lives for such a portion. What about the poor people in Winooski? She always told me that my family would be better off if my father moved us to Albany, where there was more work. She said my mother was to blame because she wanted to be near my father; I look a lot like my father when he was my age.

My grandmother gave me an allowance, 50¢, for emptying the garbage and washing off the stoop. I couldn't get dirty or she would holler at me. There was no place to play in Albany. The park was too far away to get to alone and I always got lost. Boys used to beat me up and make fun of the way I talked, because I was from Vermont. I hated summers at my grandmother's house.

Composing As an Experience of Discovery in Itself. When writers discuss composing, they report they literally don't know what they want to say until after they have written it out. Professional writers testify to this. E. M. Forster, the novelist, describes the act in this classic statement: "I don't know what I think until I see what I've said." Denise Leventov reveals how she composes a poem: "Writing a poem is a process of discovery ... you can smell the poem before you can see it—like some animal." But well known writers aren't the only ones to describe composing as an act of discovery. A beginning writer describes her experiences with the composing process like this.

My two most favorite (and perhaps best) pieces are the two situation descriptions. The first (sickhousewife) was a real-life situation that occurred to a friend who related it to me. I thought about it for a long time before writing, but it was the most spontaneous—the words just rolled onto the paper. It was the same with the last piece—the personality profile. The situation was well thought-through before writing, and I sat down and wrote it in about thirty minutes. I did some revision of both, but I didn't want to spoil them.

In many cases, we probably "teach" too much, talk too much "about" writing. Beginning writers don't realize that all experienced writers start composing to write. Students need to become aware of this. If they plan and think too much, they may well become paralyzed before a blank piece of paper. If they understand that all writers have the same feeling when they start composing, they may have enough courage to start writing themselves.

Past Experiences with Teaching Writing Affect Composing. How were you taught writing? How were your students taught writing? Did your students learn the composing process and were they encouraged to write about their personal experiences? Or were they taught to write only expository essays and business letters and led to believe the composing process was writing down one's ideas with the teacher finding and correcting all mechanical errors in red?

See how the instruction in writing these two young women had affected their attitudes toward writing.

In college my writing (Fresh. comp.) came back covered with red (I hate red pens!) and with few positive comments. My confidence went way down. I felt I did not have the talent to write anything except term papers. I continued to keep a journal but had no desire to ever write for a course again.

I have always been a compulsive writer—of letters and journals. (In junior high I even wrote a 300 page mystery a la Nancy Drew—which I threw away when my 9th grade English teacher intimidated me with the "proper" components of a story.)

Stages in Composing. If we want our students to go through the composing process, we must have firsthand knowledge of it. Unless we have gone through the composing process over and over, produced many kinds of writing, and wrestled with the problems our students face, we are in no position to help them understand what composing in writing means.

When asked to compose in a writing class, a high school English teacher told how her experiences with writing affected her idea about composing:

Writing is hard work. How many times have we heard this? We all smile and nod and never quite believe it's the agony it's made out to be. Well, I believe it now. Any teacher who understands this about writing has just got to have more sympathy for the student who encounters the paralyzing agony of facing a blank sheet of paper without confidence, without experience, and without encouragement for at least the attempt.

All writers go through certain creative rituals and insist on setting special conditions for themselves before they can start composing. Our students are no different. And they should know, as experienced writers do, that there are several stages in the composing process, stages through which they must pass before they can produce a piece of competent writing. Although experienced writers seldom label these stages, if we are going to help our students become conscious of them, we need rough labels to talk about them.

Prewriting. We may call this first stage "prewriting," "prevision," "incubation," or "gestation." The prewriting stage may cover minutes, hours, days, or even years. During this stage, we draw upon all of our experiences and relations with human beings and with other creatures as the raw material for our composing.

Planning. All writers order their ideas and feelings before they begin composing. The ordering ranges from detailed outlines to general categories carried in the head. One novelist outlined all the scenes for his novels and then fleshed out the scenes with narration and dialogue. Other writers of fiction start with a character only and let the character "write" the novel. John Updike, the short story writer, poet, and novelist, plotted scenes of one novel he was working on in church on Sunday mornings and wrote out the scenes during the week. Inexperienced writers also have different ways of planning and report different schemes for various kinds of writing.

First Draft Writing. Some teachers of writing call this the "zero" draft. Whatever the preparation—the planning and prewriting—this is the stage when the writer takes pencil or pen to paper or starts typing. It's best to say something like this to beginning writers at the first draft stage: "Now that you have thought out what you're going to write about, just go ahead and start writing. Don't worry too much about what it looks like right now. Remember, this is just a first draft and you will, of course, be revising it."

Rewriting. Because they have no experience with composing, beginning writers believe that after they have written the first draft and made some minor corrections the composing process is over. The experienced writer knows that a new kind of work, far different from the initial creative burst, remains.

Some writers see rewriting as the heart of the composing process and go so far as to maintain that all writing is rewriting. Whether that is true or not, students need to know what experienced writers do during the rewriting stage.

We can see what experienced writers do during the rewriting stage by studying their working manuscripts. In the following passage Budd Schulberg, himself a successful novelist, marvels at the diligence F. Scott Fitzgerald displayed while he revised the manuscript of *The Great Gatsby.*

Throughout the manuscript (and on through the galley revisions) one follows Fitzgerald's tireless quest for the mot juste *as he changes* shadow *to* silhouette, quickly *to* vigorously, he interrupted *to* he suggested, a sort of joy *to* a joyous exhaltation, looked *to* glanced, My house was on the tip of West Egg *to the more direct* I lived at West Egg.

As the inexperienced writers come to realize all successful writers revise, they should accept revision as a necessary step in composition, not some excruciatingly painful and useless assignment created by the teacher. Better yet, the students may now assess realistically the polished pieces experienced writers create, respecting the work they have accomplished during the rewriting. No longer are they intimidated by pieces that appear to be so perfect they do not understand the process by which they were produced.

Editing. Perhaps for experienced writers, there are only three general stages to composing: planning, writing, and rewriting—until one stops. For some writers, the rewriting never ends; as one writer commented on his rewriting, "I never stop rewriting. I just let the piece go."

For inexperienced writers, we should add the final stage of editing, of preparing the manuscript for print. But there are varieties of print. For our purposes, editing means bringing a manuscript to as nearly a perfect state as possible. We, and our students as well, should be satisfied with nothing less than what professional editors call "good, clean copy."

Students may edit their pieces for the school newspaper, the literary magazine, or for an anthology to be printed in ditto or mimeographed form for distribution to other students in a classroom. It is essential, in fact, that students do prepare some pieces for "print," so they can see the necessity for editing.

A final word which may anticipate a question: If the composing process is so tough, so time consuming, why bother with it? Why try to persuade students to do something so obviously difficult? It's not easy to give answers to these questions for people who have never tried writing. The most we can do is to be truthful about the exhilaration one enjoys from writing.

Here is what one high school English teacher had to say about the rewards of writing:

The writing assignments were great. I didn't produce much of value but I worked hard trying to say something in a fresh, exciting way. The work was necessary to understand the process. I now have a deeper respect for those who are creative and able to express themselves.

And an elementary school art teacher found the satisfactions from writing much like those to be enjoyed from painting or drawing.

The variety and approaches to writing that were utilized proved to be a very valuable personal experience. I discovered to my delight, the satisfaction received in expressing oneself on paper. Although most of the pieces I wrote came from personal experience, I found their development in words to be a very creative process. I approached many of our writing assignments in the same way I would create an idea in art. It was enlightening to see this comparison in two different "academics." This in addition to the heightening of my self-confidence in verbal expression were the greatest benefits derived from our assignments.

The "satisfaction" and "delight" the inexperienced writer receives from her composing are not far removed from the "happiness" the professional writer Erica Jong enjoys while she writes poetry.

With the process of writing the poem, there is a kind of connection which sustains one. Then the poem is done and one is alone again. Other people may enjoy the poem later, but the poet can hardly relate to it. The poet is happy only while writing the poem.

If only one could write all the time! If only there were not all those hours of non-writing to get through!

Varieties of Writing

Experienced writers don't need outside help with finding a topic to write about, what we call "subject." They have trained themselves to observe, listen to what people say, to read, to use their other senses, and to verbalize what they experience. But inexperienced writers, especially at first, do need help with discovering topics about which they can write.

I'd like to advocate a method for inciting students to write something like this. We might have them try writing on a wide range of topics in a number of forms, such as the critical and persuasive essay, figurative language, or short fiction. Only we won't tell them they're trying a certain type of writing. We'll show them student models—which will be far less likely to intimidate them than professional models—give them a minimum of directions about the assignment, and say, in effect, "Now, why don't you try a piece something like this? See how it works out. If you don't care for this particular assignment, though, then try something you do like better." After they have completed the assignment, we can label the form of the particular piece by saying in a casual manner, "Good work. If you're interested, we call this kind of paper a persuasive essay."

So we set up a series of assignments for the students to "try." Whatever they produce will be accepted and not condemned. Since they won't be overly worried about whether we will criticize harshly what they produce, they will gradually begin to assume responsibility for what they write. They will become more independent and more liable to defend what they create. At the same time, once our students begin to assess their own writing, they become their own severest critics. What they need more than ever at this stage—before they have gained confidence in their writing ability—is encouragement and deserved praise for the attempt, not criticism which they may see as attacks on them as persons.

As they continue with the "tries" in writing for which there is little risk, they gain confidence in their writing ability and are willing to try more and more ambitious writing, to take greater chances because they have only themselves to worry about liking their work.

What follow are some of the varieties of writing young adults can produce:

Spontaneous Writing. With spontaneous writing the student is told to write whatever he wants to without thought of "correctness" or a grade for a set period of from twenty to thirty minutes. This assignment is almost always successful in getting the student started at composing.

Gripe or Gratitude (Persuasive Essay). In the persuasive essay, the writer attempts to persuade an individual to do something for him. In writing of gripes and/or gratitudes the student must focus his writing on a particular audience, and he writes easily on a topic he feels deeply about.

Reaction to Something Read or Seen (Critical Essay). All persons have opinions about movies, TV programs, or books they have read and will react willingly as long as they are not overly concerned with the "proper" elements of the critical essay.

A Newspaper Story. Students may try different types of newspaper writing like the editorial, letter to the editor, sports story, human interest story, or feature story. From such assignments, the students become aware of the varieties of prose in daily newspapers and decide, on the basis of firsthand experience, which kinds they like or do not like to write.

Figurative Language. It is a mistake to separate "exposition" from "creative" writing. Figurative language pervades all successful writing, whatever we label it. When the students observe and become sensitive to figurative language, they are learning skills of writing which will serve them in all future composing.

Sense Recordings. Students can make notes of sights, sounds, feelings. The medium of the Haiku poem is ideal for sensory recording.

Character Description (Short Fiction). As the students describe, in writing, people they know intimately, they are acquiring skills of writing fiction. When they add conflict and dialogue to character description, they usually write, mostly unaware of the proper "form" of fiction, a short story. The skills of using narration and dialogue to show character relationships, like the use of figurative language, can be used with most kinds of writing.

Skills of Writing

Some teachers of writing believe students learn the skills of writing as they write. So the argument goes, as they write, they teach themselves to correct mechanical errors. Other writing teachers maintain students must practice writing skills in exercises and that when they write complete compositions, they will transfer those skills learned from exercises to writing error-free compositions.

The answer to how beginning writers acquire command of the skills of writing, I believe, lies somewhere between these two positions. Experienced writers, as usual, don't need anyone to tell them to revise sentences or to correct mechanical errors; they have learned to do so by much practice and constant attention to the writing process. The inexperienced writer, though, needs to become aware of certain categories of writing skills, especially in the rewriting and editing stages. But he must also be aware of the relative importance of a command of the mechanical skills of writing; it is a necessary part of the writing process but should never be mistaken for the process itself.

Here are some of the types of writing skills which beginning writers might need to practice in exercises.

Passive and Active Verbs.

Directions: Rewrite the following sentence so the passive verb is active.

Original: On Sundays, the table is surrounded by everyone, and a pleasant meal is enjoyed by all.

Revised: On Sundays, everyone sits at the table and enjoys a pleasant meal.

Openers.

Directions: Rewrite the following beginning sentences from a student composition. You may add words or clauses to do this.

Original: It was Wednesday night.

Revised: It was Wednesday night, and I was being followed down the street by a six-foot-ten-inch gorilla.

Overuse of Adjectives and Adverbs.

Directions: Revise the following sentence, cutting out adjectives and adverbs to improve the sentence.

Original: I blankly stared out into the distant sea.

Revised: I stared out into the sea.

Better Sentences

Although the ability to create a variety of well-formed sentences may appear to be one of the skills of writing, we might better consider it in a separate category.

We might ask, "Why separate exercises on creating varied sentences? Don't students learn how to write longer and more complex sentences by just writing?" Yes, they do. Research shows that with traditional instruction in writing, twelfth grade students do write longer and more complex sentences than do fourth grade students. But research also shows that with special language instruction in what we call *sentence combining*, students may advance in their ability to write longer and more complex sentences twice as fast as they normally would, showing two years of growth in sentence complexity in one year.

What do we mean by sentence combining? It is a term used to describe a process of combining short, basic sentences into longer, more complex ones. Sentence-combining problems reflect complex rules for producing sentences which transformational grammarians have developed over the last several decades. But what makes problems in sentence combining useful in the class-room is the fact that anyone can learn how to combine a wide variety of complex sentences without knowing any of the complicated terminology of transformational grammar.

In this sentence-combining problem, one basic sentence is embedded within another as a relative clause.

Base Sentences:	People should live with other garlic eaters.
	People eat garlic (Who)
Result:	People who eat garlic should live with other garlic eaters.

Students learn very quickly how to do this exercise and others like it. And they report they enjoy doing such language "puzzles," especially if they see the problems as games and have no trouble in working out the solutions.

We must make two reservations about sentence-combining problems. First, syntactic fluency is not all there is to writing well. No writing instruction program can be built on sentence-combining problems alone. Secondly, syntactic fluency should not be equated with writing style. Yes, experienced writers write longer and more complex sentences than do inexperienced authors. But experienced writers also show rhythm with their sentences, balancing short and long sentences, and students should learn how to use a variety of sentences in their writing.

Talking About Writing

What you say or write to students about their writing is crucial to how they approach writing, whether or not, in fact, they will go on composing in writing when they are no longer compelled to. What we say about their writing and how we say it is the basis of our relationships with our students as we all approach writing.

I have found the best way to talk to my students about their writing is based upon an assumption which goes something like this: "I know writing is hard, but once you learn how to write, it can be one of the most satisfying and exciting things a human being can do. Let me help you become an able writer. I will do my best to show you ways to improve your writing. I will teach you what I have learned about writing from study and extensive writing myself. But don't always count on me to tell you what or what not to do while you write. You must learn to make your own decisions about your writing. That's the only way you'll ever become a competent and maybe even an outstanding writer."

Here are some general guidelines which I have found useful to consider when talking to inexperienced writers.

Especially at the beginning, all of our comments are aimed at helping the inexperienced writers gain confidence in themselves as persons and as writers.

We must praise a great deal. We find at least one interesting word, phrase, or idea to note. Since the initial pieces are mostly "free association" and first draft writing which the student has produced simply to get something down on paper, they don't deserve extended comments anyway. For such initial, ego-boosting pieces, we might say or write comments like these.

Good start. Good observation. You might want to go on with this description.

You feel deeply, Susan, and have the ability to share your feelings with us. You may wish to describe this more fully.

You generate a lot of excitement here with your honest responses. Good work.

We don't need to make extensive comments on all aspects of the student's writing.

Remember that our comments are intended chiefly to help the student learn how to rewrite his compositions himself, not to provide detailed corrections. We want to place the burden—and excitement—of revision and proofreading on his shoulders, not keep them on ours.

We want to keep our comments in perspective. We note important things in our students' writing like honest reactions, fresh observations, sustained point of view, precise use of words, good openers, expert use of dialogue, or the generation of excitement.

But, of course, we don't react to all of these at once. We comment, of course, about lesser matters as well but convey the impression that we know they are of secondary importance. In this category of less important elements, I would include such matters as handwriting, spelling, capitalization, punctuation, and formal standard usage. Here are some of the things we might say.

You have really looked at the young tree in the courtyard and described it well. Now can you think of fresh, new ways to talk about it?

I get the impression that you really didn't know how to end this piece. Endings are always hard. You may want to try working this one over.

By the way, your handwriting is hard to read. Try to write larger, and don't cramp your letters together.

You seem unsure of how to use commas. Check with your handbook. There are only a few basic punctuation conventions. You should know them.

The next time double space and give yourself wide margins. This is hard to read, and it's hard for you to revise.

We should help our students see writing as the art of making choices. If I were to arrive at one phrase summing up writing, I would say, "making choices." As teachers, we move from suggesting rather simple and straightforward choices to recommending complex, overall choices that students might consider. But, as we offer alternatives, we never forget that our recommendations are only that, recommendations they may consider but may accept or reject on the basis of whether the substitutes seem right for them.

Here are some types of comments which may prod our students into making choices in their writing.

Have you noticed that you've used many formal words? I've underlined some. Why not substitute less formal ones? Do they sound better?

In the second paragraph you really get warmed up. You might cut out the first paragraph and find out how the second paragraph sounds as an opener.

Many of your sentences are long and involved. Why not try to break them up into simpler ones? How do they look and sound now?

What you have written is more poetry than prose. It's filled with images of specific plants and animals. The similes and metaphors are striking. Why not redo as a poem? Compress. Sharpen the images. Make sure the metaphors work. Don't try for regular verse, but break your lines where they seem natural for you. What you've written has so much promise, it's worth a try.

We should help our students find their voices.

As our students find out what they know best and feel most deeply about, they will be discovering their writing "voices." If we assist them with writing honestly, we shall find that virtually all the other problems encountered in writing will take care of themselves.

Here are some comments aimed at helping inexperienced writers discover their individual voices.

You love your grandfather very much, and your feelings come through. You might want to go on with this if for no other reason than to put down your memories on paper.

You really feel strongly about this issue, don't you? And you know what you're talking about, too. You might go on with this topic. Your special knowledge makes the subject fascinating.

I had never thought of fishing being so beautiful. You may like to work some more on this piece. You certainly describe the whole business with authority and flair.

Your voice comes through in this piece! And it's a strong, clear voice. Good work. Don't be afraid to show us who you are, what you stand for in your writing.

What happens when you move forward to fundamentals in teaching writing? What can we expect if we help our students write? If we support and encourage them? If we help them find that writing is a process, an act that can be broken down into its component parts and learned? If we talk to them about their writing so they see us as honest and trusting readers? If we train them to see their writing as the art of making choices with language? If we help them to discover through language what they are and what they might become?

Several things are likely to happen. I can almost guarantee it.

Our students will be able to write competently. Because they are writing about topics close to them, they will care more about their writing. They will write complete sentences; employ correct usage; spell, capitalize, and punctuate effectively; write legibly; and use acceptable conventions of format. Or they will themselves correct errors in these matters. And, interestingly enough, they will have no more trouble than the average adult with filling out job applications, driver license applications, or assorted questionnaires.

Our students will begin to observe life more fully. They will begin to see the world as the trained writer does. They will filter experiences through their senses and then analyze what they see, smell, touch, hear, and taste. They will work out structures from masses of seemingly unrelated details. They will bring some personal order to the chaos that surrounds them.

Our students will have a realistic idea of what the writing process is. Since they are now familiar with the frustration, loneliness, and pure drudgery of writing well, they will no longer fear the act. Also they will have a better understanding of what admired writers go through before they finish an essay, poem, short story, or play.

Our students will show confidence in their ability to write when they need to. Few of them will continue writing away from a situation where someone requests them to produce. But, since they have now written a variety of pieces, they are no longer paralyzed by the admonition, "Write a composition!"

Our students will know themselves better. They have learned—as have other writers before them—that they actually didn't know what they wanted to say until they had written it out. And they have discovered that one of the surest paths of self discovery is through words, especially through written words.

And finally our students will experience the joy of creativity. If we mean by creativity the ability to use words in a novel way to instruct or move other human beings, then all of us can create in words. It's a marvel to behold student after student, in his own unique way, construct sentences that are original, sometimes elegant, and frequently breathtaking.

· 9 ·

COMPOSING FOR THE LEFT HAND

Writing Activities for the Intermediate Grades

Robert W. Blake (1978)

The Right Hand, the Left Hand, and Luck

We all have dim feelings of the left hand being somehow sinister, unlucky, or at least odd. In fact, the word "sinister" comes to us from French by way of Latin, in which "sinister" meant literally "left" and therefore evil or unlucky. This was so because in augury—the ancient practice of foretelling the future by signs and omens—anything that took place on the left side was inauspicious.

Conversely, the word "dexter" in Latin, meaning "right" was lucky because signs that appeared on the right side were advantageous. People today who are "dextrous" are either skilled with the body and hands or are mentally alert. And persons who are "ambidextrous" are unusually agile; they have right-handedness with both the right and left hand.

But what has this to do with writing, you may ask. Or with pupils in the intermediate grades?

Please bear with me.

So the accumulated centuries of custom have established those activities related to the right hand as being lucky, skillful, and useful. But at the same time, folk wisdom also acknowledged a strange power flowing from the left hand. After all, "The left hand is the dreamer."

But is all this business with the right hand and the left hand reflecting two very different facets of our being only a bunch of old wives' tales?

If it is, then it appears that the old wives knew more than we gave them credit for.

The Right and Left Parts of the Brain and Two Ways of Behaving

For over a century, neurologists have been collecting evidence about how the "two modes of consciousness" as represented by the two hemispheres of the brain appear to operate. Only within the last decade or so, though, have neurosurgeons and psychiatrists confirmed that two dissimilar ways of behaving are directly related to two different parts of the brain.

Robert Ornstein (1972) summarizes the fairly recent state of thinking on the subject. The cerebral cortex of the brain consists of two parts, called hemispheres, which are joined by a bundle of interconnecting fibers known as the "corpus callosum." The two hemispheres control the opposite sides of the body. Thus, the right hemisphere controls the left side while the left hemisphere controls the right side.

All well and good, if the two hemispheres regulate general physical activities. They do. But that's not all they affect. The two hemispheres also control how we perceive our world. Even though both hemispheres may share the responsibility for various human activities, for most normal people the two parts of the brain have separate functions.

What do we know about how the two parts of the brain operate? The left hemisphere of the brain—it affects the right side of the body, remember, symbolized by the right hand—analyzes and thinks logically, especially with words and mathematical symbols and handles information sequentially. This is how Ornstein describes the function of the "right hand": "This mode of operation of necessity must underlie logical thought, since logic depends on sequence and order. Language and mathematics, both left-hemisphere activities, also depend predominantly on linear time." (p. 67).

So what remains for the right hemisphere to take care of? It regulates the left side of the body, of course, symbolized by the left hand. The right hemisphere handles information, not in sequence, like the other side of the brain, but grasps reality all at once, as a whole. We are told that it has little concern with language and appears to help us orient ourselves in space, directs manual activities related to painting and sculpture, and work with crafts, requiring handling of objects. Our ability to remember faces seems to lie with the right hemisphere. Ornstein describes activities of the "left hand" as follows: "If the left hemisphere can be termed predominantly analytic and sequential in its operation, then the right hemisphere is more holistic and relational, and more simultaneous in its mode of operation" (p. 68).

In essence, what do the findings generally reveal? That our brains are divided into two parts. That the left hemisphere of the brain controls the right side of the body, the right hand, so to speak, and that it deals with those mental activities that we might label as—and here I use Ornstein's word—*intellectual*.

That the right hemisphere of the brain controls the left side of the body, the left hand, and that it is responsible for activities that we might label—again Ornstein's choice of words—*intuitive*.

In case we might assume that one part of the brain directs activities which are "better" than the other, Ornstein cautions us that the two hemispheres indeed complement each other, that in every day life we simply choose the mode of consciousness appropriate for dealing with a particular situation. In fact, when we integrate the two modes of consciousness, when we combine intellect and intuition, we are most likely to achieve at the highest possible level.

Intellect and Intuition in Writing

That's what men of science say about the two modes of consciousness. What is uncanny to me is that professional writers, discussing what happens when they write, describe in their own terms two states of awareness amazingly like the two modes of consciousness pictured by the scientists. A great many writers—too many to be discounted—talk about two stages in the composing process. One is unconscious, personal, irrational, intuitive, the stage of writing a first draft at top speed, of trusting their personal muse or daemon or feelings to lead them where it will. Another stage is conscious, impersonal, rational, and intellectual, the stage of revising the first draft, of analyzing and criticizing the hastily produced words which originally burst forth.

Let me give you just a few examples to support my contention.

In a recent article, Gail Godwin (1977) the novelist, describes the two stages in these terms. One she calls her "creative powers" and the other a "watcher at the gates." She cites a passage from Freud's "Interpretation of

Dreams," in which Freud quotes the German poet Schiller, who is writing to a friend complaining of his lack of creative power. Schiller suggests that his intellect may be examining too closely the ideas pouring in at the gates. Writes Schiller, "In the case of the creative mind, it seems to me, the intellect has withdrawn its watchers from the gates, and the ideas rush in pell-mell, and only then does it review and inspect the multitude. You are ashamed or afraid of the momentary and passing madness which is found in all creators ..."

While Schiller made real the intellectual mode in writing as a "watcher at the gates," other writers personify the intuitive stage. Rudyard Kipling (cited in Emig, 1964) called this mysterious, subconscious force his "daemon." Wrote Kipling: "My Daemon was with me in the Jungle Books, *Kim,* and both Puck books, and good care I took to walk deliberately, least he should withdraw. ... When your Daemon is in charge, do not try to think consciously. Drift, wait, and obey ..."

Ray Bradbury (1966a) personifies the intuitive mode as his "muse" and in an essay aptly entitled "How to Keep and Feed a Muse," describes her. "What is subconscious to every other man, in its creative aspect becomes, for writers, The Muse. They are two names for one thing. But no matter what we call it, here is the core of the individual we pretend to extol, to whom we build shrines and hold lip services in our democratic society. Here is the stuff of originality."

For many writers, this intuitive mode of consciousness is so potent that it essentially leads its own existence. Bradbury (1966b.) tells of trusting his muse's ability to create. "Above all, I have never doubted my subconscious. It is my richness. It is my bank. To doubt is to destroy. To believe is to create. I believe. I believe. I believe."

Writers often report that their independent intuition leads them to find out what they want to write. For John Updike (1966), "Writing and rewriting are a constant search for what one is saying."

John Ciardi (1966) tells of his unconscious helping him in this way: "The artist writes compulsively as a way of knowing himself, or of clarifying what he does not know about himself. He writes, let us say, for those glimpses of order that form can make momentarily visible."

And Joan Didion (1976), the novelist, says much the same thing about the power of her subconscious to reveal what she didn't know about herself. "I write entirely to find out what I'm thinking, what I'm looking at, what I see and what it means. What I want and what I fear."

Perhaps William Faulkner sums up as well as anyone this awe of his personal creative powers:

And now I realize for the first time what an amazing gift I had. Uneducated in every formal sense, without even very literate, let alone literary, companions, yet to have made the things I have made. I don't know where it all came from, I don't know why God or gods, or whoever it was, selected me to be the vessel. Believe me, this is not humility, false modesty: it is simply amazement. (cited in Welty, 1977).

Modes of Writing in the Schools

So what has all this to do with teaching writing in the schools? For composing for the left hand?

Suppose we use the right and left hand activities of the brain as a metaphor for two kinds of writing. As we have seen, professional writers, especially those of creative writing—fiction and poetry—state that they go through two distinct stages of consciousness while composing in writing. It makes sense to me, then, to call that writing which is produced during a state of consciousness called variously analytical, sequential, rational, logical, conscious, or intellectual "writing for the right hand." In the "right hand" category we would include reports, outlines, critical essays, logical persuasive essays, business letters, and formal essays.

And it makes as much sense to call that writing which reflects a state of consciousness called holistic, nonrational, illogical, unconscious, or intuitive as "writing for the left hand." Examples of writing for the "left hand" are personal entries in diaries and journals, autobiographical personal recollections, character sketches, stories, fables, myths, personal letters, emotional persuasive essays, and figurative language of all kinds.

I have a notion that most of the writing that our kids engage in in the public schools is writing for the right hand. And my strong suspicions were confirmed when I read a report of research conducted by James Britton and others (1975) to find out what kids from eleven to eighteen years of age actually wrote in classrooms. The research was conducted in British schools, but I wouldn't be surprised that if we duplicated the study in American schools we would find essentially the same results.

This, in a simplified summary, is what the researchers found. They collected over 2,000 samples of writing from school children from the ages of eleven to eighteen—roughly equivalent to students in our grades seven through twelve. The samples came from classes in history, geography, religious education, science, English, and classes in "other subjects." Before the researchers analyzed the compositions, they developed two categories for analysis, one for the kind of writing done, the *function* category, and the other for the audience for which the writing was intended, the *audience* category.

The function categories were these three: *transactional, expressive,* and *poetic. Transactional writing* was defined as writing to get the business of the world done, writing used "to record facts, exchange opinions, explain and explore ideas, construct theories; to transact business, conduct campaigns, change public opinion" (Britton, p. 88). *Expressive writing* is personal writing addressed to an audience intimately known and includes exclamations, writing about feelings, thinking out loud on paper, personal diary entries, and personal letters to friends to maintain contact with them. *Poetic writing* is writing using language as an art medium, in which words are arranged in a conscious pattern. Such writing includes all figurative language used not to inform or to persuade but to create pleasing visual or verbal effects.

The audience categories reflected how the student writers saw the audience to which they were addressing themselves. The major divisions were: 1. child to self, 2. child to teacher, including child to trusting adult and child to adult as examiner, 3. child to wider audience, 4. child to unknown audience (writer to his readers or public) and 5. child to additional categories, including virtual named audience and no discernible audience.

First, to what audience did the school children generally address themselves? Most students wrote for a teacher audience and particularly for the teacher as examiner. Were you surprised at that?

Second, what were the kinds of writing the school children generally produced? Most of the writing was transactional, writing to get the business of the world done, if you like, "writing for the right hand." Very little of the other varieties of writing were found. Expressive, highly personal writing to oneself or to an intimate friend, most of which we might call "writing for the left hand," was "minimally represented." Poetic writing, which again we may identify as "writing for the left hand," was significant during the first three years of what we would label secondary schooling, but it dropped off markedly during the last years of schooling. Furthermore, examples of poetic writing were found almost solely in English and Religious Education classes.

I would submit that most of the writing that our kids do, like British kids, is transactional writing, writing for the right hand. I would further submit that although writing for the right hand is an important type of writing, we should try to correct this over-emphasis on transactional writing in our schools and engage our children in more expressive and poetic writing activities, in writing activities for the left hand. I would even go so far as to suggest that very possibly during the composing process—a process which is to some degree followed by all writers during the creation of any kind of writing—that there are at least two distinct modes of consciousness, in which intuition and intellect in a complementary fashion produce far more worthwhile writing than what results from a single mode. I propose that the intellect, so to speak, may be used for organizing thoughts and details and certainly for rewriting and editing. But if we don't trust our intuition, our left hand, to spill out an abundance of deeply felt ideas, feelings, and images, the intellect well may have little of value to revise.

So, not only should we encourage kids to compose in writing for both right and left hands, we should help them learn that both the right and left hands are used during the composing process for any kind of writing.

Assumptions for Composing with the Left Hand

Let me offer some assumptions which I believe teachers should hold when they encourage kids to compose in writing and then some guidelines for teaching composing, especially for the left hand. Later I shall offer concrete examples of useful writing activities for the left hand that intermediate grade pupils may profit by.

These are some assumptions I believe are necessary to hold if one is to create a learning climate in which beginning writers can release their personal, creative powers.

1. *Writing is not a superstar contest.* Every person is an absolutely unique individual who happens to share common feelings and experiences with other people, with other creatures. Therefore, we can't compare the work of one pupil with that of another. And that's what marking individual compositions with letters or numerals does. We can give a grade at the end of a marking period, but we should never attempt to place writers on a bell-shaped, "normal" distribution curve.

2. *Writers are pussycats.* And we must teach them to become tigers. No one is more timid than the writer, especially the beginning writer. If we scold inexperienced writers, they will cower, slink, scamper, crawl, growl, or yowl. But if we pet, feed, and stroke them, they will purr, stand erect, and extend themselves fully. Writing is the supreme act of ego. To grow, an ego must have praise, not criticism.

3. *Writing is a process.* Nobody, contrary to all kinds of claims by instant geniuses, has ever produced worthwhile writing in one, instantaneous draft. Writing is magic, but once we learn—and trust—the steps in writing, anybody can do the tricks. Anybody! Most knowledgeable people now talk about three distinct stages in composing in writing: prewriting, writing, and rewriting. And we know that within these stages—or interrelating among them—are at least two modes of consciousness—writing for the left hand—activities which are reflected by words like remembering, flowing, being alone, feeling, associating—and writing for the right hand—which is suggested by the words outlining, gathering, ordering, examining, testing, and analyzing. If our inexperienced writers are to become successful, they need to become aware of the stages is composing in writing and become familiar with the two modes of consciousness.

4. *Writing is for lovers.* And only secondarily for wheelers and dealers. Sure, manipulators need writing to get the business of the world done. But all of us need writing to show our love of life, to glorify the world—its people, creatures, water, sky, clouds, plants, rocks, and earth. Writing lets us rejoice!

5. *Writing is chiefly from the heart.* And only secondarily from the intellect. Writing for the left hand precedes writing for the right. Writing which reveals to us and to others our fears, dreams, desires, and loves is infinitely more exhilarating and restorative than any outline or business letter.

Guidelines for Teaching Composing for the Left Hand

So how do we engage kids in composing for the left hand? Here are some general guidelines for getting them started. After that, you only have to trust your own intuition, your personal feelings from the "left hand."

The first step is to assist them in getting in touch with their most intimate emotions. Virginia Woolf once wrote that dealing with personal "shocks" produced her best writing. Joan Didion found one or two "shimmering images" to be enough to get her started on a novel. Any consideration of a first memory, a love or hate, a secret place, or a person whom they remember with strong emotions is usually sufficient to get them going.

Writing models, both student and professional, are essential for them to see how others put similar memories and feelings into words. Pictures and photographs can be used as stimuli for writing, but I believe these are useful only for the very beginning writer.

At this first stage, you might say things like these:

> What is your earliest memory? Were you terrified or very happy? Or both?
>
> What do you love most in the world? What do you hate?
>
> Where would you be if you could go to the place you love the most, your secret place? Describe it.

Second, get them started writing! Don't over-plan or over-discuss. Let the creative juices flow. Open the flood gates. Restrain the watcher at the gates. Make sure they start in the physical act of writing. Let them begin with a single word which leads to another word and then to a feeling, a memory, an image, a thought.

Here you might make comments such as these:

> Okay, start writing.
>
> Don't worry about it now (punctuation, spelling, handwriting, paragraphing, topic, etc.).
>
> Let it go. Trust yourself.
>
> Write to find out what you think or feel.
>
> What you're writing is important, good for you.
>
> Don't worry about it.
>
> Do it!

Third, now that the first draft is down on paper, help them revise. Now let the watcher at the gates take over. This is the time to rewrite, rearrange, add, delete, move around, "show not tell," use specific words, state don't imply, check for spelling, punctuate correctly, and produce a manuscript which others can read without hindrances.

And at this point you can help with remarks like these:

> What general impression were you trying to create? Did you succeed?
>
> Who are you writing for? (Who is your audience?)
>
> How's the opening? Does it grab the reader?
>
> Does the ending work? Does it tie up things?
>
> Go over every sentence. Does each one make sense? If you are stopped by any group of words, change them.
>
> Do the paragraphs hang together? Have you used transitions well?
>
> Have you explained that which is not clear? Implied that which is overstated? Added that which is missing? Cut out that which is repetitious?
>
> Are your mechanics perfect?

A Baker's Half Dozen Activities for Composing for the Left Hand

And so finally I offer you a Baker's Half Dozen of Activities aimed at helping pupils in the intermediate grades to compose with and for the left hand. These are writing assignments that I have found successful in the classroom. The not so strange fact is that adults of all ages also get a kick out of doing these writing assignments and then reading them out loud to each other.

I must give credit where credit is due. The ideas for the "wish," "lie," and "dream" poems come, of course, from that absolutely basic book on composing for the left hand, Kenneth Koch's *Wishes, Lies, and Dreams* (1970). The other activities are the result of my students' and my working together at this problem of turning kids on to the invigorating experience of writing for the left hand. For all but three exercises, I have set up the writing activities to allow for the three stages in the composing process: prewriting, writing, and rewriting.

1. List five things you love to do. (You and a student next to you read your lists to each other.)

2. List five things you hate to do, that upset you. (You and a student next to you read your lists to each other.)

3. *Writing Your Favorite Words*

Prewriting

Make a list of 20 words that you like. You can use names, words from other languages, names of cities or of countries, words that suggest sounds, brand names, names of colors, any 20 words.

You may select them for their meanings, because they sound good to you, or just because you get a kick out of them.

Now that you have 20, cross out 5!

Writing

Write your 15 favorite words in these blanks. Put them in any order that you like. If you care to, look around with different combinations.

                _____ _____

          _____ _____ _____ _____

          _____ _____ _____ _____

          _____ _____ _____

          _____ _____

Here are some samples of 15 favorite words written by middle school students.

candle burr	scrumptious artichokes
tumble smile shine	strawberry tequila hyena
saw fire water	luminous bowling atmosphere
treefort climb sway wind	sunsummer astrology horse-de-overs
eternity darkness	hydroglifics swimming Ilama
fungus	gazebo

4. Writing about Your "Secret Place"

Prewriting

Think of a place where you'd like to be more than anything else in the world.

Shut your eyes. Think about the place. Put yourself there. What do you see? Immediately before you? In the distance? To the right, the left? What do you feel? Smell? Taste? Hear?

Writing

In sentences and in paragraph form, write down your perceptions. Before you rewrite the piece, turn to this paragraph:

It is a cold and snowy night. The main street is deserted. The only things moving are swirls of snow. As I lift the mailbox door, I feel its cold iron. There is a privacy I love in this snowy night. Driving around, I will waste more time.

As you read and come to a place where you believe you should pause or where there is a mark of punctuation, draw a slash.

Now look at how the poet Robert Bly "lined" this particular poem. What is the effect of the word "deserted" being written off by itself?

DRIVING TO TOWN LATE TO MAIL A LETTER
It is a cold and snowy night. The main street is deserted.
The only things moving are swirls of snow.
As I lift the mailbox door, I feel its cold iron.
There is a privacy I love in this snowy night.
Driving around, I will waste more time.
                    Robert W. Bly

Rewriting

With your paragraph on your secret place, draw lines where you pause naturally or where there is a mark of punctuation.

Copy the paragraph over in verse form, writing each line you have marked off as a line in the poem. Write words on separate lines if you wish to make them stand out for some reason.

5. Writing a Wish Poem

Prewriting

What would you wish for if you could have anything you wanted? A new bike, a pair of skiis, a tennis racket, a new stereo? Colors like blue, aquamarine, orange, mauve? Drinks like nectar, champagne, or retsina? Places like Timbuctoo, Damascus, Shangri-la? Or real life or fictional heroes or heroines like Babe Ruth, Chris Evert, Huckleberry Finn, or Wonder Woman?

a. Writing

Write a "wish poem." Begin each line with the words "I wish _____." Include in each line the name of a color, a real life person or fictional character, and a place. Be as crazy and weird as you like. See what unusual things you can put together.

I wish I were a green Superman in Peiking.
I wish I were a red Bionic Woman in Java.
I wish I were a yellow angel in Nome, Alaska.

b. Writing

Write a "wish poem" with the whole class participating. Each person write an "I wish _____" line and have someone write the lines on the chalkboard, one after the other. Or pass around a sheet of paper with everyone taking turns writing down an "I wish _____" line. Only this time follow each "I wish _____" with the name of an animal doing something in a building.

6. Writing a Lie Poem

Prewriting

We all like to make up outlandish stories, to tell things that aren't true. In real life we usually get in trouble for doing so, but in poetry, we can tell lies and get away with it.

Writing

Pair off with another student. Each of you give the other a lie, alternating your lies until you have each given *five* lies for a total of *ten*.

I am a tomato.
I have orange hair.
I am Muhammed Ali.
I live at the South Pole.
I'm Buck Rogers from Mars.
I was once a humming bird.

I was once a pyramid.
I have a brand new Datzun 280Z.
I totalled it yesterday.
I have 72 fingers.

7. Writing a Dream Poem

Prewriting

Try to remember a recent dream you have had. Do you have a dream which keeps on happening, a "recurring" dream? Do you dream in color or in black and white? Can you "dream" when you're wide awake and with your eyes wide open, wish you were miles away and doing or being something fantastic?

a. Writing

Write a poem in which you start every line with "I dreamed _____." You can write about real dreams you have had or about what you daydream.

I dreamed I was floating down a river and all the monsters were after me.

I dreamed I was falling off a cliff, and before I could hit the ground I started to fly.

I dreamed I was on my own yacht sailing over water so clear I could see the bottom fifty feet below.

I dreamed a millionaire found me and wanted me to come and be his adopted daughter.

b. Writing

Write a poem in which you describe one dream or even a series of dreams. Here are some dream poems written by students.

Nightmare
I dreamed it was the day
of the big test
And all I could remember was
the winter solstice.

Stutson Street Bridge
When I was small,
I used to dream detail.
I dreamed I had to cross the Genesee River
and the Stutson Street Bridge was not there.

When I was small,
I used to dream absurd.

I dreamed the two banks were connected
By the foundations of a roller coaster.

When I was small,
I used to dream fear.
I dreamed I had to swing across the river
Like a lady on a trapeze or a monkey
Hand to bar, hand to bar.

When I was small,
I used to dream clever.
For just as I reached the middle
I realized how silly my dream was
And I fell into the Genesee.

References

Bradbury, Ray, How to keep and feed a muse. On *Writing, By Writers*, William W. West (Ed.), Boston: Ginn and Company, 1966a.

Bradbury, Ray, Seeds of three stories. On *Writing, by Writers*, William W. West (Ed.), Boston: Ginn and Company, 1966b.

Britton, James, *et al.*, *The Development of Writing Abilities*. London: Macmillan Education Ltd., 1975.

Ciardi, John. John Ciardi. On *Writing, By Writers*, William W. West (Ed.), Boston: Ginn and Company, 1966.

Didion, Joan, Why I write, *The New York Times Book Review Section*, December 5, 1976, 98.

Emig, Janet A. The uses of the unconscious in composing. *College Composition and Communication, XV, 1*, February, 1964.

Godwin, Gail, The watcher at the gates. *The New York Times Book Review Section*, January 9, 1977, p. 31.

Koch, Kenneth, *Wishes, Lies, and Dreams*. New York: Vintage Books, 1970.

Ornstein, Robert, *The Psychology of Consciousness*. New York: Penguin Books, 1972.

Updike, John, The growth of a short story. On *Writing, By Writers*, William W. West (Ed.), Boston: Ginn and Company, 1966.

Welty, Eudora, Review of selected letters of William Faulkner. *The New York Times Book Review*, February 6, 1977, p. 30.

· 1 0 ·

COMPOSING AS THE CURRICULUM

The Albion Writing Project

Robert W. Blake and Frederick B. Tuttle, Jr. (1979)

In the fall of 1976, we began an inservice program for "Improving Basic Writing Skills, K-12," in the Albion, New York, Public Schools. The Superintendent, Dr. Douglas Houck, with the approval of the Board of Education, wanted teachers in the Albion School District, kindergarten through grade twelve, to address themselves cooperatively to the solution of a major curriculum problem, in this case, improving the writing of students and the teaching of writing in the school system. The charge was for us to conduct a series of workshops with selected elementary school teachers from grades K-6 and with all English teachers, grades 7–12, for the improvement of writing.

This article is a description of how we devised and conducted the workshop meetings and a report of what all of us—public school teachers and administrators and college faculty—learned from the experience.

What We Planned

We first met with administrators of the school district—to find out the needs of their individual schools and to gain their crucial support—arriving at this initial outline of procedures.

Inservice Agenda

1. Conduct inservice workshops for the teachers of English language arts, K-12, including these activities:
   a. make available for study and discussion the latest research, textbooks, and special materials on teaching writing.
   b. help teachers in creating lessons which exemplify the composing process.
   c. train teachers to use discussion and planning skills.
   d. outline with teachers a program for assessing writing by students and for assessing the total writing program of the school district.
2. Develop a writing program for grades K-12.

We intended the project to be an exploratory one, in which teachers, school students, and college consultants would work cooperatively for the improvement of teaching written composition, grades K-12. At the time we found no reports of a similar proposal. We knew we would be gathering first-hand information on improving writing and teaching writing. Although there were many questions and initial disagreements, we were all agreed that an intimate understanding of the composing process was the basis of the project, that, in fact, "composing" *was* the writing curriculum. We knew, furthermore, that a key would be persuading teachers from varied backgrounds and different grade levels to develop and implement radically new practices in their classrooms. Essentially, though, we were cautiously optimistic that if we presented ideas and methods which appeared to be logical and reasonable, teachers of good faith would accept these ideas and implement practices they thought useful.

After several planning meetings with the teachers who were to be involved in the program, we arrived at this plan for the year's inservice sessions and work in the school classrooms. We decided to hold weekly two-hour workshop meetings from October through May, alternating one week with selected elementary school teachers and supervisors, K-6, and another week with all secondary school English teachers, 7–12.

Outline of Inservice Topics and Classroom Activities

Inservice Topics	Classroom Activities
1. Composing Process—prewriting, drafting, revising, and editing.	1. Teach composing process in the classroom.

Inservice Topics

2. Traditional varieties of Writing—description, narration, persuasion, and exposition.

3. Skills of Writing—use of adjectives and adverbs, active verbs, wordiness, use of concrete and abstract words, transitions, focus, and so forth.

4. Conventions and Mechanics of Writing.

5. Sentence Combining—syntactic fluency and sentence variety.

6. Workshopping—during prewriting (invention) and after successive drafts; teaching teachers and students how to "talk about" (assess) the elements of successful writing.

7. Assessment and Evaluation—by primary traits, holistic assessment, and by mechanics; arriving at a grade on the basis of assessment.

8. Develop Sample Classroom Assignments—based upon the composing process with the format of prewriting, drafting, revising, and editing.

9. Develop Competencies in Writing, K-12—types of writing for various ages, levels, and abilities.

Classroom Activities

2. Teach varieties of writing from the universe of discourse, following traditional categories (most familiar to students and teachers).

3. Teach skills of writing as separate activities or during composing process (after the first draft).

4. Teach conventions (format) and mechanics of writing (spelling, punctuation, capitalization, standard usage) as separate activities or during composing process (after first draft).

5. Teach sentence manipulation through free and signalled sentence combining exercises.

6. Present characteristics of each variety of writing during prewriting; help students understand concepts of audience, message, and writer's role and how they relate to distinct types discourse.

7. Provide teachers with a variety of ways for assessing student writing and a procedure for arriving at grades; teach students how to assess their own writing.

8. Try out writing assignments in classes and keep sample compositions with student and teacher reactions.

9. Try out types of writing assignments in classes and subjectively assess the effectiveness of the activities.

What We Did

The Composing Process. The idea of the "composing process as the curriculum" was at the heart of the program. Throughout the first meetings we had the teachers write diverse pieces of discourse, following the various stages in the composing process. And they, in turn, led their students through the composing stages with various kinds of writing, representing the traditional modes of discourse, as well as poetry.

We asked the teachers to use the following model as they prepared writing lessons. In the left hand column are the stages of composing; the right hand column shows where the skills of writing could be integrated with the composing stages.

Model for Preparing Composition Lessons

Stages in the Composing Process   *Writing Skills*

Prewriting—any activity to provide raw material for writing: questioning, free writing, making entries in journals, guided recollection, or responding to visuals. This stage is *interactive*; that is, it occurs with others.

Drafting—the first draft of any piece without concern for "correctness" at this point; writing to find out what you want to say. This is the only stage in the process which is *individual*; that is, it is done alone.

Revising—extensive changes in the manuscript, such as altering tone or point of view, moving sections around, creating new openings or endings. This stage is *interactive*.

Editing—correcting errors in spelling, capitalization, punctuation, and standard usage; producing "good," clean copy. This stage is *interactive*.

Skills of Writing—such as the use of concrete and abstract words. This state is *interactive. Sentence Combining*—taught with prepared exercises or with sentences from students' first draft compositions. This stage is *interactive*.

Mechanics and Conventions in Writing—teaching the correction of errors from exercises or with examples from student compositions. This stage is *interactive*.

Publishing—preparing polished pieces for the enjoyment of others by mounting on construction paper and posting in classrooms, publishing in school magazines or newspapers or dittoing copies for other students. This stage is *interactive*.

Varieties of Writing. We considered various outlines of types of discourse, such as Britton's, Kinneavy's, and Moffett's (see Bibliography), but eventually we settled on the traditional modes of discourse: description, narration, persuasion, and exposition, for these three reasons. First, we could gather almost all types of writing done in the schools under one of the four categories. Second, they were categories the majority of us knew well and felt comfortable with. And third, the kinds of writing ranged from personal and aimed at an intimate audience to impersonal and aimed at a distant audience.

Skills of Writing. For the most part, skills of writing, such as using appropriate diction and employing transitions, were treated during one or more stages of the composing process with emphasis on a particular skill, which was, in turn, related to a type of writing, such as the use of logic in a persuasive piece. We assented that this was the most reasonable time to teach these skills.

Mechanics and Conventions of Writing. Most of us agreed to deal with mechanics, that is, spelling, punctuation, standard usage, and capitalization, throughout the composing process, especially after the revision stage. Some teachers, however, wanted separate drill on mechanics. We did not resolve the question of integrating skills instruction in mechanics with stages in the composing process to everyone's satisfaction, but we were insistent that, although a command of writing mechanics is essential for successful writing, mechanics should never be considered as all there was to writing. We were concerned that teachers who wished to teach the mechanics of writing, unrelated to actual discourse situations, would, like too many teachers, mistake drill in spelling and correcting usage errors for writing aimed at actual audiences.

Sentence Combining. We presented to the teachers the background of research in sentence combining by Kellogg Hunt, John Mellon, and Frank O'Hare as well as an outline of sentence combining problems, grade 3–8, developed by Robert W. Blake and an article with an outline for sentence combining problems, appropriate for secondary school students, by Charles Cooper. (See Bibliography.) The teachers worked through exercises prepared by Blake and used the texts on sentence combining, *Sentencecraft* by Frank O'Hare and *Sentence Combining* by William Strong. (See Bibliography.) The problems by Blake and Cooper and the texts by O'Hare and Strong formed the basis for a sequential program of sentence combining activities for students, grades 3–12.

Workshopping. The interactive aspect of the composing process was the core of the writing program. Most teachers had not been trained to let students work with each other in the classroom, and they voiced concerns about the plan: How can students help each other write better? Won't they discuss everything *but* the writing? What will the administrators say when they hear such a noisy classroom? How can I allow students to talk together when I have a class of thirty-seven? And these were legitimate concerns, too. For "workshopping," the practice of people working together—criticizing and offering feedback for each other's ideas—in order to produce better pieces of writing than they would if they worked completely alone, the idea that "composing *is* the curriculum," was a revolutionary one.

Sample Assessment Scale

COMPOSITION# _____   Evaluator: _____

ASSESSMENT SCALE: AUTOBIOGRAPHY

	LOW				HIGH	
TONE: mixture of humor and seriousness	1	2	3	4	5	_____
PERSONAL VOICE: has many "I's" and "me's"; personal touch; first person point of view	1	2	3	4	5	_____
DETAILS: sufficient details	1	2	3	4	5	_____
REAL EXPERIENCES: happenings seem to have really occurred	1	2	3	4	5	_____
ORGANIZATION: structure clear; either chronological or use of flashbacks	1	2	3	4	5	_____
OPENING: grabs your interest right away	1	2	3	4	5	_____
ENDING: makes you want to know what happens next	1	2	3	4	5	_____
MECHANICS: (spelling, punctuation, capitalization, correct usuage); not crucial but important	1	2	3	4	5	_____

COMMENTS:

But when these teachers tried workshopping in their classrooms, tentatively and even timidly at first, when they started to trust their intuitive feelings about how writing should be taught, and when they began to have faith that kids would write about matters close to them and discuss their compositions with each other if they were allowed to, amazing things happened. Students began to point out problems in their writing and in the writing of other students, many times as well as could the teachers. The students, as we anticipated, did at times discuss matters other than those directly related to the immediate piece of writing, but, in almost all cases, the discussions were at least indirectly related to their writing. Yes, the classrooms were sometimes noisy, but the noise, the teachers reported, was that of kids excitedly discussing academic matters, and the administrators, once they accepted the principle of interaction, endorsed the method.

Assessment and Evaluation. Assessing compositions and giving grades are always ticklish topics for English teachers. We emphasized the difference between assessing—identifying the elements of a good composition for purposes of improving instruction—and evaluating—giving a grade to a finished product. Essentially, we arrived at this procedure for assessing and evaluating student writing. Teachers, working cooperatively with students would develop the features of a particular kind of writing, for example, autobiography. The students would know what the characteristics of a successful autobiography were, would have student and professional samples of the type of writing available, and would assess their own and each other's autobiographies, using a scale like this one as a guide.

We found several advantages for this type of assessment. The students knew features of a successful piece of composition before they started writing. After they had created their own piece, they, using the scale, could help each other identify problems in their compositions. The teachers, furthermore, could help the students improve their compositions without worrying about the negative effect grades would have on successive drafts of a composition.

We suggested that the grading of compositions be handled this way: Each student kept his or her personal folder in a filing cabinet in the classroom. Toward the end of a marking period—when a grade was required—the teacher would look at each folder and regard three factors as the basis for a grade. First, the teacher would note effort. Had the student at least tried all the writing activities? Second, the teacher would assess the student's writing improvement over the marking period. And third, the teacher would ask each student to pick out his or her two or three best pieces and discuss them with the teacher. From these three types of evidence, the teacher assigned a grade. Although it was a lengthy process, the procedure had obvious advantages. The student was evaluated on his best work. The grade was used to acknowledge improvement. The student had a clear idea of what the basis was for his or her grade. And the teacher didn't need to mark all drafts of all compositions; he or she read only the final, finished pieces. Most grades for the writing, therefore, were high because the teachers were grading not first drafts but polished compositions.

And, best of all, few students needed to argue about their grades because they had revised successive drafts until the papers were clearly competent, and the students had a clear understanding of the basis for grading.

As well as showing the teachers how to assess and evaluate the individual compositions of their students, we led the teachers through the process of assessing student papers in selected classrooms at grades three, seven, and ten. Although we had not planned the program as an empirical study, we did show the teachers how such an experimental investigation could be conducted. Since the students were not assigned randomly to groups and there were no control groups, we were well aware of the limited value of the results.

First, we measured growth in the *average length of T-units*, an acknowledged measure of syntactic maturity, discovered by Kellogg Hunt. (See Bibliography.) Normally, researchers measure growth in T-units after carefully controlled, sequential programs in sentence combining. Although we had no such procedure at Albion, we assessed the number of T-units in pre- and post-treatment compositions to show the teachers how the T-unit was measured. We found the number of T-units had declined in compositions for all three grades, even though the decline was not significant.

Second, we measured *growth in fluency*, simply a count of the number or words in the compositions. The results showed that fluency declined for the third graders but increased for both the seventh- and tenth-grade students, with the overall fluency for all compositions in the three grades increasing over the inservice period.

Third, the teachers, after a training session, assessed the *quality of compositions* with a modified primary trait rating scale (similar to the one on autobiography previously described). The results showed that the quality of the third-and seventh-grade compositions increased slightly while the quality of the tenth grade compositions declined. The quality of the total number of compositions, however, improved slightly, although the improvement was not significant.

One important factor in the decline of T-units and the slight gain in the quality of compositions, we were convinced, was the traditional experimental design. For the pre-treatment compositions, we presented as a stimulus a picture of marching soldiers with bayonetted rifles and asked the students to write, as an example of narration, a story about the picture. For the post-treatment compositions, the teachers gave the same stimulus and assignment. Many students were unhappy with the task, the teachers reported, because they didn't like writing about the same picture twice, and they definitely did not like writing compositions in a testing situation with time for only minimum revisions of a first draft, especially when they had been taught throughout the year to take their time—at least two or three class periods—to produce a third or fourth draft composition. (For a more valid type of experimental design for assessing compostions, see Cooper, 1975, in the Bibliography.)

Developing Sample Writing Assignments. After the introductory workshop sessions, the teachers devised writing activities for their students, following the Model for Preparing Composition Lessons (previously presented), with skills instruction integrated throughout the composing stages of prewriting, drafting, revising, and editing.

Here are two sample writing assignments for the third and seventh grades.

Sample Writing Assignments

Writing Activity/Description
Grade 3
Linda Spierdowis

Prewriting
1. Pupils read silently and orally story about an imaginary bird.
2. Pupils discuss the bird with each other and with the teacher.
3. Pupils dramatize the story of the bird.
4. With lights turned off, pupils close their eyes to "see" their own imaginary birds. Pupils describe orally their birds.
5. Pupils draw a picture of their imaginary bird.

Drafting
1. Teacher writes on board, "I saw a bird. ..." and asks pupils to finish the sentence on scrap paper.
   Workshop Activity
   Each pupil reads his sentence to another pupil.
   Skills Instruction
   The teacher uses flash cards to show pupils interesting descriptive words.

Revising and Editing
1. Pupils rewrite their sentences, concentrating on creating interesting sentences.
2. Each pupil reads aloud his sentence to another pupil and then to the entire group.
3. The teacher reads the sentences and makes oral suggestions to each pupil about improving the sentences (sentence combining).

4. Pupils rewrite their sentences, correct mechanical errors, and copy the sentences onto the pictures they had drawn.

> Writing Activity/Description
> Grade 7
> Mark Williams

Prewriting
1. Discuss basic definition of description and techniques involved in writing description.
2. Read sample descriptions by Richard Wright.
3. Study large mounted photograph of descriptive scene.

Drafting
1. Students list details from photograph.
2. Students change details to words representing images.
3. Students refine image list.
4. Students write spontaneous rough drafts in class (subjects devised by teacher and students).
5. Students write rough drafts in paragraph form.

Skills Instruction
1. Discuss guidelines for organization.
2. Review passive versus active verbs.
3. Discuss use of dictionary and thesaurus.
4. Do sentence combining activities.
5. Define image.

Workshop Activities
1. Students discuss writing with other students they feel comfortable with.
2. Discuss feeling of trust related to sharing one's writing.
3. Students read compositions aloud in small groups and present the best in the group to the class as a whole with justification.

Revising and Editing
1. Students revise their own compositions.
2. Students meet with the teacher to discuss problems of mechanics in final revisions.

3. Students prepare their final drafts.
4. Students submit their final drafts to the teacher.
5. Teacher reads and reacts in writing to the final drafts.

Developing Competencies in Writing K-12. We started this ambitious task by making an outline for each of the grade levels and asking the teachers to fill in the types of writing they presently required of their students under the categories of description, narration, persuasion, exposition, and poetry. By the end of the school year, we had refined the outline so it was sequential and logical and included examples of lessons for all grade levels.

What We Learned

In one school year, we discovered much about designing a program to improve writing and the teaching of writing in a school system, grades K-12. But we also learned some rather important lessons about working cooperatively on problems of teaching and learning, and with what happened when we assumed that "composing was the curriculum" and conducted workshops based upon this assumption. We discovered, essentially, that many concepts critical to the success of the program took us—teachers, students, administrators, and college professors—a long time to internalize. We had to live with these ideas, argue about them, practice them, and assess and refine them before we could accept their usefulness and make them the basis for future actions. Here are some of these difficult but important ideas.

The idea of the "composing process." Teachers and students found it troublesome to accept the uncomfortable truth that all worthwhile writing takes a great deal of time and involves at least four stages: prewriting, drafting, revising, and editing. As the teachers committed their students to the process of composition in the classroom, they found they needed to revise their traditional notion of "covering" a large body of "content." Instead of drilling in mechanics, assigning the time-honored "theme a week," and having students read and analyze pieces of literature, the teachers learned it might take two weeks of class work on the composing process for students to produce polished compositions. And students found it hard to comprehend that revising meant not just "copying it over in ink," but that revising meant changing major portions of their initial drafts and rewriting papers several times until a piece "sounded" right.

The idea of students "sharing" drafts of composition with each other and with their teachers. Before the workshops most teachers and students held to the belief that writing was chiefly a solitary pursuit, with the student writing a composition ultimately to be "judged" by a teacher. They found it difficult to adopt the notion that students and teachers could actually help each other in improving successive drafts of compositions.

The idea of "assessing" writing without numerical or letter grades. At first both students and teachers felt the need for a grade on each paper they wrote. Eventually, however, teachers said students would rewrite and polish papers without regard for immediate grades, once they became used to the idea that teachers were reacting to their papers in a positive fashion rather than marking their compositions negatively on the basis of how many errors in mechanics found. As a matter of fact, the students began to enjoy writing for the excitement it brought them rather than solely for a grade.

The idea that one could "talk about" the essentials of a piece of writing without even mentioning mechanics—like spelling, punctuation, and standard usage. Both students and teachers were first frustrated with trying to describe a piece of writing except in terms of mechanics, but after instruction in and discussion of the elements of particular varieties of writing, like narration or persuasion, both students and teachers found they could analyze the components of various classes of writing soundly and confidently.

The idea that there may be at least two very different "modes of mental activities" going on while one writes—one we might label as intellectual and conscious and the other emotional and unconscious. Both students and teachers needed to be encouraged to trust their unconscious as they let ideas pour out in prewriting activities and in initial drafts. Then, they learned, they must use their conscious intellect to revise and rework the results of their spontaneous first drafts.

The idea that "cooperation" by a group of interested professionals to solve a complex, pedagogical problem—like teaching written composition in an entire school system—is more productive than the work done by individuals trying to solve such problems by themselves. We all worked hard at creating a spirit of encouragement, cooperation, and sharing of ideas. As the workshops and writing went on, and the teachers became more self assured, they contributed substantially to the proceedings, produced many successful writing lessons, and helped to outline a rough draft of a district wide, K-12, scope and sequence program for improving basic writing skills.

Bibliography

(Selected articles, books, and materials examined by the participants. Some of the references have been brought up to date since the original program)

The Composing Process

Blake, Robert W. "Composing for the Left Hand: Writing Activities for the Intermediate Grades," *Facilitating Language Development*, Report of Third Annual Conference on Language Arts. Buffalo, New York: State University of New York at Buffalo, 1978.

Elbow, Peter. *Writing without Teachers*. New York: Oxford University Press, 1973.

Emig, Janet. *The Composing Process of Twelfth Graders*. Urbana, Illinois: National Council of Teachers of English, 1971.

Varieties of Discourse

Blake, Robert W. and Laurie Taillie, "Quiet and Warm Like Sunshine: Teaching High School Kids to Write Poetry." Typescript, no date.

Britton, James, *et al*. *The Development of Writing Abilities (11–18)*. London: Macmillan Education Ltd., 1975.

Kinneavy, James L. *A Theory of Discourse*. Englewood Cliffs, N. J.: Prentice-Hall, Inc., 1971.

—— John Q. Cope, and J. W. Campbell. *Aims and Audiences in Writing*. Dubuque, Iowa: Kendall/Hunt Publishing Company, 1976.

Koch, Kenneth. *Wishes, Lies, and Dreams*. New York: Vintage Books, 1970

—— *Rose, Where Did You Get That Red?* New York: Random House, Inc., 1973.

Moffett, James. *Teaching the Universe of Discourse*. Boston: Houghton Mifflin Company, 1968.

Revising Writing

Blake, Robert W. "The Writer as Writer and Critic: How to Be a Schizophrenic and Still Not End Up in Bedlam." *Indiana English Journal*, Vol. 9 (Spring, 1975). No. 3:3–9.

Murray, Donald M. *A Writer Teaches Writing*. Boston: Houghton Mifflin Company, 1968

—— "Internal Revision: A Process of Discovery." *Research on Composing*, ed. Charles R. Cooper and Lee Odell. Urbana, Illinois: National Council of Teachers of English, 1978.

Shaughnessy, Mina P. *Errors and Expectations*. New York: Oxford University Press, 1977.

Sentence Manipulation

Blake, Robert W. "Outline of Syntactic Structures, Grades 3–8," Mimeographed, no date.

Cooper, Charles R. "An Outline for Writing Sentence-Combining Problems," *English Journal*, Vol. 62 (January, 1973), No. 1: 96–102, 108.

Hunt, Kellogg W. *Grammatical Structures Written at Three Grade Levels*. Urbana, Illinois: National Council of Teachers of English, 1965.

Mellon, John C. *Transformational Sentence Combining*. Urbana Illinois: National Council of Teachers of English, 1969.

O'Hare, Frank. *Sentence Combining*. Urbana, Illinois: National Council of Teachers of English, 1971.

—— *Sentencecraft: An Elective Course in Writing*. Boston: Ginn and Company, 1975.

Strong, William. *Sentence Combining: A Composing Book*. New York: Random House, 1973.

Workshopping

Blake, Robert W. "How to Talk to a Writer, or Forward to Fundamentals in Teaching Writing," *English Journal*, Vol. 65 (November, 1976), No. 8:49–55.

Cooper, Charles R. "Responding to Student Writing," *The Writing Process of Students*. Buffalo, N.Y.: State University of New York at Buffalo, Department of Curriculum and Instruction, 1975.

Judy, Stephen N. "Writing for the Here and Now: An Approach to Assessing Student Writing," *English Journal*, Vol. 62 (January, 1973), No. 1:69–79.

Odell, Lee and Joanne Cohick, "You Mean, Write It Over in Ink?" *English Journal*, Vol. 64 (December, 1975), No. 9:48–53.

Assessment and Evaluation of Writing

Beaven, Mary H. "Individualized Goal Setting, Self-Evaluation, and Peer Evaluation," *Evaluating Writing*. Urbana Illinois: National Council of Teachers of English, 1977.

Blake, Robert W. "Assessing English and Language Arts Teachers' Attitudes Toward Writers and Writing," *The English Record*, Vol. XXVII (Summer—Autumn, 1976), No. 3–4 : 87–97.

Cooper, Charles R. "Measuring Growth in Writing," *English Journal*, Vol. 64 (March, 1975), No. 3:111–120.

—— and Lee Odell. *Evaluating Writing*. Urbana, Illinois: National Council of Teachers of English, 1977.

Diederich, Paul B. *Measuring Growth in English*. Urbana, Illinois: National Council of Teachers of English, 1974.

· 1 1 ·

SETTING UP AN EFFECTIVE WRITING PROGRAM IN THE SCHOOLS

Robert W. Blake (1981)

What's the Problem?

Kids can't write. Everyone knows that. The National Assessment of Educational Progress tell us that. Articles in popular periodicals tell us that. College and high school English teachers tell us that. And assorted gurus on the educational scene tell us that.

But to make an intricate problem even more complex, most of what the "everyone" knows about writing and teaching writing just isn't so. Furthermore, to make the subject even more complicated, the half-truths "everyone" holds are frequently contradictory. So before we consider the features of a successful writing program, we should lay to rest some of the more persistent fictions about writing and teaching writing.

Myths About Writing and Teaching Writing

1. *Only a few especially gifted and talented people can write well.*
   Just not true.
   Everyone, except those who are physically and psychologically disabled, can learn how to write effectively. And the sooner we discount this myth the better we can proceed with the task at hand.

2. *You can't teach writing.*

   Nonsense.

   You can't, of course, teach the talent and perseverance it takes to become even a journeyman professional writer, but you can teach others the skills writers employ.

3. But, And here's a zinger.

   On the one hand, we hold the myth that you can't teach writing, *but anyone with a course in college composition, a few acceptable literary research papers under his or her belt, and a college degree can tell students what's wrong with their papers.*

   A dangerous and harmful assumption.

   Not anyone can teach writing, and no one should try without special training. Just as experienced writing teachers can do a lot of good, it deplorably follows that individuals uneducated in teaching writing can do a lot of harm.

4. *Writing is grammar, spelling, capitalization, punctuation and neatness.*

   A misleading half-truth.

   Sure, these elements are part of writing, but only a piece, and the writing teacher knows writers pay attention to such matters in the last stages of the writing process, when they edit final drafts. Teachers who equate "writing" with mechanical concerns confuse a low level part with the whole of the composing process. But more of this later.

5. *Writing is always a lonely, solitary pursuit.*

   This is what gives writing such a bad name.

   Teachers who operate from this assumption give writing assignments, have students write away from the class by themselves, "correct" first- or second-draft papers for mechanical errors outside school, and hand back the red-pencilled papers in class with little time spent on discussing how to make the drafts polished, finished pieces.

   A frustrating and unfortunately not very productive business—for either teacher or student.

   Again, more on this later.

6. *There's only one kind of worthwhile writing, at least for the schools, and that's expository writing.*

   Another reason why writing has such a bad name.

   Regrettably, most school and college teachers believe this myth. As if accomplished writers didn't intuitively employ myriad kinds of writing—description, narration, persuasion, and figurative writing—in their expository essays.

7. *Teaching writing is a simple business.*

A simplistic and harmful notion about teaching writing.

But I said before, didn't I, one of the myths was, "You can't teach writing." And now I say, "Teaching writing is a simple business." Illogical? Sure Myths frequently are.

According to this myth, all you have to do is have students choose a topic, gather ideas, prepare a three-part outline with beginning, middle, and ending, turn in a first- or second-draft paper based on the notes and outline, and correct the mechanical errors.

Such a myth doesn't reflect except in the most superficial manner how writers turn out polished pieces. Nor does the notion take into account the characteristics of compositions as different, for instance, as the explanation of a process is from a persuasive essay aimed at a general audience.

8. *Teachers should grade all first- and second-draft papers after they proofread them for mechanical errors.*

Another perilous and self-defeating activity.

When they grade all drafts of papers, teachers who have confidence in this myth convey the mistaken idea that a first draft is all there is to writing.

Besides, when teachers grade all writing, they confuse two related but separate activities, *assessing* and *grading*. By assessing, I mean to make remarks, to give feedback—either orally in conferences or in writing on a paper—which suggests ways for improving a composition. With assessment, the intent is not to grade. When you stop to think about it, what writer would logically expect any drafts, except the last, to be judged? And by grading, as contrasted to assessing. I mean giving a grade. After students have revised and edited compositions, teachers may grade them. Or they can even wait until the end of a ten- or twenty-week marking period to assign grades for the student's progress during that period.

In other words, teachers—as well as students—should constantly assess each others' written compositions. And, since schools require grades periodically, teachers need to give grades, but they should grade only finished papers and report marks at the end of an instructional period.

9. *The writing teacher's major role is to correct mechanical errors in student papers.*
A misguided notion.

If writing teachers see their major function as rooting out mechanical errors in papers, illuminating the mistakes in red, and subtracting points from papers on the basis of these errors, whether they know it or not, they establish an adversary relationship between them and their students. When just the opposite should be the case.

Rather than being the person who "corrects," writing teachers should establish themselves as "trusted readers," as "writing coaches" who firmly but humanely prod and coax students to write better. And, incidently, the writing teachers, when they see themselves as "trusted readers," naturally create a classroom atmosphere in which students also become, not critical, sarcastic opponents of each other, but themselves become "trusted readers," individuals who are trained to encourage and give informed feedback to those serious about their writing.

What Makes an Effective Writing Program?

So, if we know how *not* to teach writing, the implication is apparent that we know how to teach writing.

And it's true. We do know how to teach writing. We have available the results of study by first rate minds on the subject, useful materials, and the conclusions drawn from innovative research to give us helpful information for setting up writing programs in the schools.

But before we become too euphoric about our possibilities, some *caveats* are in order.

First, learning to teach writing—like learning to write itself—is a way of life. You can't learn how to teach writing by reading a book, by attending a one-day workshop, or by taking a crash course in "speed writing." Contrary to what many popularizers of teaching writing hold, there are no dazzling tricks in this business. Permanent, worthwhile ones, anyway. If you're going to be a writing teacher, you need to make some resolutions difficult to keep. You'll spend the rest of your life at it. You'll be refining skills until the day you expire. And you'll live by a set of convictions which will govern your every thought and action when you put pencil to paper.

Second, because writing is such an incredibly complex business, improvement in it is glacially slow. Teachers of writing know they will not *see* progress in their students' writing overnight. They are prepared to work for weeks and months and even years before they can see marked improvement.

Third, not only can writing be taught, it must be taught. We learn many skills outside the classroom, but, with few exceptions, writing is not one of them. Some vastly talented and breathtakingly motivated people appear to learn how to write by themselves, but even they are instructed by feedback from relatives, friends, and editors throughout most every stage of their writing. The point is that for the rest of us benighted creatures, we need a trained person to teach us how to write.

What Makes Up an Effective Writing Program?

If then you're willing to set up an effective writing program, what's the next step? How do we know when we come across a good program? How do students act in one? How do teachers behave? If we walked into a classroom where students were writing well, what would be expect to find? Here. I submit, is what students and teachers should be doing.

Essentials for an Effective Writing Program

Students	*Teachers*
1. regularly write complete compositions—not canned exercises—on subjects they discover for themselves and about which they feel strongly (within guidelines set up by the teachers) to real audiences, sometimes including the teacher in those audiences.	1. regularly write themselves, sometimes on the topics they give their students, other times on subjects of their own choice, but the fact remains they write constantly. If they don't, they have no understanding of how to teach writing or the special problems their beginning writers will encounter.
2. write varied forms of discourse, including description, narration, persuasion, exposition, essays about literature, and poetry.	2. write varied forms of discourse.

Students	*Teachers*
3. spend considerable time in the classroom preparing for the first drafts by performing activities like these: thinking, remembering, asking and answering questions, contrasting, reading and taking notes, brainstorming, free-writing, writing dialogue, role playing and recording what happens, and playing with sentence structures.	3. set up activities in the classroom in which the students can gather a richness of material from which to write.
4. arrive at a focus—a discernible thesis—and a structure—no matter how simple at this stage—for a proposed piece of writing.	4. assist students in writing out their focus, thesis, or "lead"—as newspaper writers call it—and in outlining a simple structure for their planned piece.
5. display confidence in getting at the task of creating a first draft, with a minimum of frustration, without worrying about revising and editing at this stage.	5. encourage students to trust their instincts to write first drafts straight through.
6. regularly revise their first drafts by changing openings and endings, adding details, showing not telling, varying sentences, using precise words, and using transitional devices.	6. arrange for activities in the classroom in which students can learn how to revise.
7. regularly edit their revised compositions by proofreading and correcting mistakes in mechanics such as spelling, punctuation, capitalization, standard usage, and conventional manuscript format.	7. allow for students to proofread in class their own and each others' revised compositions.
8. do exercises as a class in common problems with mechanics, such as standard usage or spelling, or individually do exercises as needed in mechanics.	8. diagnose problems students have in mechanics of writing and assign class exercises for common problems or activities as needed for individuals.

Students	Teachers
9. regularly interact with each other and with the teacher at all but the first draft stages of the writing process to receive immediate feedback from various audiences on how to improve their writing.	9. set up classroom situations with pairs of students, small groups of from four to five students and with the whole class so students can read their papers and get immediate feedback; teach students how to interact in groups; teach students how to ask useful questions aimed at helping them improve their writing.
10. act as "trusted readers" for their classmates, encouraging them in their writing but realistically identifying areas for improvement.	10. establish a classroom atmosphere in which each student, as well as the teacher, assumes the role of "trusted reader."
11. frequently bring their writings to final form by publishing them in school newspapers, literary magazines, or in dittoed booklets produced in classrooms.	11. provide opportunities for students to publish their finished writings.
12. read professional and student models of the same kind of writing they are producing to see how "other writers" solve the problems they are confronting.	12. have students read and analyze various professional and student writing models, not as literary critics, but as writers reading other writers' works.
13. expect to have their writing "assessed" at every stage; assume that their fellow students and teachers will give them immediate feedback on how to improve their writing drafts.	13. along with students in workshops, "assess" student writing at every stage by giving immediate feedback on how to improve the writing.
14. expect to be graded on their finished compositions—not on their successive drafts—expect to be given a grade for their improvement in writing over a marking period.	14. do not grade drafts of compositions; do grade final, finished pieces; and do grade for writing improvement over a marking period.

Students	Teachers
15. frequently produce writing which has not been assigned and expect their classmates to read and respond to it.	15. create a classroom atmosphere toward the value of effective writing which encourages students to write well independently of the teacher.

How To Get It Done

So you want to improve writing and the teaching of writing in your schools? Here, I believe, is what must be done.

1. *Get support from the top.* The evidence is clear from many sources that kids can't write. Therefore, it's not too hard to make a case for the need to improve writing and writing instruction in our schools. But to initiate any program, you must first get support from the top, from the school board and the superintendent. A few teachers can teach writing well in their individual classrooms, but to bring about change in a whole school, you must have the top administrator behind you.

2. *Get outside help.* Again, working teachers, no matter how well intentioned and hard working, cannot set up alone and manage an effective program for improving writing. They need outside help. This means individuals knowledgeable about writing, who themselves write regularly, who know how to teach writing, who are expert in curriculum development, and, importantly, who know how to get teachers—frequently independent and proud individuals—to work together on a major curriculum problem over a long period of time.

Unfortunately, such outside consultants who can do such a job are scarce, for they jealously guard their time for their own writing and would rather write themselves than take on the difficult task of changing people's guarded attitudes toward teaching writing.

3. *Plan to have the program take at least a year, preferably two.* There must be a regular, long term plan of at least a school year for such a program to be successful. One- or two-hour workshop sessions held at least every other week are a minimum. Selected teachers may first work with the outside consultants, but eventually all teachers who will be responsible for improving writing need to be involved in the workshop gatherings. If the groups are too big, they may be split into smaller groups.

4. Set up specific goals to be reached by the end of the school year. If the teachers are given released time, then you have a right to expect them to come up with tangible products at the end of school. Here are some basic goals which might be set for a one-year inservice program.

Basic Goals for a Writing Program

The teachers, with the help of the outside consultant, will

— study, analyze, and discuss the meaning of the latest research, textbooks, and special matters on writing and teaching writing and select the most useful ideas and materials.

— create lessons which exemplify the composing process, try them out with school children, and revise them on the basis of feedback.

— practice using discussion and planning skills and develop guidelines for future interaction.

— outline a program for assessing writing by students and for assessing the writing program for their grade level or for the total school.

— develop a tentative scope and sequence of writing activities for grade levels and for various groupings of students within grade levels.

— devise a tentative list of basic writing competencies for each level and for various groupings of students within grade levels.

But Why Do It?

And a good question, too.

Teaching writing is a hot topic but not a very jazzy one, like the current catch phrases, "disadvantaged" or "gifted and talented"—as if we're not all handicapped in our own fashion and each of us creative in our own way, too.

But if "teaching writing" is not a flashy slogan, it is a topic which gets at what makes people human—the ability to control written language—and when we initiate a scheme to teach writing better we have a chance to help all students—not some special group isolated for quick transfusions of big federal bucks—to learn a top level, human skill, one they can use for the rest of their lives.

So, then, we're at the bottom line: why help people learn how to control written language?

First, kids need to know how to write to get the business of the world done. They need to fill out forms, write business letters, and write papers to persuade and explain. They need to gather information and write reports. The world of commerce, contrary to what the mathematicians and computer whiz bangs say, runs on the expertly handled written word.

Second, kids need to learn how to write well because writing is an amazingly useful intellectual invention. When we take notes, we remember. When we outline, we see structure. When we write down something, we can look at what we have written and rearrange, recast, and thus reexamine in a strangely critical way what we have written. And as we put into words something initially but dimly perceived, we come to understand our intangible thoughts and feelings.

As an aside, if we don't give all our school children the opportunity to learn to write effectively, we deprive them—in the keenest sense of the word—from becoming productive members of our society. And the gap between those who are *able*—meaning those who can control written language—and those who are *not able*—signifying those to whom written language is an incomprehensible, magical system—will widen and increase the alienation in our land.

Third, kids need to write a lot because in some miraculous way, as they do, they will come to learn about themselves in a way no other medium provides. When we write about our early memories, about descriptions of our secret places, when we recount in writing stories told to us by our loved ones, when we respond in writing to what we read in newspapers and magazines and see in the movies and on TV, we learn in a deeply profound way who we are and begin to perceive, however faintly, the potential we have for becoming.

And finally, although writing is not flashy stuff it can be exciting. Kids need, if for no other reason, to learn to write well so they will not be cheated out of the exhilaration of being able to perform with skill and, possibly even with elegance, the complex, exacting, and intellectually demanding task we call writing.

A STARTER'S KIT FOR SETTING UP A WRITING PROGRAM: A BASIC LIST OF USEFUL MATERIAL ON WRITING AND TEACHING WRITING

The Composing Process

Blake, Robert W. "Composing for the Left Hand: Writing Activities for the Intermediate Grades," *Facilitating Language Development*, Report of Third Annual Conference on Language Arts. Buffalo, New York: State University of New York at Buffalo, 1978.

Elbow, Peter. *Writing without Teachers*. New York: Oxford University Press, 1973.

Emig, Janet. *The Composing Process of Twelfth Graders*. Urbana, Illinois: National Council of Teachers of English, 1971.

Varieties of Discourse

Blake, Robert W. and Laurie Taillie, "Quiet and Warm Like Sunshine: Teaching High School Kids to Write Poetry." Typescript, no date.

Britton, James, *et al. The Development of Writing Abilities* (11–18). London: Macmillan Education Ltd., 1975.

Moffett, James. *Teaching the Universe of Discourse*. Boston: Houghton Mifflin Company, 1968.

Revising Writing

Blake, Robert W. "The Writer as Writer and Critic: How to Be a Schizophrenic and Still Not End Up in Bedlam." *Indiana English Journal*, Vol. 9 (Spring, 1975), No. 3:3–9.

Murray, Donald M. *A Writer Teaches Writing*. Boston: Houghton Mifflin Company, 1968.

Shaughnessy, Mina P. *Errors and Expectations*. New York: Oxford University Press, 1977.

Sentence Manipulation

Blake, Robert W. "Outline of Syntactic Structures, Grades 3–8," Mimeographed, no date.

Cooper, Charles R. "An Outline for Writing Sentence-Combining Problems," *English Journal*, Vol. 62 (January, 1973), No. 1:96–102, 108.

Workshopping

Blake, Robert W. "How to Talk to a Writer, or Forward to Fundamentals in Teaching Writing," *English Journal*, Vol. 65 (November, 1976), No. 8:49–55.

Cooper, Charles R. "Responding to Student Writing," *The Writing Process of Students*. Buffalo, N.Y.: State University of New York at Buffalo, Department of Curriculum and Instruction, 1975.

Assessment and Evaluation of Writing

Blake, Robert W. "Assessing English and Language Arts Teachers' Attitudes Toward Writers and Writing." *The English Record*, Vol. XXVII (Summer-Autumn, 1976), No. 3–4:87–97.

Cooper, Charles R. "Measuring Growth in Writing," *English Journal*, Vol. 64 (March, 1975), No. 3:111–120.

———— and Lee Odell. *Evaluating Writing*. Urbana, Illinois: National Council of Teachers of English, 1977.

Diederich, Paul B. *Measuring Growth in English*. Urbana, Illinois: National Council of Teachers of English, 1974.

Setting Up a School Writing Program

Blake, Robert W. and Frederick B. Tuttle, Jr. "Composing as the Curriculum: The Albion Writing Project." *The English Record*, Vol. XXX (Spring, 1979), No. 2:9–14.

· 1 2 ·

ASSESSING ENGLISH AND LANGUAGE ARTS TEACHERS' ATTITUDES TOWARD WRITERS AND WRITING

Robert W. Blake (1976)

Many of the problems English and language arts teachers have with teaching writing surface in their statements about their attitudes towards writers and the act of writing. If they assume, for instance, that teaching writing consists of having students write compositions from an outline and then in discovering mechanical errors in a first draft, what they say about teaching writing will reflect this assumption. If, on the other hand, they feel that one should treat a first draft as professional writers do, as initial copy to be revised and reworked, then their comments about teaching writing will be quite different.

We might assume that English and language arts teachers who held the first assumption about the teaching of writing—after practice in creating varieties of writing and in discussing their writing with others—would change substantially their attitudes toward writers and writing. It should follow, moreover, if they then reported feelings which reflected how experienced writers actually compose, they would become more secure in their ability to teach others to write and, on the basis of their modified attitudes, change what they do in the classroom.

With these assumptions as a basis, I decided to develop and try out an attitude scale on writers and writing with graduate students in a concentrated, five-week summer session course, "Teaching Writing Composition, K-12." In the class were six high school English teachers, one high school social science teacher, seven junior high school English teachers, five elementary school language arts teachers, one high school remedial writing teacher, one college learning skills center teacher, and one high school teacher who taught English as a second language in the American School in Rio de Janeiro, The classes lasted for one and one-half hours per day, five days a week for five weeks.

This is what I wished to do. I would prepare an attitude scale of some forty items dealing with writers and the process of writing, have the college students take the scale at the beginning of the course, do an analysis of the items in the scale to find out which discriminated between those students who were top scorers and those who were bottom scorers on the scale, conduct a course on the teaching of writing which would include varieties of writing and would realistically reflect the writing process, and then find out whether or not the attitudes of the students had changed on a revised scale as a result of the course. I was aware, of course, of how difficult it is to change anyone's attitudes over such a short period of time, but like all curious teachers, I wanted to find out whether or not what we did in a course on teaching writing would actually make a difference in what the students thought about writing after the course was over.

A word about what I believe my audience to be. The paper is addressed to you English and language arts teachers who may or may not have had a beginning course in educational measurement. I'll describe how I set up the attitude scale and treated the data so that if you wish you can create your own attitude scale from my directions. No doubt you will wish to add your own items, delete those you think are inappropriate, or reword mine for use with a different group. In any event, this report is not intended for the educational measurement specialist, who would no doubt be impatient with my narration.

First, I made up a list of statements, both negative and positive, about writing, drawing on what professional writers have to say about how they compose and on my own experiences with writing and teaching writing over a period of twenty years. The statements I grouped into three categories.

There were 18 items in the first caategory, which I called the *Skills of Writing*. Included in it were items like these:

Skills of Writing

	Positive Statement	Negative Statement
Topic: Strong Verbs	I emphasize active verbs in my writing.	Passive verbs make writing style smooth.
Topic: Varied Sentence Structure	I believe it is necessary to revise the sentences in my writing so that they are varied: some short some long, and so forth.	The ideas in writing are important, not the kinds of sentences used.
Topic: Audience	I believe it's important to have an audience firmly in mind before you begin to write.	When I write, I write for myself only and don't think at all about the people who might read what I write.

Other statements in the category of *Skills of Writing* elicited attitudes towards the use of words to refer to concrete things, wordiness and repetition, overworked phrases (cliches), figurative language, and mechanical errors like spelling, punctuation, and capitalization.

The second category I called *Varieties of Writing,* and statements in this category, of which there were 16, were designed to reflect a person's willingness to write pieces from the universe of discourse other than traditional expository prose.

Varieties of Writing

	Positive Statement	Negative Statement
Topic: Letter Writing	I get a kick out of writing letters.	I almost never write letters.
Topic: Character Sketch	I like to write about people I know well.	It doesn't make much sense to try to describe a person in writing.

Statements about other *Varieties of Writing* dealt with short stories, plays, letters to a newspaper editor, and poems.

In the third category were 6 statements, dealing with attitudes toward different *Kinds of Writers*.

Kinds of Writers

	Positive Statement	Negative Statement
Topic: Fiction Writers	I admire writers of fiction.	I don't think short story and novel writers are very useful.
Topic: Poets	I believe the poet is a valuable member of society.	Poets don't contribute anything of importance to our culture.
Topic: Newspaper	I'd like to be a writer for a newspaper.	A newspaper writer's job doesn't seem like much to me.

I then arranged the positive and negative statements in the form of a Likert-type attitude measure in this fashion.

Directions: For each of the following statements about writers and writing, encircle the abbreviations for the words which best describe your opinion about the statement.

	Strongly Agree	Agree	Undecided	Disagree	Strongly Disagree
Trying to write poetic language is a waste of time to me.	SA	A	U	D	SD
I'd like to be a writer for a newspaper.	SA	A	U	D	SD

The positive statements were assigned scores of Strongly Agree—5; Agree—4; Undecided—3; Disagree—2; and Strongly Disagree—1. The negative statements were given reverse scorings with Strongly Agree—1; Agree—2; Undecided—3; Disagree—4; and Strongly Disagree—5. The highest possible score was thus 200, and the lowest possible score, 40.

I gave the "Attitude Scale: Writers and Writing" to the students on the first meeting day. In order to find out which of the forty items discriminated between those students who scored high on the scale and those who scored low, I ranked the papers from highest to lowest, took the scales of the top twenty-seven percent (six papers) and the lowest twenty-seven percent (again six), and did an item analysis of the forty items. This is how item analysis works with the first two items.

Item Analysis of Test Items

Statements from Attitude Scale	Total pts. awarded by 27% of low-scoring students.	Ratio	Total pts. awarded by 27% of high-scoring students	Ratio	Discrimination Index
I almost never write letters.	21	.70	19	.63	-.07
Trying to write poetic language is a waste of time to me.	22	.73	28	.93	.20[1]*

* Item retained because of high discrimination.

First, I added up the scores of each of the items for the low-and high-scoring students independently. The six low-scoring students had on the first item "I almost never write letters" 21 out of a possible 30 points, the ratio of which is .70. The six high-scoring students had 19 out of 30 points, the ratio of which is .63. When we subtract the ratio for the low-scorers from the ratio of the high-scorers, we get the Discrimination Index of -.07. This item discriminated all right, but in a negative fashion, in a direction contrary to that which I expected. The high-scoring students, in other words, liked to write letters even less than did the low-scoring students, and therefore this item was discarded as useless.

As you can see, the next item, "Trying to write poetic language is a waste of time to me" was highly discriminating. The ratio for the low-scoring students, 21 out of a possible 30 points, was .73 and for the high-scoring students, 28 out of 30 points, was .93. When we subtract the ratio of the low-scoring group from the ratio of the high-scoring group we arrive at the Discrimination Index of .20. Usually, acceptable items must show a Discrimination Index of "equal to or greater than" (the mathematical symbol for this relationship is -) .20 (-.20), but since I wanted 20 items for a final, reliable scale, I accepted 3 with Discrimination Indexes of .16 and 1 of .17. The remaining 16 were at .20 or above.

As far as items discriminating within the categories, there were 7 out of the 18 which discriminated in the category of *Skills of Writing,* 10 out of 16 in *Varieties of Writing,* and 3 out of 6 in *Kinds of Writers.*

At the end of the course, the students took the entire Attitude Scale of forty items again, and we discussed their personal reactions to each item. Generally, the items that did not discriminate and were discarded seemed to be one of two kinds.

First, some did not reflect a clear case for good or poor writing; neither low-nor high-scorers could agree on them. For instance, I thought Mark Twain's epigram "As to the adjective: when in doubt, strike it out" would be a fine item, but it showed no discrimination between low-and high-scorers; the score was 12 to 12, with a .00 difference. The negative statement for using adjectives fared even worse: "An expert writer makes his writing come alive with descriptive adjectives." The score was 12 for low-scorers and 9 for high-scorers, with a .10 difference. Possibly a good number of the high-scorers believed professional writers use many descriptive adjectives. Or I had simply worded the items poorly.

For other statements, both low-and high-scorers agreed to the extent that there was little difference between the items. Both groups, for instance, concurred with this item: "I make sure I proofread carefully my writing for mechanical errors in punctuation, spelling, capitalization, and word usage" to the tune of 21–26, with a Discrimination Index of .03. And likewise with the statement, "I emphasize active verbs in my writing"; the lows had 19, the highs 21, with a Discrimination Index of .10.

Using a split-half technique and the Spearman-Brown Prophecy Formula, I computed the reliability coefficient of the final scale of twenty items, which is .852. (You can look up the process and formula in any educational measurement textbook.) A homemade scale like this, I am told, which has a coefficient of .85 or better, is quite reliable. In layman's terms, this means that if students re-took the attitude scale they would score on it in about the same position; they would not have any marked up's or down's. When any test is reliable, in other words, it is consistent.

After the students had taken the Attitude Scale for a second time at the end of the course, I selected only the twenty items that discriminated best and compiled the scores for them on the pre-and post-Attitude Scales. Three students had losses of 3, 2, and 1 points, but the remaining nineteen students showed gains on the post-Attitude Scale of 20 items was 74.95, and the average score for the post-Attitude Scale was 81.36, with an average gain of 6.41.

This is the final scale of 20 items.

ATTITUDE SCALE: WRITERS AND WRITING

Last Name	First	MI
	Date	

Directions: For each of the following statements about writers and writing, encircle the abbreviations for the words which best describe your opinion about the statement.

	Strongly Agree	Agree	Undecided	Disagree	Strongly Disagree
1. Trying to write poetic language is a waste of time to me.	SA	A	U	D	SD
2. I'd like to be a writer for a newspaper.	SA	A	U	D	SD
3. I'd rather do almost anything than write a scene for a play.	SA	A	U	D	SD
4. Writing poems seems kind of useless to me.	SA	A	U	D	SD
5. I believe it is necessary to revise the sentences in my writing so that they are varied: some short, some long, and so forth.	SA	A	U	D	SD
6. I admire writers of fiction.	SA	A	U	D	SD
7. Effective writers use many general terms and abstractions.	SA	A	U	D	SD
8. I like to write something every day.	SA	A	U	D	SD
9. I believe the poet is a valuable member of society.	SA	A	U	D	SD

	Strongly Agree	Agree	Undecided	Disagree	Strongly Disagree
10. I would like to be able to write poems that could be published.	SA	A	U	D	SD
11. I believe it is necessary to revise what I write.	SA	A	U	D	SD
12. Being able to write a short story isn't one of the things that I want to do in life.	SA	A	U	D	SD
13. I enjoy writing figurative language like similes, metaphors, and personification.	SA	A	U	D	SD
14. I like to write about people I know well.	SA	A	U	D	SD
15. I would like to be able to write a short story that could be published.	SA	A	U	D	SD
16. The writer who uses those phrases developed over the years appeals to more people.	SA	A	U	D	SD
17. The ideas in writing are important, not the kinds of sentences used.	SA	A	U	D	SD
18. The best writing is produced in the first draft.	SA	A	U	D	SD
19. Once I have written down what I have to say, I don't want to go over it again.	SA	A	U	D	SD
20. I don't ever write anything unless I am forced to.	SA	A	U	D	SD

For the category of *Skills of Writing* with 7 items, the average score for the pre-test was 25.00, for the post-text 28.05, with a gain of 3.05. For the category of *Varieties of Writing* with 10 items, the average score for the pre-test was 36.32, for the post-test 40.23, with a gain of 3.91. And for the category of *Kinds of Writers* with 3 items, the average score for the pre-test was 12.18, for the post-test 12.27, with a gain of .09. It was obvious that the third category of *Kinds of Writers* contained too few items for it to measure any significant attitude change. More items should be added to this category, or it might just as well be dropped.

So what can we say about the Attitude Scale: Writers and Writing? After an intensive five-week course in the teaching of written composition, a group of twenty-two experienced elementary language arts and secondary school teachers, by a convincing majority, changed their attitudes toward writing and writers.

It is difficult to isolate the particular activities during the course which caused the students to change their attitudes, but on the basis of written and oral comments from the students, I believe some of the following activities may have contributed to the changed attitudes.

First, the students came to know the composing process intimately and intuitively. We spent little time in talking *about* writing. Rather they produced pieces of writing every day or so. They went through the stages of prewriting, first draft writing, and rewriting and came to have a realistic idea of what all successful writers do when they compose. Many students reported they had a better understanding of what writing was really like and they stated they would have more sympathy for their students as they wrestled with the composing process. Such changed ideas might have appeared in the changed attitudes.

Second, the students all wrote a variety of pieces, including spontaneous writing, a critical reaction to a movie or television show, a persuasive essay (letter to a newspaper editor), newspaper writing (editorials, news stories, sports stories, and feature articles), autobiography (earliest memory), figurative language (similes, metaphors, sense reporting, refreshed observations, haiku, concrete poetry, free verse), and character description and short fiction. Many of the students had written little previously except for critical analyses, expository pieces, and first draft essay examination papers. Some reported difficulties with creating similes and metaphors, but the same individuals were delighted to find they could write effective figurative language if they persisted. In fact, many students preferred the writing of poetry and fiction to exposition and said that they now understood better what poets and novelists did. Again, their revised ideas about writers might have influenced their changed attitudes on the scale.

Third, I gave the students discrete exercises dealing with the skills of writing to do and to discuss with other members of the class. These skills included such items as good openers, active and passive verbs, wordiness and repetition, overworked phrases (cliches), the use of vivid verbs, and the use of words to refer to concrete things rather than to abstractions. I also gave them some exercises—not a fully structured program, though—with creating better sentences through sentence combining. Students reported they were unaware or had forgotten that there were these skills of writing and were pleased to find that as they revised sentences they improved their writing. As a result they became more confident in their ability to control their composing. Some items in the final attitude scale reflect such changed attitudes toward the skills of writing.

Finally, the writing workshop feature was a crucial element of the course. Each day when the students had written a piece, they read their writing aloud to each other in a group of from ten to twelve students. I've found that in groups of more than twelve or so even adutlts seem inhibited about reading their writing orally. In the writing workshop situations, we insisted that all comments had to be positive and supportive; there should be no criticism which would crush the writer's confidence, especially at the beginning of the course. And all comments had to be aimed at improving the writing, not at tearing it apart. Very shortly, the students learned how to encourage each other by making comments like these: "What a great figure of speech!" "I like that description of your grandmother. I'd like to hear more about her." "What would happen if you changed the point of view of that story? Why don't you try to tell it from the little boy's viewpoint rather than from his mother's?" and "You have many formal words and complicated sentences. How would the piece sound if you used simpler words and broke down the long sentences into shorter ones?"

And as they learned how vulnerable a writer feels when he reads his work to others, the students reported that they now had a great deal of empathy for their students as they went through the writing process and promised themselves to be less critical in a negative sense and more supportive of their students, work. Although such changes in attitudes were not reflected in the attitude scale, I consider the writing workshop activities and the attitudes reflecting these activities to be crucial for teaching individuals to write.

There are, of course, obvious limitations to the Attitude Scale. It was aimed at experienced teachers of the English language arts, most of whom had been English majors in college. The initial scores were therefore fairly high, with some gains slight. And the instruction which was to influence attitude change occurred over a relatively short period of time.

Some of the items, furthermore, which did not discriminate for these individuals might be discriminating for a different group. The item, "I make sure I proofread carefully my writing for mechanical errors in punctuation, spelling, capitalization, and word usage," for instance, did not discriminate because it appeared that all teachers considered theis necessary for good writing. A group of ninth grade students might react differently to such a statement.

And finally there was no control group of students who might have taken the Attitude Scale before and after a different kind of writing course or even a group which took the Scale without any writing course at all. All we can finally say is that this group of particular individuals, in this situation, generally changed their attitudes about writing after a series of experiences with writing and reacting to writing.

So much for the Attitude Scale itself. There are other ways to find out how people feel about experiences. One way is to ask them. So at the end of the course, I asked the students to respond in writing to this question:

As a result of the experiences that you had with the course—reading books, writing different pieces, reading out loud your writing in groups, listening to student reports on techniques for encouraging public school students to write, and reading the instructor's comments on your writing—how do you feel about writing and the teaching of writing? Is the feeling different from the feeling that you had at the beginning of the course? If so, will you please explain?

Here are comments that are typical of those made by the students.

I feel much better about my own writing. You really convinced all of us that we have it in us if we take the time. Since I have more confidence in my own writing. I therefore feel more competent to teach others writing.

It happened. I've changed. I've improved as a writer simply because I am writing and am conscious of all the elements we've established as keys to good writing. "Show don't tell." "Exorcise English." "Accentuate the active." "Reach for the refreshing." "Grab with the opener." I'm listening to myself again and filtering my experiences through all my senses, consciously searching for the small surprises which my perceptions can create.

At the beginning of the course I was also discouraged with my job [high school remedial writing teacher] and felt at times it was hopeless. Through interaction with other teachers and my work on a writing program, I have reversed my feelings. I honestly believe I can do a better job teaching writing than I did last year.

In general my feelings towards writing haven't changed. I knew it was hard work and difficult to maintain. I knew we taught ineffectively in many areas. The course and the writings did help me solidify the areas of weakness or foolishness, however, and give me encouragement to continue myself and the programs I use to reach the kids. It made me feel I was on the right track and not alone.

I think I am more aware of the necessity to relax and enjoy what the students write. I don't mean lowering standards—accepting shoddy work—but accepting the work for what it is and enjoying it. Being aware of what goes into writing, I am more aware of what I want out of it.

I have a tremendous amount of improving and editing to do but have a concrete awareness of some of my faults. I also feel more capable of teaching and assessing other people's writing. I hope that I will have the ability to criticize gently but effectively and be able to accept another's writing as the best expression of what he feels without forcing my feelings into his writing.

Is the "Attitude Scale: Writers and Writing" a valid one? Over a period of many years, I have read what professional writers say about writing. And I have myself struggled with moving from half formed thoughts, to first drafts, to revisions, and finally to pieces in print, so I think I have an accurate idea of what is involved in the writing process. Do the statements in the scale reflect written composing? And do they represent attitudes which reflect accurately what beginning as well as experienced writers do as they compose? I believe they do.

You might use such an attitude scale in at least two ways. First, you can use the scale, or one adapted to your purpose, to find out where your students are with regard to practices in writing. If you find they have negative attitudes towards the Skills of Writing, for instance, then you could provide instruction which would change these attitudes.

But more importantly, I think, you could use such a scale to help students consider their beliefs about writing. Then if they are able to contrast their beliefs with those expressed by experienced writers, they may strengthen attitudes which make sense and discard those which don't.

But why bother with attitudes about writing in the first place? Because how we feel is so closely tied up with what we think and do; our attitudes, expecially our unconscious attitudes, mirror our actions. If this is so, then we and our students can profit from a close examination of our attitudes toward such a complex task as composing in writing. And if we find that our attitudes reflect unrealistic practices, then perhaps we shall be willing to change our attitudes *and* our practices, If an attitude scale on writers and writing and the consideration of its items can help a teacher or student change for the better what they feel and do about writing and the teaching of writing then it may be of some use.

Note

I should like to thank my colleague in measurement and evaluation. Morris Beers, for helping me with this project to paraphrase a close friend of his, he asked me to produce more data than I thought I needed.

SECTION IV

POETRY IN THE CLASSROOM

The first three pieces in this section on poetry were part of a three-part series that the "English Journal" published in 1990, 1991, and 1992, respectively. In the first, on poetry and the "reconstruction of reality," Robert poses the question, "Why do they [poets] spend so much agony and time at a chore which most people hold as useless?" Drawing upon the original Greek word for poetry, "that which is created," Robert reveals to us what many poets, like Atwood and Robert Penn Warren, say are their reasons for writing poetry in the first place.

The second in this series "One way to write a poem" takes us through an exercise in writing poetry, "Early Memory, "that Robert found gave even beginning student-poets the confidence to believe that "spontaneous writing would lead to something … to continue to work on."

The last article situates poetry in our culture as a tool; an outlet; a method that allows us, as human beings, to struggle with some of the "great moral issues of our time." Essentially, here, Robert challenges to us to question the premier place of the "logical-mathematical" in our schools and society as the dominant mode of thinking and, hence teaching and learning. Robert reminds us that, "poetry is a way of learning and knowing that far antedates rational thinking and abstract thought."

In the next, and last, piece in this section, Robert shows us how high school students can (and do) read and respond to poetry in the classroom, as he shows us that while it may be easier to "tell" students the "correct" meaning of a poem, it is much more worthwhile to "show "students how to respond, highlighting the processes they use in revealing both the mental and emotional experiences they follow in what he called, "the response process."

Robert's treatment of poetry from a "reconstruction of reality," to the moral aspects of poetry, to creating actual poetry, and then responding to it, both mentally and emotionally, comes to us, 25 years later, once again, at a crucial time for teaching and learning in our schools. Again, accountability measures and a standardization of curricula by outside accreditation bodies are putting a heavy emphasis on writing for "workplace ready." That is, writing is seen as a vehicle to transmit the logical-mathematical (that Robert so convincingly shows us is only ONE way of knowing) knowledge that is so prevalent in U.S. businesses today—that of short informational and/or persuasive pieces (think: memos, fact sheets, instruction manuals). Indeed, the New Common Core State Standards de-emphasizes poetry altogether, so that by the time students are in high school, they are expected to have had little, if any, exposure to poetry at all, leaving room for a full 70% of their writing classes to focus on non-fiction.

· 1 3 ·

POETS ON POETRY

Writing and the Reconstruction of Reality

Robert W. Blake (1990)

When one writes poetry, one reconstructs reality. Throughout this series of three sections to be published separately here, I'd like to explore what I mean by the words "poetry," "reconstruct," and "reality." The original Greek word for poetry simply means "that which is created," good enough to cover broadly all of what is meant by literature. "Reconstruct" means literally to "construct again" from observations and memories a new version of reality. And by "reality" I mean all of the miraculous world we can perceive through our senses and our minds.

In this first section, "Poets on Poetry," I shall first consider what poets themselves have to say about poetry: how they write poems, why they write poems, and what poetry is good for. In the second section, "One Way to Write a Poem," to get at the process of writing a poem, I use testimony from the most faithful witness I know, myself, as well as drafts from students.

In the third, concluding section, "The Morality of Poetry," I argue that although the logical-mathematical way of learning and knowing is the prevailing mode of thinking in our culture—and therefore is taught almost exclusively in schools—poetry as a way of knowing is another valuable way of thinking and, in many significant ways, far superior to abstract thought. Through poetic knowing, we learn about our feeling selves, learn how to give audience to others and become members of a culture, and ultimately learn how to use words, in the company of others, to reconstruct reality.

Poets on Writing Poetry

Most poets are more serious about writing poems than they are with telling anybody how they do it, but as I looked through what some said about writing poetry—here and there among all the stuff they produce in response to interviewers—I find short, offhand comments about how and, when pressed to the wall, why they write poetry. But these poets can't really tell me how to write poetry. Only I can learn that for myself by doing. As Theodore Roethke (1975) says in "The Waking," "I learn by going where I have to go" (1,133, 1,134). No, I can't learn how to write poetry by eavesdropping on others, but I can feel reassured—have my own timid and tentative thoughts validated—by what they say about writing poetry which sounds so familiar to me that I smile, nod my head vigorously, and mumble, "Sure, they do it, too. That's what they do." I feel a kinship with them; I feel that I'm not alone in this world of people who don't much care about words and how they're used or for what purposes. I feel that I am one of a band of brothers and sisters who actually are concerned about words, how they can be jockeyed back and forth, how they can help me make a design out of my life, and how I can use them to reconstruct my own version of reality.

Obsession with Words

Saying that poets love words—have an inexplicable attraction to them—is not a strong enough statement. Poets are obsessed with words. They listen to them, then write them down. Look up their meanings. Track their origins through etymologies of unabridged dictionaries. Test them against their personal versions of reality. They arrange them, uproot them, and transplant them next to other words to see how they go together and grow.

> Distractions are substitutes for the fearful experience of facing one's self alone.

Many poets begin the first step of poetic writing simply with the sound of words. Margaret Atwood perceives poetry initially as an aural activity, poetry as music. "My poems," says Atwood in an interview with Joyce Carol Oates (1978), "usually begin with words and phrases which appeal more because of their sound than their meaning, and the movement and the phrasing of a poem are more important to me" (15). Poetry, for Atwood, is not a rational activity but one based upon the sounds of words. "For me," continues Atwood, "every poem has a texture of sound which is at least as important to me as the 'argument.' This is not to minimize 'statement'" (15).

For Galway Kinnell, the oral and aural dimensions of poetry are so crucial that he memorizes poems, both his and those of others, because he believes a poem does not really enter the reader until he memorizes it (Beckman 1983, 16).

Need for Solitude

Most poets don't mention this aspect of their lives much because I guess they just take it for granted. Robert Penn Warren tells us, "Ideas come to me when I am relaxed. Poems in particular. I compose them in my head, memorize them, then I write them down" (Tucker 1981, 41). In his half tongue-in-cheek "Godfatherly Rules of Writing a Bestselling Novel," Mario Puzo (1978) lists these as "Rules":

- Moodiness is really concentration. Accept it because concentration is the key to writing.
- A writer's life should be a tranquil life. Read a lot and go to the movies.
- Never let a domestic quarrel ruin a day's writing. If you can't start the next day fresh, get rid of your wife. (71)

William Stafford (1973) starts writing poetry every morning, often before the light. He tells us,

When I write, I like to have an interval before me when I'm not likely to be interrupted. For me, this means usually the early morning, before the others are awake. I get pen and paper, take a glance out the window (often it is dark out there), and wait. (44)

Why the need for solitude? I suspect because only when we are quiet, without distractions—distractions that too much of the time are substitutes for the fearful experience of facing one's self alone—are we able to free our captive thoughts and feelings and learn how to let the images we have swirling in the unconscious bubble up and coalesce into bright, uninvited pictures, images, and patterns. Only when I block out sights and sounds immediately on my mind's surface can I allow what is deep within me, what is original and strikingly precious, to come up like a great fish rising from the depths, its presence felt first only as a slight tremor in the water, then as an indistinct shadow, and finally as a fully formed, awesome, multicolored creature bursting into the sun of my consciousness.

A Tempered Confidence

By "tempered" confidence, I mean the assurance poets have learned from constant practice that when they absent themselves from diversions, allow themselves to become tranquil, empty their minds to let unthought ideas, forgotten images, and scarred-over feelings appear, words, singly and in patterns, mysteriously, almost by their own volition, come forward. If certain conditions are met, the poet knows poems will take shape, will be born, but to the word "confidence" I must add "tempered" to describe this "humbled arrogance," this "battered cockiness" because I know how fragile the conditions for producing a poem are. I am confident when I say to myself "if I am quiet and empty my mind of intruding distractions, I believe a poem will appear." I'm tempered, though, and not a little timid because I'm not quite sure I really do *know* a poem will appear. Although one always has unfolded in the past, I'm bare-bone, deep-in-my-marrow, really afraid that the poem this time just might not materialize. A timid confidence, I'm afraid, is what I share with other poets.

Stafford, who appears more confident than I usually feel, calls this state of mind, "receptivity." He says,

> But I do not wait very long in solitude, for there is always a nibble—and this is where receptivity comes in. To get started I will accept anything that occurs to me. Something always occurs, of course, to any of us. We can't keep from thinking. Maybe I have to settle for an immediate impression: it's cold, or hot, or dark, or bright, or in between! Or—well the possibilities are endless. If I put down something, that thing will help the next thing come, and I'm off. If I let the process go on, things will occur to me that were not at all in my mind when I started. These things, odd or trivial as they may be, are somehow connected. And if I let them string out, surprising things will happen. (44)

An unexpected gift, an unearned benefit, a "grace," if you will, which comes as a result of this tranquility, this meditation, this cleansing of distracting thoughts and images, is the inevitable fact that the images rising from one's unconscious converge, grow together, connect, form patterns, and achieve a form of their own. As Stafford puts it, if poets allow themselves to become receptive to words,

> [a] strange bonus happens. At times, without insisting on it, my writings become coherent; the successive elements that occur to me are clearly related. They lead by themselves to new connections. Sometimes the language, even the syllables that

happen along, may start a trend. ... I know that back of my activity there will be the coherence of my self, and that indulgence of my impulses will bring recurrent patterns and meanings again. (45)

So poets I know are essentially obsessed with words separately and in patterns, how they sound, how they look, and what meanings humans imbue them with. In order to be receptive to words, though, poets arrange considerable blocks of solitary time, sometimes time at regular intervals and sometimes at random intervals, during which, like wine tasters—who rinse out the lingering essence, the scent and taste and color of a wine from their mouths and nasal cavities with a swirl of clear water to flush out lingering perceptions—to let in new thoughts, images, and feelings, which, by a will of their own, form into coherent webs of meaning.

Why Poets Write Poetry

That's something of what poets say they do as they create poetry. There's not really much to go on because poets, I suspect, don't believe many people—except other poets—have the slightest interest in exactly how they do what they do. Most people are interested only in what they produce rather than in the process by which they create poems, especially if it's tied to a literature anthology or Pulitzer Prize. But *I'm* interested in what they do. Why do they expend so much agony and time at a chore which most people hold as useless? I really want some response to this one because it will help me understand what poetry is all about. People, I know, do what they do for a number of reasons: they serve hamburgers to buy rock-and-roll tapes, baby-sit to buy stonewashed jeans, assemble cameras to eat and pay the rent, sell stocks and bonds to live in a colonial house with a two-car garage, two cars, and three kids—a boy, girl, boy—with a golden retriever, and become administrators and politicians so they can wield power over great masses of people. I understand why these people do what they do. But why do poets write poetry when they can't buy a summer house on Cape Cod with it or snort coke for breakfast or hold power over people and inflict insufferable indignities on them in the names of religion, politics, or education? I already know why I write poetry (although I'm sheepish about telling people my reasons), but I really want to know why other people write poetry. Anyway, here's what some poets say about why they write poetry.

When asked why she writes, Atwood answers,

I suppose I think it's a redundant question, like "Why does the sun shine?" As you say it's a human activity. I think the real question is "Why doesn't everyone?" (Oates 45)

In answer to the question, "Why do you write?" Robert Penn Warren answers with another question,

Why do you scratch when it itches? It's a compulsion. It's a statement. I know a thousand stories, everybody knows a thousand stories. ... I've carried a novel for as long as twenty years. And some poems longer than that. Sometimes a line will hang around for years. (Tucker 1982, 38)

> "I think the real question is, 'Why doesn't everyone?'"
> —Margaret Atwood

Shirley Hazzard (1982) writes, she says, because, for her, literature

is a matter of seeking accurate words so that tone, context, sound and syntax are ideally combined, without a show of contrivance. That is the proper and agonizing business of literature, in which much of the writer's suffering originates: "the intolerable wrestle with words and meanings," as T. S. Eliot called it. Every writer who is serious about his craft experiences a sense of profaning pure meaning with unworthy words. (11)

These, then, are a few answers to why poets write poetry. It's natural—" Why doesn't everybody?"; it scratches an itch; it uses words to convey truthfully the human condition; and some poets are compelled to write in order to be witnesses to how we humans behave.

What's Poetry Good For?

Related to the question of why poets write poetry is another question that I am dying to learn about: What's the good of poetry? Although I'm strangely invigorated when I write poetry—even after a long day of teaching and desk work, even though I'm told it's a natural act, even though it does relieve an itch, even though poetry conveys the human condition, what, really, is it good for? I know what writing poetry does for me, but I need to hear what other poets say poetry is good for. Most poets create poetry simply because they are compelled to do so, they tell us, and never stop to think much about the reasons for their suffering and travail, but now and then, some poets—when they are not writing poems—stand off and try to put into words their notions of the value of poetry.

Atwood seems to be the sort of person who writes poetry because she simply and directly needs to and doesn't stop much—unless asked—to think about what poetry's good for.

> I'm not sure what the function of poetry is. ... poetry acts like a lens, or like a thread dipped in a supersaturated solution, causing a crystallization, but I'm not sure that's it either. (Oates 44)

For John Ashbery, poetry is for telling people about things they might not have thought about before. Says Ashbery, "I believe in communicating, but I don't believe in communicating something the reader already knows" (Lehman 1984, 64). If that's true, he has been asked, what *do* you want to communicate? And he replies,

> I guess the answer is that I don't really know until I'm actually in the process of writing, and after that happens, I forget what it was. But my aim is not to puzzle and terrorize readers but to give them something new to think about. (Lehman 64)

The joy received from poetry, for Ashbery, is something more than message.

> The pleasure one gets from reading poetry comes from something else than the idea or story in a poem, which is just a kind of armature for the poet to drape many colored rags. These are what one really enjoys but can't admit it, since there *is* this underlying urge to analyze and make sense of everything. But what is "making sense," anyway? (Lehman 82)

Madeline Beckman reports in an interview with Kinnell that for him the poem represents "the sacred character of human life" (15). Kinnell believes a sacred force exists in everything, the force even showing itself in destruction.

> When one animal eats another, that definitely had to do with the interchange of life, the dependency of one living creature on another. ... I think the problem with us today is that we have gone crazy. Human destruction is of a different order from every other form of destruction ever known on earth, because it's an act of madness. ... The original and continuing function of poetry has been to counteract technological madness and to reconcile the human being once again with existence. (Beckman 15)

For John Updike (1976), the reason for poetry (all art) is this:

> My first thought about art as a child, was that the artist brings something into the world that didn't exist before, and that he does it without destroying something else.

A kind of refutation of the conservation of matter. That still seems to me its central magic, its core of joy. (79)

And finally, Czeslaw Milosz (1983), the Nobel laureate, tells us that, for him, poetry is the passionate

> pursuit of the Real. No science or philosophy can change the fact that a poet stands before reality that is every day new, miraculously complex, inexhaustible, and tries to enclose as much of it as possible in words. That elementary contact, verifiable by the five senses, is more important than any mental construction. The never fulfilled desire to achieve mimesis, to be faithful to detail, makes for the health of poetry and gives it a chance to survive periods unpropitious to it. The very act of naming things presupposes a faith in their existence and thus in a true world, whatever Nietzsche might say. Of course, there are poets who only relate words to words, not to their models in things, but their artistic defeat indicates that they are breaking some sort of rule of poetry. (57)

Poets, I gather, see the value of poetry in various ways. Poetry is like a lens or prism through which one views the world in a heightened way. Poetry is for telling people what they hadn't noticed or thought about before. Poetry is for displaying unexpected yet pleasing patterns of words, like "multicolored rags." Poetry is using precisely chosen words to reveal what people and living creatures are really like. Poetry is for representing the sacredness of human existence. Poetry creates something that didn't exist before without destroying something else in the process. And poetry is for naming all the concrete things in our universe and, by naming, acknowledging their existence and ultimately placing them in an intuitively perceived order, which I call reconstructing reality.

Works Cited

Beckman, Madeline. 1983. "Galway Kinnell Searches for Innocence." *Saturday Review* Sept.-Oct.: 14–16.

Hazzard, Shirley. 1982. "The Making of a Writer: We Need Silence to Find out What We Think." *The New York Times Book Review* 14 Nov.: 11, 28–29.

Lehman, David. 1984. "John Ashbery: The Pleasures of Poetry." *The New York Times Magazine* 16 Dec.: 62 +.

Milosz, Czeslaw. 1983. *The Witness of Poetry*. Cambridge: Harvard UP.

Oates, Joyce Carol. 1978. "Margaret Atwood: Poems and Poet." *The New York Times Book Review* 21 May: 15, 43–45.

Puzo, Mario. 1978. "Mario Puzo's Godfatherly Rules for Writing a Bestselling Novel." *Time* 28 Aug.: 71.

Roethke, Theodore. 1975. "The Waking." *The Norton Anthology of Poetry*. New York: Norton. 1,134–35.

Stafford, William. 1973. "A Way of Writing." *Responding: Three*. Lexington, MA: Ginn. 44–46.

Tucker, Carll. 1981. "Creators on Creating: Robert Penn Warren." *Saturday Review* July: 38, 40–41.

Updike, John. 1976. "The Paris Review Talks to Writers." Qtd. in *The New York Times Book Review* 21 Nov.: 79.

· 1 4 ·

POETS ON POETRY

One Way To Write a Poem

Robert W. Blake (1991)

In the first article in this series (1990, "Poets on Poetry: Writing and the Reconstruction of Reality, *EJ* 79.7, 16–21), I related what I've learned from some poets about how they view poetry—how they write, what poetry is to them, and what it's good for. Now I'd like to tell about one task I set for my students to help them with the frequently strange and foreboding job of writing a poem. To do this, I'll detail the assignment and show how one student worked through this particular task with evidence from her drafts. But since I won't be able to report what went on in her head as she went through the incredibly complex process of creating a poem, I'll also chronicle the process I followed as I composed along with the students.

Early Memory

Once one becomes a practicing poet—receives a life sentence of solitary confinement with words—one discovers prompts, cues for writing poems anywhere if one is receptive. One of the enduring starts for various kinds of writing—autobiography, narrative, as well as poetry—is that of an early memory. I first came across the idea in "Endpaper," by Jerome Agel in the *New York Times Magazine* (1975, 26 Oct.), called simply "First Memory." Nine people reported on their earliest memories. Arthur Miller, for instance, re-created this one:

> I was probably 2 or 3; I don't know. I was on the floor; my mother, in a long woolen dress that reached to her ankles, was speaking into a wall telephone. I tugged at her hem: a shaft of sunlight crossed her shoe. (111)

Mikhail Baryshnikov told this story:

> I was very young and it was a very sunny day in Riga, Latvia, and my mother and I were outside. I couldn't walk very well yet and I was holding onto my mother's skirt for support and looking up at her. I remember that she was wearing a dress of chiffon with yellow and purple flowers. I remember her ashblonde hair and bright blue eyes and thinking how incredibly beautiful she looked in the sunlight. (111)

I imagined such a prompt would be a natural for students to start off writing. All of us, of course, have memories, so no one would have the anxiety of having nothing to write about. (Later, I read in an interview with Bernard Malamud something to the effect that writers have two funds of experiences to draw from: early childhood and the rest of their lives.) Furthermore, such very early memories call forth bright images, conjure sharp senses, and awaken profound feelings. Such a task would produce great raw stuff for writing, I thought. I first asked students to write literally about the first time they could remember anything but found that for the students these memories, although vivid and intense, were invariably brief and slight. Later, I asked for an early memory, not necessarily for *the* earliest memory, and directed them to remember a time when they were "either terribly frightened or enormously happy." But then I recalled Thornton Wilder's play *Our Town* (1958, *Adventures in American Literature*, New York: Harcourt) in which Emily resolves to return to the life she had known and decides to pick a "happy day." Mrs. Gibbs tells her, "No. At least choose an unimportant day. Choose the least important day in your life. It will be important enough" (Act III, 395). Is it that any single day would be miraculous enough for a heightened consciousness of living?

When I asked students to use the early memory as a prompt, I found that what they wrote could have gone off into any number of directions to become an autobiographical piece, a story, or a poem. So to move them directly from the early memory to a poem, I asked them to follow these general movements. First, to the task.

Prewriting Task

Think back to a time in your early childhood when you were terror-stricken, unbelievably happy, or when you were just conscious of your life being wonderful. Close your eyes and put yourself back in that time. Think about questions like these:

- Where are you? In your house? At school? In the fields or in the woods?
- What time is it? Early morning, noon, or late at night? What time of year is it? Summer? Fall?
- Who's there? Your father or mother, brothers or sisters, other relatives, or good friends? What are their names? How old are they?
- Is there an animal there? If so, what kind of creature?
- What sounds do you hear? People's voices? Other sounds?
- What do you feel? Taste?
- How do you feel? Contented and happy? Frightened? Do you hate what's happening? Are you strangely miserable? Or are you so happy you can sing? Why are you feeling this way?

Try to connect your feelings to an object or image, like a strawberry ice cream cone, a flashlight beam, a cigarette glowing in the dark, or a streak of lightning seen through a window at night.

Now jot down your images and feelings as they come to you. Don't worry about the "correctness" of what you're writing. Let the words coming from your pen or pencil carry you to new pictures and associations.

Charlotte's Process

Here's how one student responded to this prompt. Charlotte originally wrote out this first draft in pencil, diagonally across lined paper. I'll show what she wrote with crossouts and notes to herself in the margin.

Reflection
I see my grandmother,
bent, eating
strawberry ice cream
with a shaking hand;
I see a flash of light
my father on hands & knees
Reading the comics to me,

and I, engrossed
burning myself on his
his lighted cigarette end
I remember fright—
an imagined face in
a dark window,
the comfort of arms & explanation
to show me safety.
thunder & lightning
a mother's fear; an
aunt & uncle's reassurance

Don't justify
enlarge on one
story—high action
end going upstairs

As we can infer from the crossouts and notes to herself in this initial revision, Charlotte started out with the general statement, "I can not grasp fully ..." but crossed it out, beginning with the direct "I see my grandmother," then crossing out "in a" and using the straightforward verbal "bent." She also deletes the word "end," possibly since the lighted end is the only part of the cigarette which can burn. At first, it appears she decided to move her original beginning "I can not grasp fully" to the end but then later decided to delete it altogether, possibly on the basis of her own decision not to "justify" the meaning of the poem. According to her note, she originally intended to end the piece by "going upstairs," but evidently decided not to do this.

She then took this handwritten revision of a first draft, revised it extensively, and typed this next revision.

First Senses
I see my grandmother bent over
And taste the
Strawberry ice cream she eats
With a shaking hand.
I see a cone of light.
My father, on hands and knees
Reads the comics to me,
And I, wide-eyed,
Burn myself on his cigarette.
I see fright—
A face in the dark window!
And feel the comfort of arms.

When we contrast this version to the previous one, we see the major changes Charlotte has made. She has her grandmother "bent over," instead of only "bent," but significantly Charlotte herself now "tastes" the strawberry ice cream her grandmother once ate. Such a change would make the image more direct and personal by connecting her to her grandmother through the intimate sense of taste. Next she changes "flash" of light to "cone" of light. Could it have been that to Charlotte the word "flash" represented an image of an intermittent light—unlike a beam of a flashlight— while the image of a "cone" more accurately represented the picture of the light thrown by the flashlight? Also, "cone" neatly relates to "ice cream cone." She then substitutes "wide-eyed" for "engrossed," and we can

> She ruthlessly deletes several lines to condense her poem.

only applaud this move because the word "engrossed," although it represents an impressive display of vocabulary, is an "academic," "general" word, "telling" rather than "showing." The phrase "wide-eyed," furthermore, shows us a clear picture of a child's face, and the phrase also has the merit of being simple and direct as well as more accurate than the original word. She changes the participle "burning" to the simple and direct verb "burn" in the line "I burn myself," thus substituting a more powerful verb for a less forceful participle. At the same time, she repeats the structure of the pronoun "I" with a simple present-tense verb related to the senses: "I burn myself" continues the structures of "I see my grandmother" and "[I] taste the strawberry ice cream." She changes "I remember fright" to "I see fright" and deletes the "telling" word "imagined" from the phrase "an imagined face in a dark window." An "imagined fright" is just as "real" as an actual fright. In a major revision, she deletes the last five lines, all but the phrase "comfort of arms" and ends with that phrase in the line, "And feel the comfort of arms." The effect of this judicious cutting is to continue the structure of the pronoun followed by a present-tense verb of [I] "feel" and to omit the "telling" phrases "& explanation to show me safety," "Thunder and lightning," "a mother's fear," and "an aunt and uncle's reassurance." By cutting out these lines and letting the line "And feel the comfort of arms" stand for the other lines, she intuitively—we presume—makes use of the poetic device of synecdoche, letting the part represent the whole, allowing the "comfort of arms" to stand for the aunt and uncle's reassurance and love they show by holding her when she sees fright in a window and hears thunder and sees lightning. Furthermore, by creating the phrase "I see fright" instead of the prosaic "I remember fright," she uses the powerful poetic device of metonomy, by which one idea is evoked by some word which relates to another associated thought or feeling.

Charlotte's revised poem is a considerable achievement. Following the composing process, she has first put herself in an early time in her life, evoked intuitively from her unconscious feelings and thoughts which the early memory reawakened, jotted down hastily a first draft, without concern for "correctness" of any kind, and then went about the business of revising her first draft. By contrasting the first draft to the subsequent revisions, we observe the changes she makes and marvel at the aptness of the revisions. She changes verbals to simple, present-tense verbs. She deletes unnecessary words. She intuitively uses poetic devices to let a word signifying the part stand for the whole, and she uses one word to stand for a word associated with that word. She ruthlessly deletes several lines to condense her poem. She repeats a simple sentence to convey how the senses summon forth an early memory: "I see," "[I] taste," "I see," "I burn myself," "I see fright," and "[I] feel the comfort of arms." She most appropriately changes the title of the poem from "Reflections" to "First Senses" to reflect this center of interest. And finally, by evoking through bright images the deeply embedded memories of her grandmother, her father, and other relatives who comforted and loved her, she reconstructs a lasting reality for herself and others to enjoy.

From Charlotte's writing of this poem through several revisions, we note how she moved from unconscious memories to a sharply focused reconstruction of reality, but we can only infer from the versions of the poem what went on in her mind as she did this. Now I'd like to describe how I followed through the same process, recounting my own progress—with all its fits and starts, side trips, back trackings, and meanderings—as I moved from an early memory through drafts of a poem.

My Process

While I was drafting an early memory with my students, I started with "Kenny and Curt [my older brothers] and I were on the roof of the second floor apartment where we lived in Manchester, Connecticut," but I didn't continue because it was too painful a memory to deal with, and I didn't want to make it public. It was about a time when my

I then looked over what I had written to see if I could find what Peter Elbow calls the "center of gravity."

brothers and I found ourselves in an apartment alone. I was about six years old. I can't remember where my mother and father were. I remember only they were not there and hadn't been for a while. I also remember the only things we had to eat in the place were some small sample boxes of breakfast cereal. No milk and no sugar to go with it. We were sitting on the roof of the second-floor apartment. I should have been thrilled because we were doing something forbidden. (Now that I have told about this fearful time, I am finally ready to write about it and possibly will do so sometime in the future. But the first time I reconstructed the memory was when I freewrote about the memory with my students.)

What follows is about a much happier time than the one I have just referred to.

> I loved the store my father had bought in Russell, Massachusetts. He and my mother played tennis with other people. My father was tall and thin. Mother was small with very dark hair. We went swimming in the river behind the house. We swam jumped off the boulders into the river and pools of the river. And we climbed up onto the hot rocks and gradually moistened the rough surfaces with our wet bodies until we could stretch out under the sun. Then we would jump up, leaving our wet shadows on the rocks, to jump into the water again. I was wrinkled with water and tingling with, frantic with laughing and shoving and shouting and exhausted.

I then looked over what I had written to see if any of it made sense, if I could find connections, if something—a word, a feeling or image—would reveal itself to me, if I could find what Peter Elbow, in *Writing without Teachers* (1973, New York: Oxford UP), calls the "center of gravity" (35, 36). In the left-hand margin of the handwritten, penciled draft, I wrote next to the "We went swimming in the river behind the house" "How did I get there? Who was with me?" I circled the two *jumps* in the "we would jump up" and "to jump into the water again." Needless repetition. I needed to find substitutions for them. At the bottom, I wrote what I felt was the focus of the draft: "pleasure, happiness, joy."

The next move was to take the focal point of the swimming with my mother and jumping off rocks into the river as the matter of the poem. I wrote out sentences in paragraph form as a first version and then, where I felt there should be pauses or spaces, I inserted horizontal lines. In this way, I could make a spontaneous lining of the potential poem. What was unusual for me, at this very early stage, was that I already had decided on a title, "Aquarium," which seems to suggest things actually living in water, becoming, if not fish, then some sort of amphibians. Here is that next version.

Aquarium
Mother was small with black,/black hair. We jumped off the boulders into/holes the
rocks. We climbed up onto the hot rocks and/wet the coarse surfaces/ with our seal
bodies and lay there under the sun./ When my heart would stop pounding, I would/
jump up,/leaving my shadow on the rock,/pedalling into the water again./ I was wrinkled with water and/ mad with shoving/and/laughing.

With the lined version to guide me, I copied over the poem to see what its
shape would be. This is the result.

Aquarium
Mother was small with black,
Black hair.
We jumped off the boulders into
Holes in the river.
We climbed up onto the hot rocks and
Wet the coarse surface with our

I needed to be confident
that my spontaneous
writing would lead
to something I could
continue to work on.

Seal bodies and lay there under the sun.
When my heart stopped pounding, I would
Jump up,
Leaving my shadow on the rock. I
Pedalled fiercely into the water, wrinkled and
Half mad with shoving
           and
Laughing.

But I didn't like the overall shape, the design of the poem. I thought the
business of isolating certain words—"Jump up" and "Laughing"—although, of
course, I set them apart on the page to emphasize them—was just too obvious, just too cute. Also, I didn't like "coarse surface" because "surface" was
an abstraction, not a word dealing with a concrete object, something I could
relate to with my senses. And, finally, I wanted to compress the lines into a
shape which didn't advertise itself as blatantly as did the present one.

Here is another version, not the final, by any means, because I'm still
not happy with the poem, but this variation does show a movement from
first thoughts and images through several rearrangings to a more finely tuned
reconstruction of reality.

Aquarium
We would jump off boulders into river
Caves and climb back into the sun,
Wetting the coarse stone with our seal bodies.

When my heart stopped pounding, I would jump
Up, leaving my shadow on the rock. Wrinkled
And half mad with shovings and laughings, I
Would pedal fiercely into a hole in the water.

What I have reported here is how I used the task I gave students to create a poem, one that even in its unfinished stage, is satisfying to me and gives me pleasure. I chose a common situation, one basic to all human beings, an early memory, and set myself—and my students—the happy task of putting myself back into the remembered event by answering questions designed to invoke strong emotions, concrete details, and the senses. I started freewriting about the event I had chosen, telling myself that I needed to be confident enough that my initial, spontaneous writing would lead to something I could continue to work on. Once I had gotten the first rush of words down on paper, I looked over what I had written to find the focal point. Excluding everything except that which was related to my focus, I rewrote the memory, now half consciously but at the same time unconsciously, employing words in ways I had trained myself to use in creating figurative language. I found words referring to specifics to substitute for general, abstract words. I let a single word stand for several and used a word that was associated indirectly but in a surprisingly new way with an action, idea, event, or feeling. And I let the words lead me to a pattern, a structure which was pleasing to me. After this draft, I continued to draft: revising, rearranging, refining, essentially working for arrangements and illuminations that astonished me and that eventually would give me satisfaction through an organic form in which shapes, sounds, and meanings all worked together. Most significant, though, by conjuring up early memories—some painful but some reawakening moments of childhood ecstasy—and by working through the shaping of words in patterns which constantly amazed me and yet finally illuminated my person, I was able to reconstruct and preserve for me a precious reality.

This isn't the only way to reconstruct reality through poetry, but it's one way, especially for beginners, those who are terror-stricken at the thought of creating a poem or, even worse, who consider a poem a first-draft spilling out of words like "love," "animals," and "sunsets." These beginners don't even suspect that the initial draft is only the first step, possibly the "zero" draft of the stage-by-stage process of finding and forging words into a poem.

· 1 5 ·

POETS ON POETRY

The Morality of Poetry

Robert W. Blake (1992)

One of the great moral issues of our time is the place of poetry in our culture. The matter is so deeply embedded in the American mind, though, that most people are unaware that the situation even exists. These, as I see them, are the dimensions of the problem. The dominant mode of thinking in our culture is what Howard Gardner (1985), the psychologist, calls the "logical-mathematical" intelligence, first identified by Plato as abstract thinking, most acutely exemplified in the work of Piaget. Such an approach to thinking, so established in our culture and in our habitual way of knowing by the traditions of philosophic thought, rationalism, the "scientific method," and simply by the ponderous weight of inertia, has become, even to those schooled in the study of literature, the basic and only way of knowing. Few teach poetry in the schools, but even those who do so accept without questioning a stance which views poems as secret messages, technical constructs. The approaches for breaking these linguistic messages are passed down indirectly by those professors and teachers who have been inducted into a cult only after years of unquestioning obedience and subservience. For these scribes, poems are indeed linguistic puzzles to be solved: they are intricate, arcane, and accessible to only a few people with special training and aptitudes.

Although I was raised by disciples of New Criticism and initiated into the cult of formalism, I now believe that such an attitude toward poetry— especially a distortion of this position—is a destructive one.

Poetry is a way of learning and knowing, and it far antedates rational thinking and abstract thought. For many people, poetry is an accepted way of learning and of being inducted into one's culture. However, what has happened in our culture, in which citizens are prepared primarily by our schools, is that the logical-mathematical way of knowing—only one among many—has held ascendancy for so long that our basic, collective mind-set operates almost solely by the "scientific" way of thinking. There are many dangers—existing and potential—to such a situation. People who are inculcated into the logical-mathematical mind-set accept, may take for granted—as unconsciously held assumptions—that there are absolutes in life. If so, they may believe that reality can be approached only by logical, systematic steps. They believe that the questions of good and evil are totally irrelevant to mathematics, logic, philosophy, and science. They may even believe that since Darwin's theory of evolution is the accepted paradigm for human existence, its notion of the "survival of the fittest" must also hold true in society. Hence, they may conclude that individual life is not really sacred and that only the fittest members of the society should survive.

Notice how insidiously the logical-mathematical way of knowing has infiltrated and now controls our schools. Students are tracked in kindergarten and in first grade by IQ tests and other "scientifically" devised instruments. Students, in all except the most enlightened classrooms, are taught to read and write by drilling on atomistic elements of language in small steps with constant and immediate reinforcement, progressing to whole tasks only after they have mastered all of the sequential elements of reading and writing, a plan based directly on the so-called "scientific" stimulus-response theory of how creatures learn—rats and pigeons as well as humans—, a theory discredited as a valid model of language learning more than thirty years ago. As for poetry, and literature in general, if it appears at all in classrooms, how is it taught? In the elementary grades, poetry is generally presented as a way to test reading comprehension or as an innocuous, free-time relief from "serious" learning. In her well-known anecdote about how poetry is frequently taught in the elementary grades, Louise M. Rosenblatt (1978) recounts this story:

> In a series of reading workbooks for the primary grades, the first inclusion of a poem occurred in the third grade book. The poem, describing a cow standing in a stream, was introduced by "What facts does this poem teach you?" (39)

Thus the "aesthetic, emotional recreation of a poem becomes secondary to a literal, factual reading of the poetic text" (39). In the secondary schools, poetry is taught mostly as a body of accepted literary texts (few contemporary ones) the meaning of which the teacher will impart to students. If students are allowed to interpret literary texts, they are trained to "find" the received meanings of poems by analyzing them rationally, systematically, logically, inductively, and with almost total disregard for their emotional impact or moral worth.

If poetry is not a technical construct, then what is it? And how is it a way of knowing? In one way, poetry is a witness, as Czeslaw Milosz (1983) maintains. For Milosz, Europeans tend to view poetry "as a witness

> "You who harmed a simple man, do not feel secure: for a poet remembers."
> —Czeslaw Milosz

and participant in one of man's major transformations." He continues, "I have titled this book *The Witness of Poetry* not because we witness it but because it witnesses us" (4). The following event, noted by Irving Howe (1981) in a review of Mislosz's book *Native Realm*, illustrates how poetry witnesses. When the workers of Gdansk unveiled a monument to workers shot down a decade ago by Polish Communist police, two inscriptions were graven on the base of the monument. One included verses from Psalm 129. The second was made up of lines by Milosz, the lines which are translated thus: "You who harmed a simple man, do not feel secure: for a poet remembers" (3).

In another basic way poetry is a way to use words to reconstruct reality, and in a preeminent way, poetry is a way of knowing, knowing about one's culture and of inevitably and necessarily becoming a member of that culture. I have already shown in a previous article, "One Way to Write a Poem," how, after starting to write about a painful and frightening time in my life, I moved to a joyous occasion and by the use of words, reconstructed for myself a version of the reality of that time (1991, *EJ* 80.4, pp. 21–26). Through that process, I came to know more about myself. Here is another example of how the poet reconstructs reality. Milosz tells how he uses words—is truly compelled by them—to reconstruct reality. In a poem reproduced in the flyleaf of the little book *The Witness of Poetry*, he includes a short poem which starts with these two lines.

My generation was lost. Cities too. And nations. But all this a little later.

Then he reveals through the eyes of the little boy he was at that time, in the midst of this chaos, the ultimate disorder of evil, how he was able to save

shards of life to be pieced together later when he was safe and able to recreate a new reality. These are some of the holographs he preserved: a swallow
performing its rite of the second, roads winding uphill and down, pine groves,
lakes, and men with scythes in shirts of unbleached linen and dark-blue trou-
sers. He ends the poem with these lines:

> Oh but he was clever,
> Attentive, as if things were instantly changed by memory.
> Riding in a cart, he looked back to retain as much as possible.
> Which means he knew what was needed for some ultimate moment
> When he would compose from fragments a world perfect at last.

To "compose from fragments a world perfect at last." That's how a poet
reconstructs reality.

In what other way is poetry a way of knowing?

Gardner identifies what may be the preeminent intelligences, those
which control all others including the logical-mathematical intelligence.
He calls these personal intelligences: on the
one hand, the intelligence that deals with
knowing about oneself and, on the other
hand, intelligence dealing with knowing
about one's relationship to others in a
culture (237–76). Poetry, or literature
broadly viewed as poetry, is a basic way for
individuals to learn about themselves and to learn enough about their
culture to become a welcome member of it. If they fail to develop these
intelligences, they will be doomed to live out their lives as strangers in a
strange land.

> Poetry is a basic way
> for individuals to learn
> enough about their cul-
> ture to become a welcome
> member of it.

How can poetry be a way of knowing? Every culture has a code of actions,
guides for behaving, criteria for judging right and wrong. Through poetry people learn the guides to personal and collective behavior. In nonliterate cultures, the people listened to precious texts being recited orally—*The Iliad* and
The Odyssey, for instance—performed by especially trained individuals who
had memorized complete epics or whole chunks of epics. As Eric Havelock
(1963) maintains,

Poetry was not "literature" but a social and political necessity. It was not an art form, nor a creation of the private imagination, but an encyclopedia maintained by a co-operative effort on the part of "the best Greek politics." (125)

Since the people who listened to these performances needed to remember and learn from the tribal texts, the epics exhibited certain crucial features. They were rhymed and rhythmic. They were made up of a number of narratives, joined together, involving important characters and gods. The matter of the epics was concrete, specific, and realistic. And the events depicted characters behaving in ambiguous, paradoxical ways. A great deal has been made of the main characters in the Greek epics and dramatic tragedies. The "protagonists" were "heroes" of noble stature. The reason for this, according to Havelock, was not artistic, but functional. If the purpose of the Greek epics and plays was to preserve the group ways of behaving, then the chief actors—Achilles, Oedipus, Antigone—must be the kind of men and women whose actions would involve both public law and family law. They must be "political" individuals in the most general sense of the term, whose acts, passions, and thoughts will affect the behavior and fate of the society. What they do sends out vibrations into the farthest confines of the society. The reason for the heroic figure in Greek poetry and drama "is in the last resort not romantic but functional and technical" [168].)

Once people became literate in Western culture—the alphabet having been invented and people being able to read and write—philosophic thought was created. Since the acquired knowledge of the culture could now be stored in books, people no longer needed to memorize. Writing need not be rhythmic, nor did it need to rhyme. Since stories were no longer needed for remembering, abstract thought—which, for instance, would allow all the qualities of a person to be abstracted in a single assertion—was invented. Instead of illustrating the just person, with human faults and contradictions, in a variety of situations and conflicts through poetic

> "Like the hands that deal them out, [poems] show their cards now and then."
> —Valerie Martin

devices, the philosopher could sum the essence of "justice" in a single statement: justice is performing one's duty. With such a way of knowing we learn to generalize and make abstract statements. An unfortunate result of this way of thinking is that only a few, special people are capable of abstract thinking. We see the result of such a mind-set in our culture: those who are capable of logical-mathematical thought are tracked in schools for advanced education and become the elite of our culture while those who are incapable of abstract thought are tracked into another kind of education and often become second-class citizens, the servants, serfs, and pariahs of our culture.

In a truly amazing way, virtually all humans, though they may not be capable of abstract reasoning—such as higher mathematical thought—can learn through poetry. They can learn about themselves and about others and can learn enough about their culture to enter it. Valerie Martin (1988), the fiction writer, explains what her way of knowing is through stories. In the following excerpt, she refers to "stories," but wherever she uses the word "story," I shall substitute the word "poems."

> [G]ood [poems] just don't seem accidental. They look meaningful; they contain symbolic patterns; you can take them apart and find pieces that fit right back together again. They are organic like flowers; they have an internal and external structure. In fact, like the hands that deal them out, they show their cards now and then; they appear to have a subconscious as well as a conscious level.
>
> This analogy to thinking may explain why [poems] are so important to us and why they appear to be so meaningful. [Poems] think, and they do it the same way. They talk straight sometimes, right to the heart, but they have always a deep, symbolic understanding of reality that can dictate what happened on the conscious level. They speak to us, as dreams speak to us, in a language that is at once highly symbolic and childishly literal. They mirror our consciousness exactly because they are composed through a process both conscious and unconscious. (36)

What the poet sees in the modern world, says Martin, as well as Milosz, is so horrendous—a world initiated by a logical-mathematical, "scientific" mind-set—that poets (that is, all of us) can maintain our sanity only at great price. Sigmund Freud (1964) was so shattered by what our culture does to its members that he once wrote,

> It goes without saying that a civilization which leaves so large a number of its participants unsatisfied and drives them into revolt neither has nor deserves the prospect of a lasting existence. (12)

The poet Erica Jong (1974) supports this position. Writing about why she believes Anne Sexton committed suicide, she says,

> Anne Sexton killed herself because it is just too painful to live in this world without numbness, and she had no numbness at all. All the little denials, all the stratagems of our non-feeling by which most of us endure from minute to minute were unavailable to her. Words spared her for a while. With the process of writing a poem, there is a kind of connection which sustains one. Then the poem is done and one is alone

again. Other people may enjoy the poem later, but the poet can hardly relate to it. The poet is happy only while writing the poem.

> If only one could write all the time! If only there were not all those hours of non-writing to get through! (61)

Milosz characterizes our age as a "nightmare" that cannot end well, and he finds its perfect expression in the barbed wire around the concentration camps and the gas chambers. This "reality" which we face daily, writes Martin, looks like a "nightmare from which no amount of screaming can awake us. Yet we continue to need, read and pay people to write [poems]" (36). In spite of our nightmarish civilization, says Martin, "one must assume that the average person is making up [poems] all the time. Otherwise we would simply go mad from anxiety" (36).

> Through writing poetry we tell people some things they didn't know or hadn't put into words before. But we write poems in order to know.

As horrified as Milosz is, however, by our contemporary society, he remains firm in his unwavering belief in the right—and obligation—for all of us poets not to despair but to have hope.

> The fate of poetry depends upon whether such a work as Schiller's and Beethoven's "Ode to Joy" is possible. For that to be so, some basic confidence is needed, a sense of open space ahead of the individual and human species. (14)

Martin also offers hope for the human species, specifically through creating poems.

> Teaching people to write [poems] requires, first of all, that for a limited period of time they will be forced to open their eyes and ears, to take off the blinders and let the images pour in—a necessary first step toward taking life seriously and even, I suspect, a good way to start taking responsibility for themselves and for the world they can finally see. (36)

Not only does creating poetry compel us to see and thus take responsibility for ourselves but, for Anne Sexton, writing poetry—rather than being a solitary act—relates the poet to the sacred essence of all humanity. In answer to a letter from Jong, relating her terror in bringing out a second book of poetry, Anne Sexton wrote this astonishing disclosure of her purpose for writing poetry.

Don't dwell on the book's reception. The point is get on with it—you have a life's work ahead of you—no point dallying around waiting for approval. We all want it, I know, but the point is to reach out honestly—that's the whole point. I keep feeling that there isn't one poem being written by any of us—or a book or anything like that. The whole life of us writers, the whole product I guess I mean, is the one long poem—a community effort if you will. It's all the same poem. It doesn't belong to any one writer—it's God's poem perhaps. Or God's people's poem. You have the gift—and with it comes responsibility—you mustn't neglect or be mean to that gift—you must let it do its work. It has more rights than the ego that wants approval. (Jong 61)

Through writing poetry we may witness the miraculous reality around us, use words to reveal the human condition, and tell people some things they didn't know or hadn't themselves put into words before. But we write poems in order to know. At the core of myself as a person is the capacity for access to my feeling life. Logical-mathematical thought will not teach me how to read my feelings. Poetry will. At the core of my capacity as a person living, working, loving with others, and sharing a common worthwhile culture is my sophisticated ability to make distinctions among other individuals, to be able to understand their actions, to enter into their lives—if ever so slightly—to make a modest start at understanding how they view reality. Logical-mathematical thought will not teach us how to live, work, and love with others; it will not teach us how to listen to others; and it will not teach us how to give audience to the thoughts, feelings, and desires of others. Poetry will.

Freud said that the key to health is self-knowledge and a willingness to confront the inevitable pains and paradoxes of human existence (Gardner 238). Logical-mathematical thought will not teach us how to do this. Poetry will. And as we reconstruct reality from words, in the company of other poets, we shall, as Milosz says, "compose from fragments a world perfect at last."

Works Cited

Freud, Sigmund. 1964. "The Future of an Illusion." *The Standard Edition of the Complete Psychological Works of Sigmund Freud*. Vol. XXI. London: Hogarth P and the Institute of Psychological Analysis.

Gardner, Howard. 1985. *Frames of Mind: The Theory of Multiple Intelligences*. New York: Basic.

Havelock, Eric. 1963. *Preface to Plato: A History of the Greek Mind*. Cambridge: Harvard UP.

Howe, Irving. 1981. "The Moral History of Czeslaw Milosz." Essay review of Czeslaw Milosz's *Native Realm: A Search for Self-Definition*. *The New York Times Book Review* 1 Feb.:3.

Jong, Erica. 1974. "Remembering Anne Sexton (The Guest Word)." *The New York Times Book Review* 27 Oct.: 61.

Martin, Valerie. 1988. "Waiting for the Story to Start." *The New York Times Book Review* 7 Feb.: 1, 36.

Milosz, Czeslaw. 1983. *The Witness of Poetry*. Cambridge: Harvard UP.

Rosenblatt, Louise M. 1978. *The Reader, the Text, the Poem: The Transactional Theory of the Literary Work*. Carbondale: Southern Illinois UP.

· 1 6 ·

RESPONDING TO POETRY

High School Students Read Poetry

Robert W. Blake and Anna Lunn (1986)

In this paper, we shall relate what we learned from several adolescents—particularly one perceptive young lady named Emily—about the process they went through as they read a poem they had never seen before. In this study, we were concerned not with what kind of critical essays young people could produce—written products—but with what mental and emotional experiences they followed—the processes—as they met, perceived, and reported their encounters with a new poem.

Background

Before we begin our account of the study and its implications, we need to sketch out a brief background in reading, responding, and teaching literature. It seems to us that the single most powerful influence on teaching literature has been the New Criticism (sometimes called Formalistic Criticism and often mistakenly lumped together with other approaches under the label of Objective Criticism) of Cleanth Brooks and Robert Penn Warren. If we read a poem as a New Critic, we are implicitly guided by assumptions like these: interpretation means discovering the objective meaning of a piece, determining the author's intended meaning, and reading and responding objectively to the place itself, not to the biography of the writer or to the cultural or social history of the time in which it was created. As prospective English teachers were trained to read literature by this approach, it seemed to us, they were then, in several formal and many less formal ways, anointed as teachers of literature. This ordination meant that they had had the necessary special training for extracting meaning from a piece of literature, had been sanctioned as *bona fide* literary critics, and knew they now served their students as the final arbiters of the meaning of pieces of literature. Such training has apparently been successful for generations, for by it students in secondary school English classes assimilated the accepted technical apparatus for reading a piece of literature while at the same time accepting the fact that the *correct* meaning for a piece rested ultimately with their teachers. A heady situation for English teachers but a rather frustrating and not so exciting a one for students.

Over the years, as we both taught literature to high school students and instructed undergraduate and graduate college students in how to read literature as new critics, we have been irked more and more frequently by the interpretations—often logical, well substantiated, and strongly held—by our students, which we amazingly enough had never thought of and which, therefore, we assumed could not possibly be correct.

We have been helped to broaden our tolerance for student responses by the work of Alan Purves, and others, which assisted us in understanding the broad range of responses individuals can make to a piece of literature, but it wasn't until we read and listened to individuals like Louise Rosenblatt, Norman Holland, and David Bleich that we began to realize that there might be more to reading a piece of literature than determining—by no matter how careful a reading—what the *objective* meaning of a piece was. Rosenblatt said to us that reading literature was essentially a transaction between the piece and the reader and distinguished between *efferent* reading (to gain knowledge) and *aesthetic* reading (to recreate an emotional experience). Holland maintained that every person responded to a piece according to his or her highly idiosyncratic, individual nature. And David Bleich advanced this revolutionary idea—most persuasively for us—about reading literature: there is no such thing as a single, objective, unchanging meaning for a piece, and therefore an individual reads literature not to arrive at an objective meaning—or at the intended meaning of the author—but to create a personal interpretation for a novel, short story, or poem.

What did we make of such notions? That reading a piece of literature was an opportunity for a reader to create a personal and immediate response. That there was no constant, objective meaning for a piece, only individual responses, reflecting the personalities of the respondents and the influences of the culture in which they lived, (Unfortunately, there is not enough space here to consider an enormously useful idea, advanced by Bleich, of the "communal" response, by which groups, small and large, create consensus about a piece.) And that the role of the teacher of literature, it seemed logical, was not to serve as the arbiter of meaning and taste but rather to act as a specially trained and sensitive person who could show others how to create rich fully detailed, persuasive, yet confidently personal responses to literature.

If individuals, unhampered by the restrictions of distorted objective criticism, actually did read and respond to literature personally, subjectively, and emotionally, what was the nature of this process? Instead of looking at what students wrote about a piece after they had read it, why not try to find out what they actually did throughout the process of reading an unfamiliar poem in a non-directive and non-threatening situation? No one we knew of had attended to this question with high school students even though some had worked with especially educated adults. The most fully realized study of perception of poetry is that of Eugene Kintgen, who asked highly trained readers, eight graduate students in an English doctoral program and eight professors of English, to read a poem they had never seen before and as they did so to talk into a tape recorder all of their thoughts and activities (looking up a word in a dictionary, for instance) as they read and tried to come to a sense of a poem.

Rather than analyze what *experienced* readers—the "professional team players and the promising amateurs" of Kintgen's study—did as they read a poem, we wanted to discover what relatively untrained readers—in this case, two boys and three girls, fifteen and sixteen years old, from the same suburban high school but with different English teachers—did as they followed the process of reading a new poem.

The Study

We chose a poem which was unknown to the students but which they could relate to, "Every Good Boy Does Fine" by David Wagoner. Although it had a simple, traditional structure, with few challenging words and simple allusions, the poem did present some complex syntactic problems and would, we believed, provide a challenge to the readers. Here is the poem.

"Every Good Boy Does Fine"

I practiced my cornet in a cold garage
Where I could blast it till the oil in drums
Boomed back; tossed free-throws till I couldn't move my thumbs;
Sprinted through tires, tackling a headless dummy.
In my first contest, playing a wobbly solo,
I blew up in the coda, alone on stage,
And twisting like my hand-tied necktie, saw the judge
Letting my silence dwindle down his scale.

At my first basketball game, gangling away from home
A hundred miles by bus to a dressing room,
Under the showering voice of the coach, I stood in a towel,
Having forgotten shoes, socks, uniform.

In my first football game, the first play under the lights
I intercepted a pass. For seventy yards, I ran
Through music and squeals, surging, lifting my cleats,
Only to be brought down by the safety man.

I took my second chances with less care, but in dreams
I saw the bald judge slumped in the front row,
The coach and team at the doorway, the safety man
Galloping loud at my heels. They watch me now.

You who have always homed your way through passages,
Sat safe on the bench while some came naked to court,
Slipped out of arms to win in the long run,
Consider this poem a failure, sprawling flat on a page.

To remove students from the school setting, we had the taping done entirely in Mrs. Lunn's home. She explained to readers what was being requested of them with no special vocabulary or poetic terms being required. Each student was then left alone with a copy of the poem and a tape recorder and was finished when he or she had satisfied all possibilities of the poem. The time for the responses varied from twenty to thirty-five minutes.

In the directions to the students, we were careful to allow them to read and respond in a completely unthreatening atmosphere. Here are the directions.

*From *New and Selected Poems* by David Wagoner, 1969 by Indiana University Press.

Directions for Reading

We would like to see how students your age read poetry on your own. This is a poem that is probably new to you. The name and dates of the author aren't given.

Read the poem any way that is comfortable to you. You should include both a line-by-line reading and your overall interpretation, in any order you wish.

Talk into the tape recorder about the poem. Feel free to say anything you think; don't censor your ideas. Thinking into a tape recorder may seem difficult at first; it's not the way you normally read a poem. Do your best to record all your thoughts. What does this poem mean to *you?*

Several readings may be necessary. Don't rush; give yourself time to think. There is no need to be talking all the while. You are finished when you've said all that you can about the poem.

Please tell the tape recorder:

If you change your mind as you go along.

If the poem reminds you of anything in your life.

If a stray thought comes to you.

This is not a test in any way. You are not being timed. There are no right and wrong answers. The poem will affect each reader differently.

The Process of Responding

There are two ways to analyze the records of individual responses, what are called protocols.

The first is to take a single sticking point in the poem and study the various approaches to it by different readers. Essentially, the readers had no problems with the poem until they reached the words. "They watch me now," in the fifth stanza. As experienced readers, we thought the antecedents of *they* were obvious—the bald judge, the coach and team, and the safety man. It is instructive to see how each reader handled the problem of what *they* referred to, but an examination of how the readers interpreted the meaning of the pronoun of *who* in the last stanza shows us in an even more revealing way the workings of their minds. Just *who* has always "homed your way through passages/Sat safe on the bench ... Slipped out of arms ... /[and *who* should] Consider this poem a failure. ..."?

This is how the five readers responded to the "You who. ..." problem.

Martin didn't directly address the "you" question and was later puzzled by the statement "Consider this poem a failure. ..."? He came to regard "you" as the reader in general.

Anita was admittedly confused by the stanza but didn't mention syntax.

Emily, avoiding the syntax in which the *you* embedded, at first thought the boy was criticizing his own poem. Later she stated that the "who" referred to her and others who hadn't tried in life. "In the last stanza, the first three lines refer to the stanzas I mentioned, but I'm not really sure why. ... Maybe he's referring to *us* who sit safe on the bench while *he* came naked to court." She concluded by saying, "I don't think this poem is a failure, but then again I haven't always homed my way through passages and stuff like it says in the last stanza."

Carol put it this way: "Those people who did all right the first time, who didn't mess up playing on stage; those people—who made the touchdowns and remembered their uniforms—they think that he is a failure, that his poem is a failure."

Steve tried to explain the stanza as a whole but didn't undertake the *you* problem.

It is important to note that the readers' different conclusions about the meaning of the word you led to variation interpretations of the poem. Those who explored possible meanings for this key word, furthermore, were not necessarily more correct than were those who sidestepped the issue, but those readers who did investigate the problem of the pronoun antecedents provided more specific interpretations with fewer unsubstantiated generalizations than did readers who sidestepped the issue. What is also noteworthy is the fact that readers decided what the passage meant in general and then tried to fit their interpretation of the meaning of words and of syntax to this initial conception.

The second way to analyze the process of responding to poetry is to study the protocol of single reader. Emily's response was a profitable one to examine because she revealed in greatest detail her mental processes. As we listened to Emily's tape several times and read over and over again her protocol, we were able to perceive in a rudimentary fashion her functioning mind as she literally "works her way through" (her phrase) the poem and identified some eleven categories of her responding process, of which the eleven categories appear to fall into the broad elements of what we call *perceive, interpret,* and *enjoy.* We shall explain each of the eleven categories with examples from the protocol and them make some concluding remarks about the three overarching categories.

Stages in the Responding Process

1. *Reads, Rereads, and Rereads:* Emily reads and rereads words and phrases from the poem; to support her interpretations she continually returned to the text. (Read the title. Read the first stanza aloud. "I'll read the second stanza." "Maybe I'll read the whole thing through, see if I can give a finish on it.")

2. *Associates:* First she associated words and phrases with her own *personal experiences.* ("This reminds me of a boy more or less having fun just as a boy does," "I feel that way every time we play Batavia. Maybe—yeah—that's what it means. 'A hundred miles by bus to a dressing room.'") She also associated items in the poem with her *personal knowledge.* ("'Boomed … thumbs,' refers to basketball." "Then 'Sprinted … dummy,' that sounds like football practice, because the guys all have to bump into that thing or whatever")

3. *Interprets:* At the heart of Emily's response was interpretation; Emily interpreted frequently and confidently, with her interpretations falling into several sub-categories. First, she *hypothesized* interpretations. ("Maybe it sounds like. …" "It could be all about the second stanza, I guess, means that pretty much as the first two lines in the first stanza." ("The first two lines seem to be about this stanza.") She questioned her interpretations. ("… or maybe it was his—coach? No, it wasn't his coach.") She *admitted her lack of understanding.* ("I don't understand the part where it says, 'Gangling away from home.' I don't know what gangling means." "I still don't understand those two lines." "Well, I don't know too much about football. I don't know what a safety man is,") And she worked through the poem, gaining confidence through dogged persistence, she stated interpretations of words, lines, stanzas, the literal and of figurative meanings of words, of themes, and of the meaning of the overall poem. ("And now I understand this. OK! 'I saw the bald judge. …' refers back to his first contest, with his cornet solo. I understand *that* now, too. I think that [horned] means like when you're playing instrument and you take your way through." "I'm not really sure if he means it [the title] literally or if he means it sarcastically. The only reason I think it may be sarcastic is the last line, 'Consider this poem a failure, sprawling flat on a page.")

4. *She restated, paraprased lines in her own words.* ("He practices his instrument, cornet, in his garage, where he can do it as loud as he wants. …" "He was in his first contest playing a solo, and he blew up in the coda, on the stage, he was all by himself.")

5. *She frequently quoted verbatim* from the poem, ("tackling a headless dummy." "... twisting like my hand-tied necktie.")

6. *She responded emotionally.* ("Oh! Maybe the first line. ..." "OK! OK! so the first line ... "And they're all watching him! That's neat" "... Ah! OK. I understand *that*, too.")

7. *She looped back.* ("I think that first stanza all refers to him practicing. ..." "The second line here probably refers to the third stanza, 'Under ... uniform." "OK—the first line of the sixth stanza refers to the second stanza, where he was in his first contest, which refers up to the first stanza, where he practices his cornet. I think these all refer to the stanzas I mentioned, but I'm not really sure why.")

8. *She connected elements of the poem*, both perceiving structures and creating her own structures. ("This is real interesting. In these three, it says his *first* contest, his *first* basketball game, his *first* football game." "Then 'Consider this poem a failure, sprawling flat on a page.' I think these all refer to the stanzas I mentioned, but I'm not really sure why.")

9. *She generalized* by creating her own overall meaning and stating general themes. ("I think these all refer to the stanzas I mentioned. Maybe he's referring to us who sit safe on the bench while he came naked to court.")

10. *She revised* her initial interpretations and evaluations. ("I think I understand up here in the first stanza, where I didn't understand the first time." "At first I didn't really like it; I thought it sounded kind of dumb. I mean, when I first read it I thought, No, this isn't right. But it's not a bad poem, and I think it's pretty good.")

11. *And finally she evaluates* the worth of the poem, showing pleasure with her judgment. ("I think this is a good poem when you understand it." "I think it's a good title." "I think it's a good poem, and I don't think it's a failure.")

Perceive, interpret, and *enjoy*—these are the general processes Emily followed throughout her reading and responding to this poem. First, then, she entered into the poem, exemplifying what Coleridge termed the "willing suspension of disbelief." accepting in good faith the challenge to come to terms with this unfamiliar poem. Once she accepted the poem, so to speak, made a leap of faith, she proceeded step by step to interpret it, but her interpretations involved many false starts, mistaken first impressions, recursive movements, and tentative hypotheses, which she continually verified by checking with specific words and phrases in the poem. Finally, when she felt satisfied with her creation of an overall meaning for the poem, she showed a well-deserved pleasure with her performance.

What is striking to us in this superficial account of Emily's mental states is how incredibly complex the process is with even this short, fairly accessible poem. And what is equally exciting to us is the fact that Emily—with no prior instruction in the apparatus of literary criticism, with no knowledge of special terms for figurative language or the technical aspects of poetry—is able to "work through" and "understand" a poem in a way that is eminently satisfying to her.

Conclusions and Implications

1. The process of reading a poem is not a simple, easy, linear, instantaneous task. Students need to go through the process enough times to become familiar with it. To achieve a personal satisfaction, they might read a new poem, write out initial first draft impressions, discuss their reactions in small groups, and on the basis of the feedback they receive, create fully thought-out responses. A good poem, one rich in meaning and sophisticated in structure, needs to grow on us—adults and adolescents alike.

2. Few students are aware of the processes available to them for a satisfactory reading of a poem. Students who say, "I don't like this poem. It's dumb," usually mean. "I don't understand this poem, and my teachers—who always know what every poem means—always make me feel stupid." Ignorance is frightening; knowledge is reassuring. This is no more true than with the reading poetry. Although none of the adolescents in this study initially reported liking poetry, after had worked through an interpretation of the poem, four expressed a liking for it. It is significant to note that this was the first time that any of the students had read a poem entirely on their own. Several expressed surprise they could do so.

3. Individuals respond differently to the same poem, and there is nothing strange about that. Adolescents, furthermore, react differently from the way we experienced teachers do, and there's nothing wrong with that, either. High school students are different from English majors and experienced teachers in many immensely important ways. Such a statement sounds trivial, but it is terribly significant for effective literature teaching. Young people have different cultural backgrounds from ours. They bring to reading and responding varied educational experiences. Few of them have acquired the critical apparatus for reading poems it took us years to assimilate. We sometimes forget these facts, but we shouldn't. This is not to imply that adolescents are unable to read poetry successfully. They can, as Emily demonstrated. If they are, however,

to learn the critical apparatus for reading poetry confidently and have confidence in their interpretations, we must anticipate difficulties they face and adjust our teaching accordingly.

4. Within the limits of the agreed upon meanings held by a class of students and by the larger community, there are as many responses to a complex and sophisticated poem as there are students in a class. Helping high school students learn how to read and respond to poems on their own takes time. Although it is quicker and easier—on the surface—to tell students the *correct* meaning of a poem, that meaning becomes valid only for the teacher and never for the student. Students who never have the chance to interpret poems by themselves will always turn to the teacher for the *correct* meaning. Teachers who say or imply. "This is what the poem means. This is what the poet intended," leave no opportunity for students to learn for themselves the process of creating personal meaning from poems.

Or for students to join our community of readers who have learned how to work through with confidence and exhilaration the process of reading and responding to subtle, complex, and meaningful language.

Bibliography

Bleich. David. *Readings and Feelings*. Urbana, Illinois: NCTE, 1975.

——. *Subjective Criticism*. Balitmore: Johns Hopkins University Press, 1978.

Brooks, Cleanth and Robert Penn Warren. *Understanding Poetry*, rev. ed. New York: Henry Holt, 1950.

——. *The Scope of Fiction*. New York: Appleton-Century-Crofts, 1960.

Holland. Norman. *Poems in Persons: An Introduction to the Psychoanalysis of Literature*. New York: Norton, 1973.

——. *5 Readers Reading*. New Haven: Yale University Press, 1975.

Kintgen, Eugene R. "Studying the Perception of Poetry." Unpublished paper, 1977.

——. *The Perception of Poetry*. Bloomington: Indian University Press, 1983.

Purves, Alan C. with Victoria Rippere. *Elements of Writing about a Literary Work: A Study of Response to Literature*. Urbana, Illinois: NCTE, 1968.

Purves. Alan C. "Evaluation of Learning in Literature," *Handbook on Formative and Summative Evaluation of Student Learning*. New York: McGraw-Hill, 1971.

Purves, Alan C. and Richard Beach. *Literature and the Reader: Research in Response to Literature, Reading interests, and the Teaching of Literature*. Urbana. Illinois: NCTE, 1972.

Rosenblatt, Louise M. *Literature as Exploration*. New York: Noble and Noble, 1968.

——. *The Reader, the Text, the Poem*. Carbondale, Illinois: Southern Illinois University Press, 1978.

SECTION V

RESPONDING TO LITERATURE/READER RESPONSE IN THE CLASSROOM

In this section, we find two pieces—the first showing us how to use a "personal" response in forming a "learning community" among secondary students as they learned to read and respond to short fiction—and the second, describing to us how the reader response process actually works in an elementary classroom.

In, "Using the personal response to become a learning community," we are reminded of the socio-cultural nature of writing -activities; processes that help us to become "one" within what Robert coins, "a learning community."

In the second piece, Robert lists both the traditional elements found in traditional response to literature as well as those elements central to a reader response approach. Through the reading of "Jesse Bear" (Carlstrom, 1989), we are walked though the steps of implementing such a process, complete with students' actual responses, in a first grade classroom.

Today, a reader response approach to literature, is virtually non-existent in our English and ELA classrooms. Indeed, most state standards, including the national Common Core State Standards have removed it altogether. New York State remains an exception however, producing a document called, "Alignment of New York State K-12 Standards to the CCSS." Here the importance of culture remains intact as well as the importance of reader response. Listed under the sections, "Response to literature," it reads: With prompting and support, [students] make connections between self, text, and the world... to recognize, interpret, and make connections."

· 1 7 ·

USING THE PERSONAL RESPONSE TO BECOME A LEARNING COMMUNITY

A Model for Secondary Students To Learn To Read Short Fiction

Robert W. Blake (1991)

The purpose of this paper is to provide a model for secondary school students to learn how to use what I call the "personal response" to a short story–through reading, writing, and discussing–to become one within what I term a "learning community." I want students to read widely, on the one hand, particularly those stories and books they choose and enjoy. But that's not enough. If they read literature by themselves and don't share their responding with anyone else, they fail to internalize in any sequential, progressively refined way the varied approaches to reading and responding to literature. Most importantly, though, since reading literature is a social and cultural activity, they miss out on the opportunity–which only a sensitive, knowledgeable, and well trained teacher in a school setting can provide–to become, through literature, part of a special group, a learning community.

The foundation of this model for reading and responding to short fiction includes three major elements. First, is the **personal response**: I want students to learn how to read, respond, and evaluate short fiction through the personal response. Second is **writing as a way of responding**: I want them to learn how to use writing to aid them in the task of making personal sense out of texts. And third is a **learning community**: I want them to learn how to make use of the power of the group response to a literary text as a means of becoming expert and sensitive readers within a learning community.

First to the matter of reading. All of the elements of the model support an overall "personal response," a generalized way of perceiving a literary text which persuades the reader to find out what the main character learns about other characters, what the main character learns about herself, and which leads the reader, as a result, to discover more about her own feelings and those of others. (I am indebted to Howard Gardner's notion of the "personal intelligences" from his book *Frames of Mind: The Theory of Multiple Intelligences*. For Gardner, there are two personal intelligences, the **intrapersonal**–becoming sensitive to one's own feelings–and the **interpersonal**–learning to read the emotions and motives of others. We learn the personal intelligences by interacting with others, through group rituals, and through the study of literature.)

Initially students need to enjoy reading a short story, after a minimum "set up," at first, quickly for the sheer pleasure of it, for the total emotional impact. They need to learn it's all right to have feelings about short stories and to relate them to other individuals in the classroom. (The notion that one's immediate response to a literary text is an emotional one is most directly and clearly stated in the work of David Bleich. See his *Readings and Feelings: An Introduction to Subjective Criticism* for an account of how he used subjective response activities with college students and his **Subjective Criticism** for a full, scholarly treatment of his position.)

Once they have "entered" the story for a general emotional reaction, students need to learn approaches related to the personal response for reading a short story. Through the personal response, they learn to ask and answer questions dealing with what the main character learns about others in the story and her relation to them (the "interpersonal response") and what the main character learns about herself (the "intrapersonal response"). Finally, students should become confident in expressing the worth of a story, evaluating it by **internal criteria** (How well is the story put together? How well does it hang together? and It looks as if the writer tried to create such-and-such a story. How well did she succeed? On a scale of one to ten, with ten being the best of all stories you have read, how would you rate this one? Why?) and by **external criteria** (Does the story tell us something of real significance for mature and thoughtful human beings?) (The problem of how to evaluate literature is a thorny one. Benjamin Bloom in the *Taxonomy of Educational Objectives: Handbook I: Cognitive Domain* maintains that evaluation is the highest level of knowing and that judging the value of something may be based on either **internal criteria**–"consistency, logical accuracy, and absence of internal flaws"–or by **external criteria**—"derived from a consideration of the ends to be served." For E. D. Hirsch, in his *The Aims of Interpretation*, evaluation of a literary text may be based on **intrinsic** or **extrinsic criteria.** One set of intrinsic criteria relates to distinctive elements of a work, the genre to which it belongs. How well, for instance, does a short story exhibit the essential features of a short story? But, one might ask, whose notion of a short story do we follow, Poe's or Chekhov's? Another set of intrinsic criteria relates to how well the literary text accomplishes what the author intended. The other general method of evaluating a literary text is by extrinsic criteria, Plato being one of the first extrinsic critics, who judged a literary work by whether or not it was useful or harmful for the state. For a final word on this matter of evaluating literature, I turn to what two "New Critics," Cleanth Brooks and Robert Penn WArren, say about this subject in their book, *The Scope of Fiction*. For Brooks and Warren, a literary text may first be judged by **intrinsic criteria:** "Rather, it is their [the authors] first article of faith that the structure of a piece of fiction, in so far as that piece of fiction is successful, must involve a vital and functional relationship between the idea and the other elements in that structure–plot, style, character, and the like." (xi) In addition, a story may be judged by **extrinsic criteria:** "In the second place, they [the authors] would agree that to be good, a piece of fiction must involve an idea of some real significance for mature and thoughtful human beings." (xi) On the basis of such considerations, I believe I am safe in asking secondary school students to judge stories by modified versions of both internal criteria (How well is the story put together?) and by external criteria (Is the story about something of real importance to us?)

Only by reading many stories and becoming confident in their ability to judge short fiction, will students become effective readers, not only of stories but of all kinds of mature prose. They will be able to read for a general impression. They will be able to comprehend how a worthwhile short story reveals personal and social truths. And they will develop their "taste" (literary appreciation) in literature by reading many stories and by evaluating the worth of the stories they read.

The second major element of the model deals with students learning to use writing as a means of "getting at" their readings of worthwhile stories. Through writing about literary texts, they learn to express emotions they are timid about revealing to others, they learn to explore their own experiences and how the story illuminates the meanings of these associations, and they learn to put into words thoughts they may have only dimly perceived. There are several kinds of writing tasks about a story which help us to realize this overall aim. One is a pre-reading writing task about an event like one of those in the story to get the student into the "feeling" mode of the story, to prepare for a full entry into the "aesthetic experience" of the story. Another writing task is for students to write out an initial, ten-minute, spontaneous response to a short story, after having read it quickly for a personal, overall perception of the work. Other writing tasks are to write an "affective response" (I laughed, I cried, I felt really upset when I read the story), an "associative response" (As I read the story, it made me think of a time when something like what happened to the main character happened to me.), or a "Literary importance response" (What's the most important word, passage, and feature of the story for you? Why?). After having written drafts of responses to the story and having discussed their written reactions with their classmates, students may create, as a final writing task, a polished, critical essay. (See the author's piece, "Reading Poetry and the Reconstruction of Reality," for a description of the uses of pre-reading writing activities and of short spontaneous written responses to a literary text. Louise Rosenblatt discusses in detail the characteristics of an "aesthetic" reading of a text to re-create an emotional experience as differentiated from an "efferent" reading of a text, one whose aim is to "carry away" meaning, usually literal and factual, in her work, *The Reader the Text the Poem: The Transactional Theory of the Literary Work*. For a full discussion of the "affective," "associative," and "Literary importance" responses, see Bleich's *Readings and Feelings*.)

My third major element of the model provides students with opportunities not only to read and to write about a short story but also naturally and without conscious thought to discuss their reading and writing with their classmates, in pairs, in small groups, and in the entire class as a whole. As they do this, several things are bound to happen. Students become aware of the great pleasure of sharing their emotional responses with others. (I just read this story, and I really want to talk about it!) They comprehend how to read and interpret better by getting immediate feedback from people more like them than the teacher. (Where'd you get that crazy idea from? Look here and see what she actually said and did!) As they respond to stories, noting how the characters behave and share these reactions with other students, they also learn to read the feelings of others and to adjust their behaviors to those of the members of the group. (In a word, they become socialized.) And they understand how to read their own feelings and motives. (Hmm. So characters in the story feel the same way I do. If that character can have those feelings, then maybe it's all right for me, too.) As the students read what they have written and discuss their interpretations in groups of other students, they begin to see each other as individuals–as real people–they learn to use the responses of others to fine tune their own response. They learn to learn from others, how to accept feedback and use of it what they can to improve their reading and writing and even to adjust their behavior. And they learn to become "trusted readers," individuals who listen attentively and give non-judgmental, useful reactions to the interpretations and written responses of their fellow learners. They learn to have confidence in each other. They even learn to like each other and become one of a learning community. By a learning community, I mean a group of learners which has these characteristics. Although each of the students is a distinct, unique person, at the same time each one feels she is one of a cohesive group. Each person includes all members of the class. Each one sees all of the others as separate, real persons. Each one feels able to speak out honestly in small groups and in the class as a whole about authentic problems of reading, writing, listening, and discussing. Each believes and respects each other, making the class a safe place where each person is not afraid to respond openly, to try out new interpretations, to make mistakes, but to learn from her mistakes. As a result, each individual becomes fearless in her willingness to read and listen and respond emotionally and intellectually to what she sees and hears. This does not mean that any of the students are destructively critical. Rather each person learns to describe pointedly, concretely, and specifically how she perceives what other students write and say in class. (It seems to me that we are learning only slowly how students might act together in groups in which they read worthwhile literary texts, respond to what they have read in special, enlightened ways and, as a result, come to learn about their own thoughts and feelings, the motives of others, and about their place in a culture. Jerome Bruner, many years ago, in his *Toward a Theory of Instruction*, stressed the crucial importance of dialogue between teacher and students and the students' need for a minimal mastery of social skills in order to learn. Peter Elbow describes a "writers' group" as a community of learners in his *Writing Without Teachers*, and M. Scott Peck describes the idea of "community" in religious and therapeutic groups in his book, *The Different Drum*. Robert Slavin, furthermore, recounts the advantages of groups of students working together cooperatively rather than competitively in his book *Cooperative Learning*, although I believe his notion is fundamentally different from my idea of a learning community. No one, however, has provided a full account of what happens to a number of students as they read, write about, and discuss their responses to worthwhile texts and eventually become one with an uncommon group, a "learning community.")

Reading, Writing, and Interpreting a Short Story

In order to illustrate how the model may provide the basis for classroom activities, let me use as an example a worthwhile story appropriate for secondary school students, in this case, "Raymond's Run" by Toni Cade Bambara. (The story appears in a Pocketbook collection of Bambara's stories Gorilla, My Love and has been anthologized in at least one secondary school literature textbook series.)

I choose "Raymond's Run" because it is a rich, expertly told tale of pride, competition, respect, excellence, love for one's fellow human beings, and self discovery of one's values and future goals. Squeaky—or Hazel Elizabeth Deborah Parker, as she's know to her enemies—exemplifies the humanistic belief that people make full use of their personal talents only when they use them to aid others less knowledgeable or less gifted physically than they are. As a close friend told me as we discussed the story, in Zen Buddhism the truth is expressed this way: "No one is enlightened until all are enlightened."

As a teacher, I may not use all the following writing and discussion activities nor ask all of the suggested guide questions, but since I have thought them through, jotted them down, and therefore turned them over in my mind, I now have command of them below my level of consciousness as a intuitive guide for what I do in the classroom.

To the Students (Pre-Reading Writing Task)

Think about a time when you helped somebody else learn to do something like a math problem or write a composition or hit a tennis ball or learn to water ski or snow ski. How did the person feel when she had learned to do the task? How did you feel?

For ten minutes, write about such a time. Don't worry about spelling or punctuation or even handwriting. Your writing won't be corrected or marked in any way. The task is just for you to get down on paper your memory of such a time and how you felt about it.

Another way to get the students "into" the story is to engage them in a short, freewheeling discussion of the nature and value of competition with questions like the following:

To the Student (Introductory Discussion)

Do you like to run races? Do you do the dash or distance races? Do you play football, basketball, or soccer? Do you like to win? Even if you don't always win or even compete much, do you have friends who play sports and compete?

What is competition? Is there competition only in sports? Can we compete in activities other than sports? When one becomes really good at something, should she try to help others be good, too, or should she keep her secrets to herself?

A football coach once said something that still upsets a lot of people: "Winning isn't everything. It's the only thing." Is competition bad for people because it prevents cooperation? Or does competition with talented and serious contestants compel us to become better?

Anyway, this is a story about a girl about your age who was a good runner. One of the best. After you have read the story, see if you can figure out why the title emphasizes a boy's run. But don't worry too much about such a question as you read the story the first time. Go through it now for the fun of it.

To get you going, I'll read the opening out loud to you of this tale of a little girl who is a hot-shot runner.

For students who have a hard time reading a story by themselves, I may read the whole story to them. Now that I or my students have read aloud the story or they have finished it on their own, I turn to other matters.

After we have read the story for an overall effect, I ask them to write in draft form their initial reactions to the story. I want them to become used to making intuitive, first impression interpretations of short stories and to trust that initial interpretation.

To the Student (Initial Writing)

Now that you have read "Raymond's Run" quickly just for fun, I'd like you to take out a piece of paper and free write for ten minutes what the story means "essentially" to you. Your papers won't be marked, and your spelling and other matters won't be corrected. Just write out as fast as you can without taking your pencil or pen off the paper what the story means to you personally. Also, don't worry about what the "correct" meaning of the story is supposed to be. Don't even worry about what I think the meaning is. Okay. Start writing.

After the students have written spontaneously about what the story means to them, I ask them to read loud their preliminary responses in pairs or in groups of from four to five students.

To the Student (Small Group Discussion of Initial Reading)

Now I want you to read out loud your draft response on what the story means to you. After each of you has read out loud her response, you should consider these questions and your responses to them. 1. What do I think the meaning is? 2. Why do I think so? Think about your own reasons for why you believe in your meaning.

Now that they have read or heard the story read out loud, responded intuitively to the beginning reading, and discussed their primary interpretation with their fellow students, I turn to a more systematic re-reading of the story, designed to help them in stating reasons for supporting their first reading. To that end, I engage them with personal response questions aimed at how they felt about the story, what the main character learned about other characters, what the main character learned about herself, and how good the story was.

To the Student

You have read the story quickly for enjoyment, written a personal response and discussed it with your small group of fellow students. Now it's time to turn to a closer rereading of the story. With your discussion group, talk about answers to questions like these which deal with three aspects of the story.

–How do you feel about the story? What memories does it bring to mind?

–What does the main character learn about other characters? What does the main character learn about herself?

–How good is the story?

–How do you feel?

a. How did you feel as you read the story, talked about it, and later thought about it? It's okay to express your feelings after you have read a story which made you laugh, upset you, or made you stop and think. In fact, if you let out your feelings as you read, you'll gradually come to enjoy stories more and more. These are the sorts of phrases you might start with when you reveal emotions while reading a story: I felf (happy, sad, upset) as I read the story. I (laughed out loud, cried, felt lonely, was depressed) after I finished reading the story.

b. What memories came to mind as you read the story? We sometimes feel closer to a story when it relates times like the ones we have lived through. These are the sorts of phrases you might start with to help you remember incidents you are reminded of by the story: This story reminds me of a time when I _____. Another thing this story reminds me is _____. This story brings back memories of a time when I _____. And this line, this part brought back memories of _____.

What Does the Main Character Learn about the Other Characters?

1. What do we learn about Squeaky's father? Look at the fourth paragraph. How old is he? What sport is he good at?
2. What does Cyntha Proctor say about herself just before something hard like a test or a spelling bee? What is the difference between what Cyntha says and actually does about practicing piano?
3. How does Rosie act? Squeaky says she "is too stupid to know there is not a great deal of difference between herself and Raymond and that she can't afford to throw stones." Do you know the saying, "People who live in glass houses shouldn't throw stones?" What has this to do with Rosie and Raymond?
4. What's Gretchen like? What does she do when Squeaky meets her, Mary Louise, and Rosie on Broadway? How does she act at the track meet? At the starting line? When she finishes the race?

What Does the Main Character Learn about Herself?

1. The story is called "Raymond's Run," but it is told by Squeaky. What do we find out about her from the story? On the surface we learn she's a tough kid. She can beat up most kids her size. She can cut down almost anyone with her tongue. She won't wear dresses like the other girls. She won't join in the May Pole dance. She's a good runner, but she boasts and brags about it. And she

won't let any other kid beat her at the fifty-yard dash even though she's won it year after year.

Before deciding Squeaky is a nasty kid, though, we need to think about these questions:

–How does she protect Raymond from other kids?

–How did she help Mary Louise when Mary Louise first moved to Harlem from Baltimore?

–What does she do when she thinks there will be a fight between Gretchen and her?

–How does she act when Raymond yanks at the fence "like a gorilla in a cage"? Is she embarrassed? Does she make believe she doesn't know him? How does she plan to help Raymond in the future? What does she mean when she says of herself, "And I've got a roomful of ribbons and medals and awards. But what has Raymond got to call this own"

2. What's in a name? The girl telling the story has many names. First, she says she is called Squeaky. The big kids call her Mercury. Rosie asks whether she is Raymond's "mother." She calls herself Miss Quicksilver and a "poor Black girl." She gives her "official" name to Mr. Pearson: Hazel Elizabeth Deborah Parker. All the names are different, but each tells us somethign about Squeaky. When is each used? What does it tell us about her?

3. Squeaky doesn't want to get dressed up for the May Pole dancing and "act like a girl for a change." Why not?

She thought she was a fool when she was a strawberry in a Hansel and Gretel pageant. What does she mean when the thinks, "I am not a strawberry. I do not dance on my toes. I run. That is what I'm all about."

At the end of the story she smiles at her supposed enemy, Gretchen. Read over the last paragraph and think about these questions: Is there a special way girls should act? That boys should act? Or just the way people should act?

Squeaky says to herself, "I run. That's what I'm all about." What do you like to do the most? Have you ever thought about what you are all about? If so. what did you come up with?

But Squeaky does more than just run, doesn't she? She thinks a lot about other people. And she understands herself pretty well, doesn't she? Is she "something honest and worthy of respect?" Why?

4. Think again about the title, "Raymond's Run." The story tells us something about Raymond, sure. But it is really about Squeaky and what happens to her as she watches Raymond run along with her during the fifty-yard dash. What does happen to her at this time? What does she learn about herself?

Evaluating the Text

As a final act of reading and responding, students should first individually and then as a whole group evaluate the text. They should learn how to do this in several ways. First, they can respond to the question of How well is it put together? Does it work out to be a "satisfying while?" When I read it over more carefully a second time, what are the clues the author has planted? Did she put it together well? Does everything–virtually each word–contribute to the overall effect? Next, they can attend to this question: Of all the stories you know, on a scale of 1 to 10–with 10 being the highest–how would you rate this story? And finally, they can react to these questions: What does the author reveal about how human beings behave? Is this information of real significance to us? In what ways?

I ask them to evaluate the story for several reasons. First of all, evaluating is the highest form of knowing, requiring a broad knowledge base and well developed critical faculties. I want them to get into the habit of evaluating literary texts, based upon internal and external criteria, so they'll develop these critical abilities to the extent they use them below the level of conscious awareness, intuitively, hardly thinking about them at all. Evaluation, based upon a close reading through personal responses, will also help them learn to develop reasons for supporting their initial, emotional responses. I want them to evaluate literary texts constantly to gradually wean them away from the teacher's authority as official interpreter. Only when they no longer turn to the teacher for the "authorized" interpretation of literary texts but respond emotionally and unashamedly to a moving short story, understand their personal motives for feeling as they did, confidently put into words these reasons so they as well as others can understand their convictions, will they become mature readers of ambiguous and ever increasingly sophisticated literary texts, becoming part of a learning community of readers.

Becoming a Learning Community

Now that the students have discussed the above questions within their small groups, I have them as an entire group relate the responses they had within their small groups. In this way I move toward a "communal response," a process by which the individual students in the group, through the give and take of an uninhibited yet supportive environment, arrive at a generally agreed upon interpretation of the story. In practical terms, I ask for a "chairman" of each group to report on what the consensus of the group was concerning the interpretation of the story, I ask for volunteers, or I call on individuals from each group, making sure I give as many persons as possible in each group a chance to speak before the whole class. The "communal" response is valuable for several reasons. The students, by expressing their interpretations about the story in a small group in which they feel confident and by listening to the reactions of their peers, learn how to interpret more fully and more richly. At the same time, as they respond in small groups and in the class as a whole, they discover that what they have to say is important to others. And as they continually move from personal reading and responding to small and large group discussion of many varied interpretations, they come to learn intuitively that interpretation of literary texts is ultimately social and cultural–that all individual reponses to literature are shaped by the personal and psychological background of the individual reader as well as by the cultural and historical setting in which the piece of literature is embedded. And finally, as students, year after year, engage socially in interpreting literary texts–freely giving responses to literary texts and honestly describing, without meanness of spirit, what they perceive as the responses of their peers–they become part of a special community, a learning community. Only in such a setting can students learn to read and interpret increasingly sophisticated literary texts and perfect the personal knowing and feeling skills so highly prized in any society.

Works Cited

Blake, Robert W. 1989. "Reading Poetry and Reconstruction of Reality: How College English Majors Read a Poem." *Reading, Writing and Interpreting Literature: Positions and Pedogogy*. Albany, NY: New York State English Council.

Bleich, David. 1978. *Subjective Criticism*. Baltimore, MD: The John Hopkins Press.

——. 1975. *Readings and Feelings*. Urbana, IL: National Council of Teachers of English.

Bloom, Benjamin, ed. 1956. *Taxonomy of Educational Objectives: Handbook I: Cognitive Domain*. New York: David McKay Company, Inc.

Brooks, Cleanth and Robert Penn Warren. 1960. *The Scope of Fiction*. New York: Appleton-Century-Crofts, Inc.

Bruner, Jerome S. 1966. *Toward a Theory of Instruction*. New York: W. W. Norton & Company, Inc.

Elbow, Peter. 1973. *Writing Without Teachers*. New York: Oxford University Press.

Gardner, Howard. 1983. *Frames of Mind: The Theory of Multiple Intelligences*. New York: Basic Books, Inc.

Hirsch, E. D. Jr. 1976. *The Aims of Interpretation*. Chicago: The University of Chicago Press.

Peck, M. Scott. 1987. *The Different Drum: Community Making and Peace*. New York: Simon and Schuster.

Rosenblatt, Louise M. 1978. *The Reader the Text the Poem: The Transactional Theory of the Literary Work*. Carbondale, IL: Southern Illinois University Press.

Slavin, Robert E. 1983. *Cooperative Learning*. New York: Longman.

· 1 8 ·

READER RESPONSE

Toward an Evolving Model for Teaching Literature in the Elementary Grades

Robert W. Blake (1996)

Abstract

We are moving from a "traditional" method toward a "reader response" approach to teaching elementary school children to read and respond to worth-while literature within the context of a learning community. After describing the present state of teaching literature in the elementary grades, one first grade teacher and her small group of children's interactions with a delightful picture book are chronicled. Elements of an evolving reader response approach conclude this article.

We are living through a disturbingly unsettled but wonderfully challenging time for teaching literature in the elementary grades. Moving from an era when children learned to find a single, "correct" meaning in a text by a step-by-step, systematic method, we have entered another period in which children are learning to read literature in a radically different way; that is, by creating, rather than finding, their own personal meanings within a learning community.

That a worthwhile literary text compels the reader, watcher, or listener to experience a story both emotionally and intellectually is, as I view it, one of the principal features of reader response. When a person approaches a literary text in the traditional manner examining it logically and rationally as a linguistic puzzle to be solved, she assumes the perspective of the scientist, acting as a detached observer. On the other hand, when an individual allows herself to apprehend a text with all her senses, she invariably becomes involved in the story and is able to see how it is related to real life. The *feeling* and *memory* responses, key aspects of reader response, are the most powerful techniques for compelling children to see literature as an extension of reality, not as a perfunctoty, frequently meaningless school exercise.

> ... Children are learning to read ... by creating ... their own meanings ...

Signs are many that such a sea of change is occurring. Here are a few examples. Some teachers have moved from "process writing" in their classrooms to "process" literature instruction (David, Doney, Kreider & Titus, 1990). Elementary school teachers report that they are employing successfully response and dialogue response journals (Hancock, 1992). The use of "real" books for literature-based reading instruction results in "... stunning levels of success with all types of students and particularly with disabled and uninterested readers" (Tunnell & Jacobs, 1989, 470). Furthermore, teachers who employ literature based reading instruction in their classrooms find their students perform better on standardized texts than do students who use traditional approaches to reading literature (Multis, Campbell & Farstrup, 1992).

Although some elementary school teachers are using literature in their classrooms, their chief aim, though, appears to be improving reading comprehension, rather than having children respond to literature. In reaction to this trend, some educators argue that literature study itself is a worthwhile activity. Purves (1993), for instance, proposed that "... we think of the place of literature in a literature program. A literature program should not be a reading program with tradebooks, which is currently the case in many elementary schools. ... It should have the elements of a Literature program" (p. 356).

Walmsley (1993) observed that the elementary language arts programs have been dominated by reading instruction, usually delivered through a commercial reading system. The literature children previously encountered was made up of excerpts, frequently revised from the original texts to make the language simpler to read and the subject matter less controversial. When Walmsley interviewed in depth a sizeable number of teachers, remedial and special education specialists, school librarians, and administrators, he discovered that teachers found it difficult to articulate any purposes for literature other than it was "fun" or "it's for teaching reading skills;" he discovered "...

little evidence of a coherent, articulated district philosophy, with respect to literature's role in the language arts program, across grades or across different levels of reading and writing ability" (Walmsley, 1993, p. 510). The teachers, he reports, had virtually no idea of the "big picture" of literature instruction; how reading and literature are related, the role of writing in reading literature, or a systematic set of methods for teaching literature. At the same time, teachers revealed they had little formal training in literature study, especially when compared to their extensive backgrounds in reading. In sum, Walmsley (1993) concluded from the teachers' remarks that there was an absence of a philosophical underpinning for literature instruction.

> More recently, Langer (1994) presented the results of a study of how children and teachers understand literature by a reader response orientation and related what strategies teachers actually used in their classrooms. Langer, like Walmsley, found elementary school teachers were unclear about how to teach literature by traditional methods but were also unable to articulate what reader response literature instruction meant to them.

However, the field [literature instruction in elementary grades] has not provided adequate guidelines or strategies to allow teachers to build "new bones"—internalized routines and options to take the place of plot summaries and leading questions guiding students toward predetermined interpretations—new bones that can guide their moment-to-moment decision making as they plan for and interact with their students (Langer, 1994, p. 204).

How Reader Response Works in a First Grade Classroom: Practice Exemplifying Theory

To demonstrate reader response theory in actual use with a small group of first grade girls and a boy, let's observe how Mrs. Kelly's children read, discussed, and wrote about a delightful picture book. From an examination of the children's and teacher's activities, I identify what I believe are essential elements of reader response and show the differences between traditional and reader response instruction. As a result, we can infer general guidelines and classroom strategies for classroom instruction.

In April, Mrs. Kelly invites four of her independent readers to take part in an informal experiment with beginning reader response. The activities will be new for both the children and their teacher. They start by reading the picture book, *Jesse Bear, What Will You Wear* (Carlstrom, 1989). The books recounts one day in the life of a preschooler, Jesse Bear. Jesse starts off his morning in a conventional fashion by "wearing" clothes, but soon—in an amazing, meta-phoric leap—he sees himself as "wearing" flowers, sun, sand, carrots and peas, celery, an apple, juice, and later, when he takes his nighttime bath, bathtub water. As he snuggles into his bed with a teddy bear tucked under his cheek and the moonlight streaming through an open window, he sleepily catalogues what he will end his day by "wearing": "Sleep in my eyes/ And stars in the skies/ Moon on my bed/ And dreams in my head/That's what I'll wear tonight" (Carlstrom, 1989, n.p.).

A joyous, reassuring picture book of a day in the life of a happy, secure little boy—in the guise of a small bear. The dedication of the book, "To Jesse David, the real Jesse Bear, with love—N.W.C." makes clear that the tale of Jesse Bear is the story of the author's own little boy.

The bright, detailed watercolor illustrations show a happy family of a baby bear, mama bear, and a papa bear, living in a idyllic cottage with a picket fence and a flower-covered arbor, with Jesse Bear taking baths in a claw footed tub and ending his day contentedly in a little boy's enchanting bedroom. The text rhymes. The characters are appealing and familiar. Although the life of the bear appears idealistic, a way of life possibly foreign to many children today, it may serve to portray not what life actually is but the way it might be.

For their first reading of the book, Mrs. Kelly has the children sit on the floor together in a circle. Each child reads their own copy of the book to silently. Then they all read the book together out loud. Although such a first reading in unison is not easy, Mrs. Kelly makes the experience pleasurable. The children and teacher obviously enjoy themselves.

After the initial, silent reading and second reading aloud, the children now talk in the whole group about their introductory impressions of the book.

Krysten:	The whole book rhymes and I think it is neat.
Jolene:	I like Jesse because he was a bear and because my sister's name is Jesse.
Lindsay:	I read the book before and after and I think it is funny.
Bryan:	(In a low voice. He seems intimidated by these articulate girls.) I think the book is good.

Now Mrs. Kelly asks for volunteers to re-tell the story. "I will," says Jolene as she raises her hand.

"Okay. Go ahead," prompts Mrs. Kelly.

"Jesse Bear had dirt on his shirt and ants in his pants."

"Would you like Jesse as a friend?" Asks Mrs. Kelly.

"I would love that."

"Why?"

"Because he looks so cuddly and cute."

Bryan pipes up, "I would like him for a friend because Jesse has neat toys."

"I'm almost like Jesse Bear," adds Krysten. "I get up, get dressed, play outside, have lunch, play some more, have dinner, take a bath, put on my pj's, and then go to bed."

All the children agree they are somewhat like Jesse Bear. Krysten even goes so far as to identify with him, seeing no difference between a little girl and a bear cub.

For the next step in the reader response process, the children are asked to go back to their seats and write a response to the book. They are also encouraged to illustrate their responses. What follows are the teacher's directions, descriptions of the children's drawings, and a verbatim account of what they wrote.

Krysten: (Krysten draws a picture of Jesse Bear in his red shirt and his jockey shorts with blue stars.)

I't all rime's. And i't says in the morning at nigte in the after noon. And Jesse Bear rime's with is clothes like with noon at nigte in the morning. And I like this story very much I injoy this book.

Lindsay: (At the top of her paper, she draws and colors a picture of Jesse's dirty shirt and a picture of Jesse with his red shirt and his blue pants.)

The book was good. Because Jesse Bear was very funny. He said I'll wear my blue pens and my red shirt. Then at noon he said I'll wear my blue pj's. At night I wear white pj's with peanda [panda] bears on it.

Bryan: (Bryan's picture shows a brown Jesse, looking somewhat like a happy seal, reclining in an immense expanse of blue water in an old fashioned, claw footed bathtub.)

I like Jesse Bear because I like the part when he's in the tub and it tells all of the time in a day and it is a good book and there is very good carters [characters].

Jolene: (Jolene's illustrations in purple, green, and red include Jesse at
                the breakfast table, Jesse reading, and Jesse in bed.)
                The book has bears in it. It had singing in it. There was a mama
                bear a papa bear in it and a little bear. Jesse was dreminge. Jesse
                was taking a bath. He had a pipe to blow bubbles with in the
                bathtub. He had sors [stars] on in the morning. He had a tesrt
                [tee shirt] on in the morning.

Elements of Reader Response in a First Grade Classroom

From the previous account of reader response with an actual group of first
grade children, we can infer the elements of reader response.

First, since Mrs. Kelly herself is taking a risk with introducing reader
response to a group of primary school children, she meets initially with a
group of four of her independent readers. Acting as an intact discussion group,
they talk informally about whether or not they like to read, what their favorite
books are, and what literature is to them. Then children silently read their
own copy of the book. After they have finished, teacher and students read the
book out loud in unison.

Now Mrs. Kelly asks the children to talk about their personal impressions
of the book. Inspired by the friendly atmosphere established, the children are
at no loss to respond about what the story means to them.

It's important to note that as the children offer their initial, intuitive
responses to the story, rather than answering questions from the teacher about
specific details, they naturally choose the details meaningful to them and necessary for their personal interpretations. Jesse Bear, for instance, has "dirt on
his shirt," "ants in his pants," he wears "blue pj's," and he has "Stars in the
morning on his jockey shorts." In effect, the children use "close reading" skills
to substantiate their conceptions of the meaning of the story, rather than the
teacher's conceptions.

What does the term "close reading" mean? The phrase is associated with
the new criticism's approach to the interpretation of literature and has become
a central feature of contemporary literary analysis. With close reading, one
moves systematically—line-by-line, section-by-section and often word-by-
word—through a text in order to arrive at its inherent meaning. This inductive method of reading a text (i.e., building up a body of evidence leading to

an interpretation) is a crucial feature of this time-honored practice. With the traditional method, one uses close reading *first* to *find* the correct meaning. With reader response, one *first* intuitively—without a systematic, inductive approach—perceives what the overall meaning of a text is essentially to one-self and then uses close reading techniques to *create* a personal interpretation, which is satisfactory to the reader.

After they have read a book silently, read it chorally, and talked unin-hibitedly about what it means to them, the children are invited to create a written response to their reading. Of course, since they are first graders, they also are comfortable with illustrating their reactions.

With great zest, the children express their feelings—in this case, good feelings—about what they've read. "I like the story very much." "I injoy this book." "This book was good." Relating feelings as an initial response to what they have read is a primary element of reader response. As the children create their own meanings for the story, pointing out specific words, lines, and fea-tures they like to support their created meaning, they are also fearlessly giv-ing opinions of the value of the book, stating simply but forcefully why they enjoyed it. From my experience, I have found that as children are constantly exposed to traditional methods of reading literature, particularly with finding the "correct" meaning of literary texts, they become less and less courageous at interpreting and inevitably become dependent upon what the teacher judges the meanings of texts to be. In this case, however, the children relate what the book means to them, evaluate its worth, and without trepidation, give reasons for their evaluations. "It all rhymes." "It deals with morning, afternoon, and night." "Jesse Bear was funny." "The book had bears." "It had singing in it,"

Not only do the children demonstrate they are able to read and respond orally to a worthwhile text in a quite sophisticated fashion, but through their written responses, they also show enormous strides in a command of written English. As a direct result of writing their responses, they discover much about the complex business of transforming sounds into written symbols, while at the same time creating a whole piece of meaningful discourse in response to a valuable book. Surely such opportunities are more substantive than writing out short answers to questions on worksheets or in workbooks. The written response to literature is another essential element of reader response. To learn what children have discovered, let's analyze their responses.

Krysten nonchalantly takes enormous risks with spelling in order to say what she wants to about the book. She hasn't mastered the spelling of such historically irregular words like "rhyme" and "night," but since she needs these words to say what she wishes—and is not shy about spelling them "correctly"—she writes them out the way she hears them. Notice she has seen the word "night" with a "g" in it but hasn't quite mastered our present day illogical but conventional spelling of it: "nigte." She spells another historically irregular word "clothes" conventionally but writes "enjoy" just the way she hears it, "injoy," showing some really clever hypothesizing about relations of sounds to their written counterparts. Finally, she hasn't worked out the conventional use of apostrophes yet, spelling "it" as "I't."

Lindsay already has a firm command of written English and is so mature she has even found it necessary to write out what characters say without having full command of the conventions of quotation marks. Notice how Lindsay uses direct quotations. "He said I'll wear my blue pens and my red shirt." To connect her life with Jesse's, she offers the information that at night she wears "white pj's," and with a fearless flourish informs us that her "pj's" have "peanda bears on it." Not only is she unconcerned about the correct spelling of "panda," she is also unaware that since the noun "pj" is plural, then the pronoun "it" should be plural "them" to agree with its antecedent, something she would likely attend to with a revision.

Bryan is competent with written English, retelling the plot of the story and ending his response with a reason for finding the story valuable, because it has "very good carters [characters]." He gives his reason for liking the book and tries hard to use written symbols to represent book-like words he has heard, in this case, probably the teacher's talking about "characters" in stories.

Jolene is virtually stricken with happiness from her experience with the book and is bursting with a desire to share with others all her reasons why. She tells why she likes it, using the words she finds significant: dreminge [dreaming], sors [stars], and tesrt [tee shirt].

In summary, the evident elements of reader response are these:

1. **Children experience worthwhile literature in a number of ways.** They read books by themselves, they read books chorally, and they have books read to them. As they perceive literary texts in several different ways, they feel comfortable with entering into them, with first experiencing them emotionally, rather than using literary texts as a means for testing reading skills.

2. **After having "experienced" a literary text, children make an initial, intuitive response to a work.** One's first, uninhibited response

invariably remains, even after extended discussion, the right one for that person.

3. **Children commonly retell a story to fix the sequence of events in their minds, to come to an understanding of plot (i.e., what happens in a story).** Although some teachers insist that children go beyond the simple recounting of plot, an ordering of the events of a story is not always a simple task. Even though the sequence of events in books for children usually occurs in simple chronological order, the plot lines in complex stories may be quite puzzling, especially with stories within stories and with flashbacks interrupting the forward movement of the narrative. Even with reader response, then, children need to under-stand the idea of narrative events and make explicit their comprehen-sion of how plot contributes to overall meaning of a story.

4. **Children use close reading techniques to find specific details on their own, to support their initial responses.** Rather than filling in blanks in texts and in workbook sheets with single words or phrases, they iden-tify concrete details with special meaning for them, choosing examples without teacher direction, thus creating their personal meaning for a literary text.

5. **Children allow feelings to arise and make use of personal memories triggered by the piece to assist them in relating the text to their lives.** Building upon one's feelings to understand a text is the activity I call the *feeling response*. Using memories and associations for connecting with a text I call *memory response*. Bleich (1975) terms these tasks, respectively, as the "Affective" and "Associative" responses.

6. **Children, at almost all ages, are able to write out responses to lit-erary texts if they are allowed to find their own voices.** They need to be nudged, coaxed, and prompted constantly to create their own responses, without worrying about what the teacher "wants" or what she may think the "correct" meaning should be. Children need to be constantly assured that it's all right to write freely, not threatened with such surface concerns as correct spelling, punctuation, capitalization, or standard usage *at this initial stage*. More importantly, though, they need to relinquish an uneasiness about what others may think about their uncensored, spontaneous reactions.

7. **Children are able to create their own Interpretations of literary texts, if we who read their written responses have assumed the stance of**

reader-response teacher and are perceptive enough to translate what they write into our "grown up" terms, like "theme," for instance.

We need to explore further how children arrive at a theme for a piece of literature. Articulating "theme," which signifies overall understanding, is another essential element of reader response. There is a commonly held belief that young children are unable to articulate themes in literary texts (Applebee, 1978). One of Applebee's major conclusions to his ground- breaking study is that children cannot generalize about "theme"—following Piaget's stages of intellectual development—until they reach adolescence. First, I believe there's a problem with using Piaget's model of intellectual development as the basis for deciding young children are unable to arrive at literary theme. Piaget's model of intelligence is not that of a scheme developed by someone grounded in literature. Piaget's model of intellectual development has been criticized because it is restricted to only one kind of thinking, that of a laboratory scientist. "Piaget tells us little about creativity at the forefront of the sciences, let alone about the originality that is most prized in the arts or in other realms of human creativity" (Gardner, 1983, 21). Piaget's model is not, therefore, wholly satisfactory for assessing children's ability to identify or state themes in literature.

Another problem I find with Applebee's conclusions is the method by which the adolescents he studied addressed literary themes. Applebee reports adolescents analyzing stories in terms of their mechanics, the logic of their structure, and by their images and symbols; in other words, adolescents study stories in a fairly formal fashion and only then do they explain their reasoning. The approach thus used reflects the new critical model, one that is logical, systematic, and "scientific." What adolescents "do" most likely reflects instruction and formulaic approaches to writing assignments. We can only wonder at how children might have responded differently to stories if they had had extensive reader response practice.

After listening to a series of three realistic fiction and three folktale books, kindergarten, second-grade and fourth-grade children were able to identify books with similar themes and were able to state in their own words what these themes were to them (Lehr, 1988). The children expressed their own ideas about the meanings of stories, and even though their general statements could not be judged as adult, their themes were appropriate to the texts. "Kindergarten children most often gave responses that differed from adult choices but were congruent with the text, suggesting that the child's perspective of meaning differs from that of an adult (Lehr, 1988, p. 337).

Real children reading and talking about what an authentic book means to them had no trouble revealing what the book's essential meaning was, its "theme," if you will. At the same time, they revealed a refined knowledge of the elements of narration even if they couldn't express this knowledge in adult terms.

8. **If we accept the assumption that learning is social** (Halliday, 1978) **and that experiencing literature is a social act** (Applebee, 1978; Berscheid, 1985; Gardner, 1983), **then children discussing what they read with others in small groups and in the class as a whole, especially with the teacher as a member of the group, is an indispensable element of the reader response approach to literature, what I term a "learning community."** [See Peck (1987) for a discussion on the elements of "community" and how it is created and maintained with adult groups]. The atmosphere of a learning community ensures that each child will have an immediate and sympathetic audience for their oral and written response to literature. This feedback, by other children and by the teacher, validates the child's response and at the same time enriches the responses of all other children. As the learning community is developed and nurtured over time, it increases trust and good feelings among the children, contributes to their socialization, and allows them to join the wider cultural community.

> ... there are signs we are moving toward a new model for literature teaching.

Figure 1 summarizes the elements of reader response by contrasting them with the salient features of traditional literature teaching.

Even though there appears to be little agreement regarding teaching literature in the elementary schools, including a philosophical base, guidelines, and strategies for classroom instruction, there are signs we are moving toward a new model for literature teaching. It is difficult, especially given the present unsettled state, to predict the exact shape this new way of teaching literature will assume. Whatever the final form assumes, the evolving model will be the result of attention to questions like these:

TRADITIONAL	READER RESPONSE
1. The teacher emphasizes the text primarily.	1. Although a worthwhile text is a necessary element, the primary emphasis is on the child's oral or written response to that text.
2. The teacher guides the child to find the "correct" meaning within the text.	2. The child creates her own personal meaning for the text, with the sophisticated help of an especially trained and sympathetic teacher.
3. The teacher directs the child to answer specific comprehensive questions about the elements of a literary text, such as setting, plot, characters, and theme.	3. The child gives an initial response to a literary piece and then uses her knowledge about literary elements to support her interpretation.
4. The traditional method is essentially objective, detached, inductive, and "scientific." Emotions and personal opinions are not emphasized.	4. Feelings, memories, associations, and intuition (perceptions arrived at without rational thought) are not only allowed but form the core of reader response.
5. The child typically shares her responses with the teacher only.	5. The child shares her responses with other children in small groups and with the whole learning community. Each child thus sees individual response grow, becoming enriched and validated by the responses from her peers and teacher.

Figure 1. Reader Response: Toward an Evolving Model for Teaching Literature in the Elementary Grades.

1. What happens as a child acrually reads literature? How do children perceive stories, poems, and plays through reader response?
2. Why is group discussion of responses to literature, both oral and written, essential to the reader response?

3. Does an understanding of literature call upon intellectual processing abilities different from those traditionally taught as components of reading?

4. And finally, why indeed engage children in reading and responding to literature? Of what inherent value is literary knowing? Is it, as many contend, a "frill"? Is it useful merely as a tool for teaching children how to read? Is its primary purpose to give pleasure? Is it to promote practice in critical thinking or are there more fundamental reasons why one should acquire literary knowing? Does literary knowledge lead to a profound understanding of one's self (Gardner, 1983)? Does a background of the important books from one's culture lead to cultural appreciation (Purves, 1993)? Is literature the repository of all the social and personal laws of a people, the guides to how one functions in a society and how one behaves in one's family life (Havelock, 1963)? Wrestling with these and similar questions will help us address the most basic of all questions related to literature: of what value is its study to the children of a society?

References

Applebee, A. N. (1978). *The child's concept of story: Ages two to seventeen.* Chicago: The University of Chicago Press.

Berscheid, E. (1985). Interpersonal ways of knowing. In E. Eisner (Ed.) *Learning and teaching the ways of knowing.* Chicago: The University of Chicago Press.

Bleich, D. (1975). *Readings and feelings: An introduction to subjective criticism.* Urbana, IL: National Council of Teachers of English.

Eisner, E. (Ed.) *Learning and teaching the ways of knowing.* Chicago: The University of Chicago Press.

Carlstrom, N. W. (1986). *Jesse bear, what will you wear?* New York: Scholastic, Inc.

David, D. L., Doney, M., Kreider, K., and Titus, M. (1990). From writing to reading in third grade: A whole language process approach. In R. W. Blake (Ed.), *Whole Language: Explorations and applications* (pp. 75–86). Urbana, IL: National Council of Teachers of English.

Gardner, H. (1983). *Frames of mind: The theory of multiple intelligences.* New York: Basic Books, Inc., Publishers.

Hancock, M. R. (1993). Exploring and extending personal response through literature journals. *The Reading Teacher, 46,* 466–474.

Halliday, M. A. K. (1978). *Language as a social semiotic: The social interpretation of language and meaning.* Baltimore, MD: University Park Press.

Havelock, E. A. (1963). *Preface to plato.* Cambridge, MA: Harvard University Press.

Langer, J. A. (1994). Focus on research: A reader-response approach to reading literature. *Language Arts*, 71, 203–211.

Lehr, S. (1988). The child's developing sense of theme as a response to literature. *Reading Research Quarterly*, 23, 337–357.

Mullis, I. V. S., Campbell, J. R., & Farstrup, A. E. (1993). *NAEP 1992 reading report card for the nation and the states*. Washington, D.C.: Office of Educational Research and Improvement, U.S. Department of Education.

Peck, M. S. (1987). *The different drum: Community making and peace*. New York: Simon and Schuster.

Purves, A. C. (1993). Toward an reevaluation of reader response and school literature. *Language Arts*, 70, 348–361.

Tunnell, M. O. & Jacobs, J. S. (1989). Using "real books": Research findings on literature based reading instruction. *The Reading Teacher*, 42, 470–477.

Walmsley, S. A. (1992). Reflections on the state of elementary literature instruction. *Language Arts*, 69, 508–514.

SECTION VI

DRAMA IN THE CLASSROOM

Who teaches drama anymore in our English/ELA classrooms? Who has time? And quite frankly, why do it, when the year-end standardized assessments that supposedly measure what are students have learned, don't even "test" for drama—neither discretely as skills, nor holistically as an entire play, for example.

And yet, in 1982 and 1989, Robert was talking about teaching drama. Himself the drama coach/teacher while a high school English teacher, Robert felt deeply connected to showing students how "the play's the thing."

In the first piece, entitled, "The Play's the Thing," he reviews the historical foundations and purposes of drama, reminding us that it is, "The oldest form of narrative, of storytelling," adding that, "A good play embodies implicitly, rather than teaching explicitly, issues which are basic to a culture's survival." Robert ends this piece by giving us a "How to" read a play using a set of systematic strategies that worked for him.

In the second and last piece of this section, Robert shows us how to adapt a play from a short story, and in doing so "teach" students a considerable amount about the English language arts. "Converting Narrative into Drama" reveals a wonderful exercise that while teaching ELA skills, does so through the beauty of literature and drama.

· 1 9 ·

THE PLAY'S THE THING FOR
MIDDLE SCHOOL STUDENTS

Robert W. Blake (1989)

Showing middle school students how to see a play as they read it is my purpose here. Even though I take for granted the inexplicable magic of live theater, I need at the outset to ask myself the following: Why teach kids to read drama? Why take valuable class time to instruct them in reading a play?

First, I know drama is the oldest form of narrative, of storytelling. When I think of "drama," what first comes to mind is something that entertains; I get images of people flocking to Broadway musicals or watching TV shows with cops and robbers or seeing movies with monsters and spaceships. But the ancient Greeks, I know, invented plays not to entertain but to enlighten; their plays were sacred community vehicles for presenting a nonliterate people with acceptable and nonacceptable ways of acting, the codes of behavior for their culture. I realize the Greeks did write comedies, but I also realize they took drama much more seriously than we do now: plays were an integral part of their lives. Although Willy Loman is not, according to Aristotle, a tragic hero, the ancient Greeks would be more at home watching Arthur Miller's *Death of a Salesman* than they would *A Chorus Line*. So a good play—one that people have seen fit to save—embodies implicitly, rather than teaching explicitly—issues which are basic to a culture's survival. These are the real reasons why school youngsters should be taught how to apprehend worth-while dramatic texts.

If the ways of behaving enacted in plays are so important, though, why not simply state them in an essay or philosophical treatise? Because that's not the way we comprehend in a lasting way. When we see humans on a stage in conflict over profound human matters, we perceive the codes of behavior made flesh and blood, and we remember and learn. Only by reading, discussing, and interpreting a worthwhile play, and then by producing it, will students learn how to read and see a play by themselves, especially young people who have no tradition of playgoing.

Why Read This Play? (Rationale)

Generally speaking, students need to learn how to read, interpret, and present a play simply because drama is a basic human activity. In specific terms, though, I need to ask myself why they should read and produce a particular play, W. W. Jacobs' *The Monkey's Paw*. First, this play is a rousing tale of the supernatural. (Although Stephen King never gives credit for it, the plot of his novel *Pet Sematary* is that of *The Monkey's Paw*.) Furthermore, the play is a model of a taut, well-made dramatic piece with three scenes, a single setting, only five characters, and every word contributing toward a single preconceived effect.

The play, however, is more than a macabre potboiler; it deals with an elemental human issue: the possible existence of fate. Although at first meeting the characters appear ordinary enough, they represent various responses to this notion. Herbert, the son, is skeptical of the power of the monkey's paw. Sergeant-Major Morris, a credible witness, is one who has observed at firsthand the powers of the occult. Mr. White, the father, believes in fate if it brings him personal gain. Mrs. White, the mother, initially uninterested in the men's debates, believes in unnatural forces the most strongly when they are called upon to return her son from the dead. This is a tightly constructed play, then, one which reveals through characters in action various views toward a supernatural manifestation of fate, with the most satisfying response to the notion of fate being—in this play, at least—that it is better not to contest fate but to live one's life ignorant of the unseen and irrational forces that can be unleashed by our meddling with the unknown.

Knowledge the Students Will Assimilate and the Skills They Will Practice (General Instructional Objectives)

After having read, discussed, and interpreted a well-made and worth-while play and presented it orally as either readers theater, acting with scripts, or actually producing it in the classroom or on stage, the students will be able to:

- respond emotionally, possibly with personal associations, to a play.
- describe the setting of a play, including its physical location, furniture, and other properties.
- explain what the characters in the play are like, based upon how the playwright describes them and what they say and do.
- tell how characters move around the stage and explain how their movements and personalities relate to the overall meaning of the play.
- describe dramatic elements of plot, initial situation, rising action, climax, and final resolution; tell how these elements are exemplified in a play; and relate their significance to the total impact of the play.
- discuss with the teacher and with other students questions (teacher-or student-created) designed to help comprehend setting, characters, and plot.
- make a statement about the value of a play, based upon intrinsic and extrinsic criteria, with the statement being substantiated by evidence from the play.
- cooperate with other students and adults in producing a play, using one of three approaches: readers theater, acting with scripts, or actual production.

How to Teach the Play (Teaching Strategies)

I need to make a number of professional judgments when I teach the play. If my students are fairly sophisticated about reading and producing plays, then I can review quickly the matters of plot, character development, theme, staging, and so forth. If the students are largely ignorant of these matters—as I suspect most middle school youngsters would be—then it's necessary to spend some time introducing and establishing these notions. In any event, I want to have the students read the play fairly quickly for an initial personal reaction and then read it over a second time more carefully and systematically, after which they will finally produce the play for an audience.

Reading the Play as a Script

To have a firm basis for future reading of plays, students need essentially to read the play as a script. I explain to the students that when a director and actors first read a play as a group, they follow the same procedure. I have the students sit in a circle or move their seats around to form a rectangular table large enough to include everybody. I assign them various parts, showing them as they go along how to read a dramatic text as a script so they might assimilate setting, character, physical appearance, mannerisms, voice, background, motivation, delivery of lines, and the overall pacing and tone of the play.

Setting

To introduce the students to setting, I draw a diagram of a typical proscenium arch stage on the chalkboard and direct them to "set the stage" by drawing in the features of the set, including walls, windows, drapes, and all furniture and other properties and their positions on the stage. Later, I might encourage interested students to draw or paint a picture of the set or to construct a model of the set design.

Characters

I tell the students that they can begin to understand the characters by visualizing what they look like from the playwright's descriptions. For instance, in *The Monkey's Paw*, the author tells us that Mrs. White is "a pleasant-looking woman," but leaves it up to the readers to create their own images of the character.

I learn most about the characters in a play, however, by what they say and do. I need to impress upon the students that from the speeches and behavior of the characters, they can gather evidence to substantiate their responses to the play and justify their interpretations of the play.

Plot

If the students are ignorant of traditional ways of viewing plot, I introduce basic terms dealing with the structure of a play. I may either run off the items with a copy for each student or write them down on the chalkboard and take a few minutes discussing them to make sure we all share generally agreed-upon meanings. I point out that a play, like any other story, has to start at a certain place, move along in a specific direction, and end satisfactorily. It has, in other words, a beginning, middle, and ending, and the parts all fit together—like any work of art—in a satisfying whole.

1. *Initial situation:* The first part of a play introduces the conflict. If the play is short, usually one major character meets a single problem or conflict about which he or she must make a decision. The rest of the play deals with how the major character attempts to resolve the problem and what happens as a result of his or her behavior.
2. *Rising action:* After the playwright has established the major conflict, introduced the characters, and provided the necessary exposition (in the best plays, subtly and unobtrusively), he or she must keep our interest in the play. This is done by introducing a series of complications following from the main character's reaction to the initial conflict.
3. *Climax:* The climax is the high point of the play, the part of greatest intensity. It is the instant at which the chief character decides to act one way or another with respect to the major conflict.
4. *Resolution:* The resolution is what happens to the main character—and to the characters who have reacted to him or her in some way—as a result of how he or she behaved when faced with the major conflict. The technical term for the final resolution in a play is the French word *dénouement*—literally translated as "untying"—which signifies an "unravelling of the plot of a play or novel" (*American Heritage Dictionary* 1973).

Reading Orally, Discussing, and Interpreting the Play

After the students have read the play out loud fairly quickly, I have them reread it in a systematic fashion. At this point, it's a good idea to have them read out loud each of the three scenes separately and discuss the play as a group, following—but certainly not restricted by—the guide questions provided below. Once they have learned how to use teacher-designed questions, they will become confident with framing their own questions as a technique for satisfying for themselves what is happening in a play.

Discussing Scene One

1. What is the setting of the play? Describe the White cottage. How is it furnished, and where are the furnishings placed?
2. What does Mrs. White look like? How does she feel about the men's wishing on the monkey's paw?
3. Describe Mr. White. What do we learn about him from Scene One?
4. Tell us about the Sergeant-Major. (First of all, what is a Sergeant-Major? What kind of a man becomes and remains a Sergeant-Major?) He says he is "tough." How do we know this? Relate the story he tells about the monkey's paw. What is the "essential meaning" of this story to you? State your understanding in a few sentences. Is this an unusual tale to be told by a tough army man? Why?
5. In an effective opening scene, the playwright includes words and events that will crop up later in the play. We call this practice *foreshadowing*. Every word, especially in a short play, counts. Note where the following details occur and, after you have read the whole play, relate their significance to the plot:
   - exactly how much money Mr. White stills owes on the house.
   - Herbert's shift at work. At what time does he usually come home?
   - what kind of job Herbert has.
   - what the first wish on the monkey's paw was.
   - why the old fakir put the curse on the monkey's paw. How the wish would come true "so natural."
   - what the bolt on the front door to the cottage was like.

Discussing Scene Two

1. What does Mr. Sampson look like? What is his purpose in the play?
2. How does the playwright keep our suspense in Scene Two after the initial conflict? What complications arise?
3. How was Herbert killed? How was his killing related to the initial conflict? Did we have a hint——a foreshadowing——in Scene Two of how he was to die? What was it?

Discussing Scene Three

1. How long has it been between Scene Two and Scene Three?
2. Why does Mrs. White, who didn't believe in the monkey's paw, now want to make a wish on it?

3. What foreshadowing do we have that if Herbert is brought back to life, it would not be a good thing?

4. What is the effect of the candle going out—"utter darkness"— as Mrs. White makes her wish?

5. Why didn't Herbert appear immediately when Mrs. White wished for him to be alive?

6. How does the playwright keep the suspense mounting toward the end of Scene Three? Describe in detail how he accomplishes this.

7. Why does Mr. White make the last wish? Explain.

8. What is the effect of the ending of the scene–quiet after "tempestuous" knocking, "a flood of moonlight. Emptiness. The old man sways in prayer on his knees. The old woman lies half swooning, wailing against the door post." Explain in your own words what is happening.

Discussing the Play as a Whole

Now that the students have read the entire play over a second time, the class needs to talk about it as a whole. Questions like the following are designed to encourage general discussion.

1. How did the reading of the play make you feel? Explain your feelings.

2. Did you enjoy the play? Why or why not? Did it hold your interest? If so, how did it do so? Did you wish to know what would happen next once you started reading?

3. Although the basic idea is an incredible one, how did the playwright make the plot seem plausible? Did the complications, for instance, proceed realistically from the initial conflict? Given the way the characters reveal themselves, was the climax appropriate? Was the final resolution—dénouement—satisfying? Did you feel at the ending that this is the way "things should be"?

4. Were the characters believable? In what ways? Was what they said consistent with what they did?

5. What do you suppose the playwright is saying about people and life in general? (You might wish to think about the friendly dispute between Herbert and the Sergeant-Major in Scene One.)

6. How good was the play? There are two ways of judging the play. First, how well was it put together? And second, does the play deal with something important for people to think about? Support your evaluation with evidence from the text.

Putting on the Play

Now that the students have read the play out loud quickly for a general impression and have reread it more carefully, following

Readers theater: The actors sit on stools before an audience in class or on a stage and read from their scripts held in binders.

Acting with scripts: The actors walk through the play with scripts in their hands before an audience in class or on a stage.

Actual production: The actors produce the play before an audience in class or on stage. The actors memorize their lines, use expressive gestures, move about the stage, wear costumes, and use properties, such as furniture and other objects.

If the students stage an actual production, they need to decide about the following:

1. Setting: Should there be flats to designate the White house or should there be just curtains and the necessary furniture and other properties?
2. Lighting: How would lighting and other special effects be used?
3. Parts: Which students would be best suited for the roles? Students who wish to play certain parts should read or try out. It may be advisable to have more than one cast for the play, to give more students practice in acting.
4. Makeup: How should the characters appear? What makeup is needed?
5. Costuming: What costumes are necessary?
6. Properties: What furniture and other properties should be rounded up?
7. Acting: The students need to learn the fundamentals of acting on a stage:
   - how to move across a stage, move upstage, and move downstage
   - how to assume stage positions
   - how to memorize lines
   - how to reflect emotions
   - how to make stage gestures
   - how to play a character realistically, such as an old lady or a military man
   - how to achieve and vary pace

Evaluation

My evaluation techniques are directly related to my purpose—teaching middle school students to see a play as they read it. Moreover, I can use my general instructional objectives directly for evaluating the students' success.

The following are various ways of assessing how well the students have learned the terms related to dramatic literature and how well they can perform the skills necessary for reading, responding, and interpreting plays. Students will:

1. Make an immediate emotional response to a play (short written response).
2. Describe or define, with examples,
   • the general elements of setting, plot, characters, and theme.
   • dramatic elements of a play, such as initial situation, rising action, climax, and final resolution.
   • the three kinds of play production (readers theater, acting with scripts, and actual production).
   • the basic elements of play production, such as setting, lighting, acting, makeup, properties, and costuming (oral recitation or short written responses).
3. Explain how the general elements of a play and the dramatic elements of a play are exemplified in a particular play (oral recitation or short written responses).
4. Describe how a particular play could be adapted to various methods of production (oral recitation or short written responses).
5. Describe how the elements of play production—setting, lighting, acting, makeup, properties, costuming—are demonstrated in a particular play (oral recitation or short written responses).
6. Identify the elements of a play and analyze how the elements are employed by the playwright in a particular play (oral recitation or short written responses).
7. Make a statement about the value of a play, using intrinsic criteria (e.g., how well the structure of a particular play holds together) and extrinsic criteria (e.g., how valuable and valid are the notions revealed in the play about how human beings behave) (written response).
8. Read a play they have not read or seen and write a response to the play, including the following:

- a personal emotional reaction
- an analysis of the general elements and dramatic elements of the play and of how the playwright has exemplified them
- a personal statement of the value of the play, basing this evaluation upon intrinsic and extrinsic criteria and upon substantiation from the text

Where Do We Go from Here?

My middle school students have learned a basic vocabulary for dealing with dramatic texts, have learned by producing a short, well-made play how the elements of dramatic literature work to produce a single powerful effect, and have learned how to use systematic strategies for reading, responding, and interpreting new plays. They are now ready—as they mature socially and psychologically—to apply their internalized understanding of dramaturgy and play production to more challenging full-length plays such as *Our Town* and *Death of a Salesman*, and with the expert guidance of a sensitive and knowledgeable teacher to turn to the great dramatic texts of Western civilization, *Hamlet* and *Antigone*. If I have been successful with my planning and instruction, they are well prepared for this most basic and crucial of human endeavors.

References

American Heritage Dictionary of the English Language. 1973. Boston: Houghton Mifflin.

Jacobs, W. W. 1910. The Monkey's Paw. In *Thirty Famous One-Act Plays*, edited by Bennett Cerf and Van H. Cartmell. 1943. New York: The Modern Library.

· 2 0 ·

CONVERTING NARRATIVE INTO DRAMA

Using the Composing Process To Integrate the Language Arts

Robert W. Blake (1982)

Having students adapt a play from a strongly dramatic short story through the composing process is a natural and powerful way to integrate the language arts. First of all, drama is an immediate and primary language art and is thus easily accessible to all students, especially those who have not had great success with academic reading and writing. Drama, furthermore, is immensely social, an activity for learning how to watch, listen, react, present, discuss, debate, and summarize. And when we use dramatic activities in the classroom, we find they lead naturally to other language activities of two general kinds: *receptive* activities, those including listening, observing, and beholding and *active* experiences, those including discussing, reading, writing, creating and presenting.

Adapting a Play from a Short Story

One way to integrate a number of language arts activities through the composing process is by having students convert a short story, in this particular instance, "This I Refute Beelzy" by John Collier, into a one act play. The story is most appropriate for our purposes. First, it is a neat little, fast moving horror tale in which a boy does in his domineering and cruel father through the aid of the character "Beelzy," whose name we take is the familiar form for "Beelzebub," the Greek appellation for the devil, which in turn is derived from the Hebrew "Ba'al ze bub," the ubiquitous and sinister "Lord of the Flies," Second, the story is supremely dramatic. It consists almost entirely of dialogue. There are only four characters, five, if we include Beelzy, whom we never see. The setting of the story is the house of a three-member family, and the action takes place during a very short time, moving from an opening expository scene through swift but deft character development to a rousing climax. In short, an ideal story to be adapted as a play.

Before engaging the students in rewriting this story as a play, we need to think about the several levels of meaning in the story and be aware of some crucial ideas. First off, on one level, the tale is a fantasy, in which the supposedly unreal occurs in the world of the actual. The story stands on its own as a rousing yarn, but on another level, the conflict between the boy and his father may represent the conflict between science or rationality and intuition and irrationality. "Thus I Refute Beelzy," furthermore, is related to the study of the "occult," a word from the Latin *occultus*, originally meaning "to cover up or conceal," which includes supernatural agencies and the knowledge of them like witchcraft, fortune-telling, ESP, astrology, tarot cards, alchemy, voodoo, spiritualism, black and white magic, palmistry, and graphology. All of these studies of the occult have one thing in common: the belief in hidden and mysterious powers.

There is no need to engage the students in an initial discussion of these matters, unless one or two have a background, and then our general information will assist us in helping them discover the richness of this apparently simple story. It's probably sufficient for their enjoyment of a horror story based upon diabolism to know that "Beelzy" appears to be the shortened form of the Greek name for the devil "Beelzebub." They should also know the meaning of the word *refute*, "to prove wrong," and be prepared to explain the irony in the inability of Big Simon to "refute" Beelzy.

Analyzing the Story

After the students have read the story by themselves or have heard it read out loud in class, they need to come to terms with what happens in it. It is best to have carefully structured questions for guided discussion and to have the students talk about the narrative in small groups, possibly even pairing students, but having no more than four or five in any one group. The small discussion is crucial because only in such groups will each student get feedback from others and in them will all students have experience in the give and take of listening, talking, reacting to feedback, and in adjusting ideas to that feedback. In other words, the students sharpen their communication skills in interacting with each other.

These are some questions we might have the student respond to, arranged simply by the categories of plot "What Happens in the Story?" character "Who Are the People?" and theme "What Are the Ideas" or "What Does It Mean?"

What Happens in the Story?

1. At the opening of the story, Mrs. Carter rings the tea bell. What is "tea?" In what country might people have tea?
2. Small Simon spends most of his time in his retreat. Describe it. Tell what Simon does in his retreat.
3. What does Big Simon do to Small Simon when Small Simon refuses to say his friend Beelzy is make-believe?
4. What makes Big Simon so angry that he sends Small Simon to his room?
5. What happens to Big Simon at the end of the story?

Who Are the People?

1. What sort of man is Big Simon? What is his "scientific and modern way" of raising a child? Is his "way" really best for the boy? Why or why not?
2. What effect does Mr. Beelzy have upon Small Simon? What do you think will happen to Small Simon with his father gone?

What Are the Ideas?

This story suggests that there are mysterious, unexplainable forces that deeply affect people's lives. Discuss the possibility of the existence of such forces. If they exist, do they operate for good, for evil, or for both? Make a list of things which are good like love, families, hospitals, schools, and charities such as the Red Cross.

Now make a list of things which appear to be evil, like hate, war, robbery, and murder. How are they explained? By the actions of people, or by the influences of forces beyond the understanding of human beings?

Retelling the Story

After they have heard the story read to them or read it for themselves and discussed it in small groups, the students can go on to retell or reshape the story in their own words, thus giving them practice in developing their ability to retell narratives. Here are some guide questions for their retelling of the story.

What would have happened if Mr. Carter had believed Small Simon and tried to help him escape from Beelzy? Make believe Big Simon knew who Beelzy was and tried to protect Small Simon from him. Retell the story. How would Mr. Carter act? How would he find out about Beelzy? What would happen when Mr. Carter met Beelzy? How would Mr. Carter get rid of Beelzy? What would happen to Small Simon?

Small groups could discuss such proposed changes in the story (or, of course, make up their own changes), outline the new sequence of events, select students to take the parts of the characters, and role play the new scenes. If they have read the story carefully—or have listened intently while it was read out loud—and discussed with other students and their teacher questions about the story, they will find such an activity a pleasant as well as profitable one.

Rewriting the Story as a Play

After this introductory work, the students are ready to convert narrative into drama, to create a play from a short story.

"This story would make a fine short play," we might tell our students as an introduction. "There is a lot of conversation, which makes good dialogue. The action takes place in one house, and it occurs within a short period of time. Here's an example at how you might start writing a play based upon 'Thus I Refute Beelzy.'"

This sample beginning shows the students how straightforward the process is when the original story is as essentially dramatic as Collier's is.

THUS I REFUTE BEELZY
by
John Collier
Adapted from the short story

Characters
MRS. CARTER
BETTY
SMALL SIMON
BIG SIMON (MR. CARTER)

The scene is the garden-room and tearoom of a tall Georgian house some-where in England. The walls are cream-washed, a coarse blue net is in the windows, there are canvas-covered armchairs on the stone floor, and a repro-duction of Van Gogh's Sunflowers is over the mantlepiece.

MRS. CARTER.	There goes the tea bell. I hope Simon hears it. I'm worried about him.
BETTY.	Oh, I see him now in the garden.
MRS. CARTER.	Yes. That's been his retreat all summer. He stays out there for hours on end.
BETTY.	He seems to be strutting up and down, making wild motions.
MRS. CARTER.	I know. Playing his game. He won't play with the other children anymore. And if I go down there–the temper! And he comes in so tired out!

To help the students in an unobtrusive way with their dramaturgy, we might ask them to pay attention to considerations like these, which deal with setting, changing description to dialogue, turning various scenes into one set-ting, and revealing how actor's and actresses should say their lines.

a. How do I turn description into dialogue? We changed the story descrip-tion of Small Simon in the garden into a conversation between Mrs. Carter and Betty.

b. How do I keep the action in one place? We moved the two women into the tearoom at the beginning of the play instead of having them walk from the drawing room to the tearoom.

c. How do I suggest to the reader or actor how the characters should talk?

First, we can use punctuation marks to show emphasis and pitch. When Mrs. Carter says "And if I go there–the temper! And he comes in so tired out!" we know that the exclamation marks mean that she is upset and that the pitch of her voice is higher than normal.

Or, we can describe how a person speaks his lines, sometimes using the direct words of the author. In this example, we have used John Collier's directions for how he wished his characters to say their lines.

MR. CARTER.   Learn from experience, Small Simon. Tomorrow, do something amusing, and you will not be bored. I want him to learn from experience, Betty. This is my way, the new way.

SMALL SIMON.   (*Small Simon speaks like an old, tired man, as little boys so often do.*) I have learned.

The students would profit at this stage from working in small groups of from two to three students, discussing with each other in a spontaneous manner rather subtle but crucial matters like appropriateness of setting, the necessity of action on and off stage, and the delivery of lines.

For those students who want to create an original play from the story, they should be encouraged to do so with directions like these:

You may wish to write a play different from the original story, one based on the version which you re-told, with Mr. Carter understanding Small Simon and protecting him from Beelzy. You will need to create new scenes to reflect your new telling of the story.

Once the students have finished their plays, they may present their finished products to an audience of other students. Obviously, the time has been well spent with their sharpening of various communication skills such as reading, writing, discussing, revising, editing, and producing a play and then with listening, witnessing, and reacting to the various versions of the adaptions.

Creating Original Fantasies: Stories or Plays

Once the students have moved through the process of adapting a play from someone else's short story, they are ready and able to create their own fantasies, either dramatic or narrative. The following introductory activity is aimed at helping them choose a commonplace situation close to their experiences, with just a hint of the macabre or occult, and to encourage them to write an original fantasy. They have seen enough tales of the supernatural in the movies or on TV or read them in stories and in comics to know the genre. For those students who need models before they can proceed, they can choose either of the sample beginnings to finish. Those who are more secure will no doubt create their own fresh fantasies.

We give them these directions and two sample beginnings to finish.

Now you may wish to create your own fantasy. Where will it happen? Who will be the people? What will happen to them?

The fantasy can take place right around where you live. And the people can be just like those that you know very well. The best fantasies are often about commonplace people, whose actions just can't be explained by reason and logic. Here are a few ideas to start you off.

a. Suppose you must pass by a fierce German Shepherd dog on your way home after school and sometimes just before dark after you have been to the neighborhood store. One night, the dog scares you so much that you say out loud, "I wish that dog were dead!"

On your way home, you meet a black cat with strange yellow eyes that seem to glow in the dark. You take the cat in and feed it. The next night you must go to the store. You bring the cat. When you are coming home, it is almost dark. The dog rushes out at you. Backing away, you fall down. The dog leaps at you.

Then you hear a screech, and a tall black creature with glowing yellow eyes comes between you and the dog.

What happens next? Write your fantasy.

b. A new boy moves into your neighborhood and is in your class at school. He is very quiet, and his eyes are wide as if he is staring at something unusual all of the time. But you and he become friends.

One day he says that there will be a grass fire in the lot behind your house that afternoon. You laugh at him, but the grass catches fire. Fire engines come to put it out.

The next day he says that there will be a fire alarm in school and that the firemen will find a blaze in the cafeteria kitchen. You listen but don't say anything. Sure enough, there is a fire at school the next day. It has started in the kitchen among some papers and boxes.

A few days later your friend tells you that one of the houses in your neighborhood will catch fire and burn. And someone may get hurt or die! Whose house is it, you ask. He doesn't know, but it is painted green with black shutters. Your house is green with black shutters.

What happens next? Write your fantasy.

The students work by themselves on their fantasies but then read them out loud to other students in small groups. After they have revised their stories on the basis of reactions by the other students, they can read them out loud or act them out before the entire class.

Learning Communication Skills by Converting Narrative into Drama

By following through these language arts activities for adapting a play from a short story through the composing process, the students have learned a considerable amount about language arts.

First, they have practiced several communication skills. They have read or listened to a strongly dramatic short story read out loud and analyzed key notions of fiction centered on plot, characters, and themes. They have retold and re-created the story in their own words. They have converted the story into a one act play. They have used models to write new fantasies or to create entirely original ones. They have started the unit with the more easily accessible skills of listening, speaking, and discussing and have moved on to the more difficult skills of reading, writing and revising.

Second, the students have followed through the stages in the composing process of gathering specific details, examples, and ideas, of drafting, of getting feedback, and then of further revising until the material has a certain polished form. Only by following this process again and again, will students learn how to revise what they say and write on the basis of feedback from other people, learn how to analyze audiences, relate what they say and write on the basis of this analysis, and quite simply, learn through interaction how to get the business of the world done.

And finally, they have directly and naturally participated in language activities more ancient than history, as old as human beings, and as basic to their welfare as breathing: creating and beholding stories and plays.

SECTION VII

ENGLISH LANGUAGE LEARNERS AND OTHER 'BASIC' STUDENTS IN THE CLASSROOM

In this section, Robert, once again ahead of his time, takes the opportunity to talk about the students no one wants to teach, and no one expects to learn.

In the first piece, he introduces us to Francisco, an English Language Learner (ELL) whom Robert calls at the time, a "non-native speaker." Attuned to the fact that what Francisco needs is "real" writing, rather than [solely] extensive remedial work on this spelling, usage, etc., he shows us with lots of peer of teacher conferencing, other ELLs, like Francisco, can understand and work well with some of the more difficult elements of writing, like purpose and voice.

The second article, "A New Look at Basic Skills," begins with Robert's proclamation that, skill and drill is quite simply, "dead wrong" in the teaching of writing. Taking us through a series of 3 workshops he designed for practicing teachers, he shows them how to "guide" students, how to only teach "skills in context," and how "unfairly and meanly" so-called basic writers have been labeled and misunderstood.

And finally, in the last piece of this section, Robert asks, "How can we help our teenagers?" Against the grain of what most teacher education programs taught then (and now), he says, teenagers are "human beings," and they can and should be "seen," "heard," and "accepted."

In my work with ELLs and adolescents over the last 20 years, I was stunned to read these pieces written in the 1980's. What did my father know then, that I only came to see after several years in the classroom in the 1990's? His empathy and understanding of both these groups of students certainly set him apart as much then, as it would today. And his ideas are instructive, today, too. Allowing basic students, those pesty and pesky teenagers, and ELLs, access to the same sort of discourse[s] we expect out of our white, middle class students still resonates as the best and most equitable type of teaching there is.

· 2 1 ·

STARTING OFF A NON-NATIVE STUDENT IN A COLLEGE BASIC SKILLS COURSE

Robert W. Blake (1982)

On the first day of Communication Skills 102, Francisco (not his real name) sits in the second row, smiling at me and at everybody around him. He is slender, and when he stands up at the end of class I see he is tall, close to six feet. He has curly brown hair, brown eyes, and a wispy mustache. I find out later that he had come to New York City a few years earlier from the Dominican Republic; he tells me this in a later narrative: "I came alone from Santo Domingo, where there is no winter; but warm sunshine weather. Like California, Santo Domingo was a day spent on the beach, relaxing and enjoying." For the last four years he has lived on FDR Drive along the East River in Manhattan, taking classes—again, as I learn later—in both Spanish and English. This is his first class in which the instruction is entirely in English. But here he is now at a small, upstate New York college in a climate and educational environment about as far removed from Santo Domingo weather and culture as he can get and still remain on earth. So on this bright September day Francisco sits, smiling, obviously eager to learn how to write English in this gringo classroom.

The communication skills course Francisco finds himself in is a remedial course for those students who—on the basis of past performance in high school—have been identified as not being ready to enter the first of the two regular college communication skills courses which all students must successfully complete before moving on to further collegiate work. Most of the twenty-five students in the class are native speakers of English. There is, however, another remedial course in communication skills each semester, Communication Skills 101, usually with two sections, for all students whose native language is something other than English. But frequently several of these foreign students overflow the two classes and the immigrants are placed in "regular" basic classes with instructors reputed to know something about teaching them how to write.

So how can I help Francisco—and two other Hispanics and one Egyptian as well—to write academic English? Should I be fluent in Spanish? It would be nice, I suppose, but I don't have any Spanish. I do, however, know some French and German and did live in Germany for a year and a half, during which time I traveled throughout Europe, making a strenuous attempt to assimilate the languages and cultures of people far different from me. Should I have special training in Teaching English to Speakers of Other Languages (TESOL is the acronym for this mouthful)? I don't, but I have taught writing at all school and college levels and have a fairly extensive knowledge of linguistics, including the grammar and phonology of English as well as the most basic notions from psycholinguistics and sociolinguistics. Most important, though, I consider myself sympathetic to the problems non-native speakers of English may have in learning how to write academic English. I go on at this length about my personal background because, contrary to what the vociferous advocates of bilingual education and TESOL hold, most English teachers in regular classrooms will find, possibly to their surprise, that their special professional training and experience have prepared them quite well to teach these new immigrants to America how to become competent writers—be they from the Dominican Republic, Puerto Rico, Viet Nam, Japan, or Egypt.

Given the present situation in the classroom and my particular training and experience, what's my first step in helping Francisco learn how to write English well enough to go on to the regular communication skills course? First, I must find out at this point simply how well he can write. To do this, I give him a two-part diagnostic test. Section A of Part II has ten sentences with common usage and basic punctuation errors. The students are directed to rewrite the sentences, in spaces provided on the test, correcting the errors as they go along. Section B contains ten common words and phrases, such as *your, there,* or *it's,* with directions to "write a sentence in which you use the word or phrase correctly." Section C addresses the skill of "combining groups of sentences by means of coordination and using proper indicators of coordination" by giving the students ten sets of simple sentences to combine. The last section of Part II deals with the skill of "combining sentences by means of subordination," directing the students to combine by subordination ten sets of simple sentences.

The second part of the diagnostic competency test—which is my chief concern within the scope of this paper—is a classroom writing assignment, leading to a piece of whole discourse and designed to ensure that "all students who intend to continue their studies at the college can complete several tasks which demonstrate knowledge and control of the writing process and the conventions of formal, written English."

In the written directions of the diagnostic essay, the students are told: "You will demonstrate competency in Part I if you can write a paragraph that (1) follows the directions carefully, (2) contains relevant examples, (3) has very few errors in spelling and punctuation, (4) includes appropriately developed sentences with clear transitions." Pretty hard reading for Francisco, I realize, but I read the directions aloud to the class—very slowly and distinctly—and answer all questions before he and the others proceed.

This is the writing assignment the students are given to complete in class within a full period. In devising this assignment, we wanted to make it specific and realistic with a clear description of the rhetorical elements of *purpose*, *audience*, and *writer's role* or *persona* the students must attend to:

Directions: You have been asked to fill out a recommendation for a friend who has applied for a job as a clerk in a bank. One section of the form has these directions.

Describe the way the applicant behaves when he/she is corrected, disagreed with, and/or given rather demanding instructions. Be sure to give specific examples of the behavior you describe.

Write a one-paragraph entry of approximately 200 words. Be sure to include specific examples. Remember also that your skill in writing may have an effect on your friend's future employment.

What Francisco wrote in response to the assignment is reproduced in figure 1.

The next step is to analyze Francisco's paper and talk with him about what he needs to work on to become a better writer. Using a simple "Student Writing Analysis Sheet," I write comments in these categories: I. Rhetorical Task, II. Relation of Parts to Whole, III. Sentence Structure, IV. Word Choice, and V. Mechanics. Francisco's "Student Writing Analysis Sheet" is presented as figure 2.

To whom may Concern:

The first thing that would like to write in these recomenendations form is. I know José Collado a ver long time. He is a excellent asset of of his community, friends, and his family. I think that there are not a easy. way of to describe the behaves of my friend Jose Collado when he is corrected by his friends of or by any other person. is it very inusual to human being ibept the corection by other person but José Collado do the opposity that we the human being loes. He acept the courtion. And too is like to follow the aper o when he is doing something wrong. Let me give a example of how José act when is corr he had being corrected by ——— someone. we were waiting Five month ago we were working together in Cawn toion grocery store. One day he was putting soda in the on the refrigerator, mR. Vallega. Luis Vallejo the owt owner of the groery came. Came and say to him of "You are doing something wrong." Jose stop and says to me the mR. Vallego "What are doing wrong?" MR. Vallejo say "I won't tell you. Then Jose say if you don't correct me I will no continuening puntting soda in. finally mR. Luis says you has to put soda in stright line, more organiz." The end was that Jose follow the corection by mR. Vallejo and after that he was one of The only person in the store who could to organiz organize the Refigerator better than mr. Vallejo. Finally I strongey believe that if you hire José Collado he will be one more asset to yours bank.

Very truly your,

Figure 1. Francisco's paper.

Student Writing Analysis Sheet

Student   Francisco

Assignment   Recommendation for Bank Clerk's Job   Date _____

Category	Analysis	Recommendations
I. *Rhetorical Task* (understand directions, recognize rhetorical aim, use conventions of mode, consistent point of view, sense of audience)	You understand the directions well. You know your audience, and you keep your point of view consistent.	Good work. Keep it up!
II. *Relation of Parts to Whole* (organization or sequencing; generalizations supported by reasons, details, examples; appropriate level of generalization; coherence)	You have a clear sense of structure. Good use of examples. Dialogue makes the paper immediate. Good use of transitions. Good balance between specifics and general statement.	Again, good work. Keep it up.
III. *Sentence Structure* (varied sentence structures, free of sentence errors, neither short and choppy nor long and stringy sentences)	Major problems with English sentences. Problems with verbs.	Need concentrated and continuing work with "English" sentences, correct verb forms.
IV. *Word Choice* (clear, concrete rather than vague language; words used accurately; single words used for longer structures; mixture of levels, unconscious word repetition)	Pretty good use of English words but need to widen your English vocabulary.	Work needed on precise English words and on expanding your English vocabulary.
V. *Mechanics* (spelling, punctuation, capitalization, handwriting, format)	Problems with spelling, punctuation, capitalization, and handwriting.	Need drill on mechanics of written English. Practice in proofreading.

Figure 2. Analysis of Francisco's writing.

So what can I say about Francisco's writing? It is of utmost importance that I am able to move past his serious problems with English sentences, diction, and mechanics to note two really significant aspects of his writing. First, from this piece, there is no doubt that he understands well the rhetorical task he has been assigned—the purpose of his discourse. He also assesses correctly the audience for whom he is writing and assumes a writer's role (persona) appropriate to convey his message to this particular audience. I'm impressed by his ability to handle maturely these crucial aspects of effective writing. Second, he has a good sense of the structure of the piece; the paper has a definite beginning, middle, and ending. He balances generalizations with specific examples and also uses dialogue—albeit not always punctuated correctly—to enhance the piece. And he employs naturally and effectively transitional devices such as "first," "let me give you an example," and "finally." In several significant ways, he is an accomplished writer.

Now to Francisco's difficulties. I can see quite clearly that he has serious problems with written English sentences, but that is no surprise since he has been writing English, especially academic English, for only a few years. The way he puts his sentences together is simply not "English." This lack of the "feel" for how English sentences "go" is most evident in his inability to control the English verb system. "I know José Callado for very long time." "The owner of the store came and say to him. ..." "José stop and says to me. ..." "Mr. Vallejo say. ..." He really doesn't have much trouble with diction—the precise use of words—but the problems he does have appear to stem from his lack of experience with English vocabulary. And finally, he has trouble with spelling, capitalization, punctuation, and even handwriting simply because he has not been writing academic English for very long. But even his spellings show a good phonetic sense of the sounds of the words. To his credit, he certainly is not afraid to use the words even though he's not completely sure of their spellings. I have no doubt he will become a better speller of English words as he writes a lot, learns how to proofread more carefully—with dictionary in hand—and learns some of the regularities and vagaries of English spelling.

Now that I have looked carefully at Francisco's writing, and talked to him about it, what do we do next? It is not within the scope of this paper to describe in detail the writing assignments, sentence combining activities, exercises in the mechanics of written English, and workshopping activities I planned for Francisco, but I can describe the general features of Francisco's program in the basic communication skills course.

1. The writing program for Francisco will be built upon my understanding of where he is at the beginning of the class. I have available a piece of his writing and can see that in a mature and confident way he is able to handle key elements in academic writing. I can also see just as clearly that he has serious problems with English sentences. I realize, furthermore, that he is a "stranger in a strange land" who needs all the personal support and encouragement he can get, even more than native speakers of English deserve.

2. Francisco's writing program will be based on what I consider a natural sequence of writing activities. He will move from writing autobiography (an early memory) and biography (a "phase" biography of a close friend or relative) to several types of traditional exposition (use of examples and illustrations, comparison and contrast, cause and effect, and a "how to" or process essay). For me, such a sequence is logical for two reasons. First, with the initial narratives, Francisco will gain confidence in his writing ability by writing about events and people he knows well. Second, he will write narrative first—in which he can follow a natural, chronological structure—before he tackles exposition—in which he must create his own arbitrary and artificial structures. (See James Moffett's justification of this kind of scheme, especially in the chapter "Kinds and Orders of Discourse," in *Teaching the Universe of Discourse*, Houghton Mifflin, 1968).

3. For all writing assignments, Francisco will create complete pieces of discourse. Although he will do exercises in usage, sentence combining, and the mechanics of written English—to complement his writing of whole narratives and essays—he will not be taught to believe that such drill in mechanics is in fact writing. I can't emphasize this point strongly enough. Many English teachers, some of my colleagues included, believe that a program for students deficient in writing skills should include heavy doses of drill and workbook exercises, gradually leading to writing single sentences and, possibly toward the end of a course, short paragraphs. No instructional plan could be worse for any would-be writer, and it's especially harmful for a so-called basic writer like Francisco. Francisco will become a competent writer—not by filling in blanks, crossing out incorrect usage items, underlining subjects once and predicates twice, and by putting together banal paragraphs, but by actually producing complete pieces of writing for specific audiences.

4. While creating these whole pieces of discourse, Francisco will, time after time, cycle through the composing process. He will interact with his classmates and me in one-to-one conferences, in small groups, and with the class as a whole during the prewriting, revising, and editing stages of composing. During the drafting stage, of course, he must work alone, and he must come to terms with the idea that although the drafting stage is a frightening and solitary one, it is nevertheless a necessary one for composing. He needs to go through the process enough times so he will learn to profit from the feedback others can give him about his writing and will not be a stranger to this process when he tackles any writing task.

5. Francisco and I will talk about his writing at every stage, from early drafts to finished products, sometimes for a few minutes but periodically for much longer times. Although he gets feedback about his writing from others, it is essential that he hear from me—a more experienced, especially trained teacher of writing—in specific terms, what is admirable in his writing but just as specifically how he can continue to improve. Short, oral conferences with Francisco are far more useful than extensive red marks on his papers—without a personal conference—would be.

6. Francisco will complete extensive and frequent sentence combining activities, discuss them with his classmates, take quizzes on the activities, and attempt to use the new structures in his compositions. Such activities will help him become aware of the range of English sentences available to him.

7. Francisco will do many exercises on the mechanics of English—standard usage, punctuation, capitalization, spelling, and on other miscellaneous problems of written academic format—and will discuss them with his classmates, take quizzes on these matters, and, I trust, learn to handle correctly items from these categories in his papers. Although he and his classmates will be taught to be scrupulous in proofreading their compositions for mechanical errors, they will also benefit from short but frequent drills on such matters.

Essentially, Francisco's program for learning how to write academic English will involve as much writing and pointed, direct discussion of his writing with me and with his classmates as we can manage within a semester. I want him to feel confident about the process of writing a whole piece of discourse, and perhaps even somewhat more comfortable than he had been before with these exotic English sentences.

I have found out where Francisco is in the development of his ability to write academic English. He and I have a fairly accurate idea of what his strengths and weaknesses are. I have set up a comprehensive program, based on my background and experience and the best information available, for helping him to improve his writing.

Now for both of us the hard work begins.

A NEW LOOK AT BASIC SKILLS WRITING INSTRUCTION

A Teacher Workshop for Basic Skills Writing in the Secondary Schools

Robert W. Blake (1983)

We all know what basic students in writing are like. They do poorly on achievement tests, especially in reading and language arts. They have poor grades. They have a poor command of the mechanics of English—grammar, usage, spelling, and punctuation. They exhibit what we call a "poor self image"; they don't do well in school, their teachers don't much care for them, and, as a result they don't care much for themselves. Because of this poor self image, they seem to be poorly motivated. They are frequently hostile and withdrawn. They have what the linguists call "language interference," which means in effect that how they learned their native language—whether it was Spanish, Vietnamese, Korean, or some other language—now interferes with their acquiring standard oral and written English. Their native language may interfere with classroom English because of social reasons—they are urban or rural poor kids who never heard standard English before they went to school. And they consistently fail writing competency tests.

Skills-Drill Approach To Basic Writing Instruction

We know then what these kids are like who are eligible for the basic skills writing class. Now what do we do with them? The ubiquitous solution is skills-drill remediation. We drill them in grammar—parts of speech, subjects and predicates, kinds of sentences. We drill them in standard English usage—subject-verb agreement, pronoun and antecedent, and verb forms. We drill them in spelling words and vocabulary lists. We drill them in topic sentences, introductions, conclusions, and five-paragraph essays. We drill them in the business letter, report writing, and the elements of a persuasive essay.

We drill them in the skills of writing and wonder why they keep on failing writing competency tests.

What's Wrong With the Skills-Drill Approach?

Why is skills-drill the wrong approach, especially with so-called "basic" students? It's dead wrong for several reasons.

The "skills" I have just noted, although they do belong to writing, are only a part of writing, and we need to be conscious of them only in the final or editing stage of the writing process. They should not be confused with real writing.

We can't teach anyone to master an activity by emphasizing only the low-level skills of that field of action—whether it be basketball, playing a musical instrument, skiing, or that immensely complicated activity of writing. We master a complex activity not by drilling continually in parts of the activity but by actually performing it. We learn how to play basketball not by only practicing lay-up's but by playing games of basketball. We learn how to play the piano not by only doing five-finger exercises but by playing complete pieces. We learn how to ski not by only practicing wedge turns but by skiing down hills and mountains. And we learn how to write by writing complete compositions for real audiences.

The skills-drill approach, furthermore, conveys the attitude that basic writers are dumb, "retards," "basics"—that something is wrong with them. In reality, there is nothing "wrong" with them; they can learn how to write more effectively with direct instruction in writing.

Skills-drill instruction is deadly dull, as any repetition of low-level skills always is. Skills-drill affects students' motivation, convinces them that writing is a boring, low-level activity, which it is to them, since that's their only experience with writing.

Skills-drill is a self defeating activity. The more they drill in skills, the more they hate writing. The more they hate it, the worse they do. The worse they do, the more they hate it. And so forth, ad nauseaum. The unfortunate fact is that basic writers, under such a regimen of skills-drill, never escape to the world of real writing.

Planning For a Basic Skills Workshop in Writing

With this introduction as a background, I should like to describe a Basic Skills Workshop in Teaching Writing for secondary school teachers which I devised and directed during the fall of 1982 at the State University of New York College at Brockport and which, I believe, had a focus radically different from that traditionally associated with instruction for "basic" writers.

The background of planning for the workshop was this. Two summers ago, I was one of ten educators from New York State who were invited by the New York State Education, Resource Allocation Plan Office, to work with State Education Department personnel to plan and develop fifteen hours of inservice training to be offered at various sites throughout the state during the 1981–82 year. As part of the program, I, with the other nine individuals, attended a five-day workshop in Albany in June of 1981, at which time Department personnel first summarized policies, procedures, and programs as they related to basic skills instruction, and then we each developed outlines of the content and a list of the materials we would be using for our sessions.

In August of 1981, I met with the superintendent and assistant superintendent for instruction of the local Board of Cooperative Educational Services to plan further for the workshops. On the basis of that meeting, I created a needs assessment form which was sent out to all the administrators in the BOCES II, Monroe-Orleans Counties district and to the Orleans-Niagara Counties BOCES district. In response to the needs assessment questionnaire, the school administrators stated that the "target audience should be secondary teachers with the emphasis being upon motivating low functioning students and devising ways by which their instruction and involvement could be more effective." The administrators also believed that a series of three all-day workshops from 9:00 A.M. to 3:00 P.M. during the middle of the week would be most useful for their teachers. I set up three consecutive Thursdays in October and November as the workshop dates to be held at one of the College dining halls, where we would have a meeting and a private dining room. I arranged to have coffee, tea, doughnuts, and Danish pastries available each morning, with a buffet lunch to be served at noon. After a final planning session with the assistant superintendents for instruction for the two participating BOCES districts, we were ready to begin.

Assumptions Underlying the Workshops

These were the asusmptions, the underlying beliefs about basic skills writing instruction, I held to be the foundation for the workshops.

1. *All individuals, even "basics," can learn how to write more effectively.* It's patently ridiculous and self-defeating to teach writing to "basic" students under the mistaken idea that some students are not able to write whole compositions but are fit only to do spelling tests, underline subjects once, write complete sentences, and produce paragraphs with topic sentences. As anybody knows who has taught real writing, everybody, except those psychologically distraught or those physiologically damaged, can learn how to entertain, explain, and persuade in writing. Writing, like speaking, is a human activity which, from instruction and through practice, humans can perform. We must assume that kids not only *can* learn how to write but *want* to; if they seem unable to or unwilling to try, we must find out the reasons why.

2. The most powerful assumption for the workshops is this: *the composing process is the model for writing instruction.* From this generative, life-giving assumption, all sorts of potent conclusions follow. Students practice the writing process in order to become so familiar with it that they lose their dread of writing. Students learn that all stages of writing excepting drafting—prewriting, revising, and editing— are interactive, that is, they not only can rely on others to help them throughout the writing steps but they need the reactions from others if their writing is to be connected to real life. As they follow through the composing process—which, by the way, is the model for all human creativity—they come to experience the ecstasy of creativity with words. This is the most telling reason against the skills-drill approach to writing instruction; no one ever experienced the thrill of creativity with written language from identifying prepositional phrases or subordinate clauses.

3. *Writing teachers need an understanding of basic theoretical statements and the results of research on writing instruction.* Although the half humorous cry "What do I do on Monday?" has a certain wry urgency to it, we need to know what to do—certainly on Monday—but also on Tuesday, Wednesday, Thursday, and Friday, long after our "fun" writing lesson from Monday has

evaporated into the air. We need to know about the research on composing by Don Murray and Janet Emig. We need to know about the techniques for evaluating writing from people like Lee Odell, Paul Diedrich, Charles Cooper, Richard Lloyd-Jones, and Kellogg Hunt. We need to know about the descriptions of kinds of writing by James Moffett and James Britton. We need to know about that original and humanistic approach to argument by Carl Rogers. And we need to know the results of recent research on teaching writing from the National Assessment and from individuals like Sondra Perl, Arthur N. Applebee, and Donald Graves. Only when we have a knowledge of what such people have discovered about teaching writing do we spare ourselves the inexcusable arrogance of sharing our ignorance with each other and with wasting ours and our students' time with re-inventing the wheel of writing instruction.

4. *Writing teachers need to write frequently themselves.* As we write, we examine our own composing processes and use feedback from others—students and colleagues—to sharpen and focus our own writing. We analyze how we write so we can pass on this knowledge of the process to our students. As we use the feedback to our writing from others, we realize the importance of feedback for our students. And we need to write frequently so we can sympathize with our students about the problems they're having with their writing. I know you have heard the advice that we should write out the assignments we give to our students. This is all right the first time around, but we should also be working on our own writing—non fiction pieces, poems, even fiction—and we should be sending these finished pieces out for possible publication. Only if we follow such a procedure, do we come to know intimately the whole writing process from idea to publication and can show our students what it actually means to be a writer.

Outline of the Three Workshops

First Workshop

The focus for the first workshop was on the foundations for a writing program for basic students and on teaching expressive writing. The following is an outline of the topics for the day.

Foundations of Teaching Writing and Teaching Expressive Writing

1. Characteristics of the Basic Writer (Sources: John Mellon, "Language Competence," *The Nature and Measurement of Competency in English.* NCTE, 1981.
Sondra Perl, "A Look at Basic Writers in the Process of Composing," *Basic Writing.* NCTE, 1981).

2. The present State of Teaching Writing in the Schools
(Sources: Results from the Third National Assessment, 1969–79. National Institue of Education.)
Arthur N. Applebee, Fran Lehr, and Anne Auten, "Learning to Write in the Secondary School: How and Where," *English Journal.* (Sepember, 1981), 78–82.

3. What Research Can Tell Us about the Teaching of Writing
(Source: Charles R. Cooper, "What Research Can Tell Us about the Teaching of Writing." Mimeographed, no date).

4. Key Elements of Effective Writing (audience, purpose, writer's role, and structure).

5. Stages in the Composing process (prewriting, drafting, revising, editing, and publishing).

6. Diagnosing Writer's Skills
Diagnosing Whole Discourse; Diagnosing Sentence Combining; and Diagnosing English Usage, Sentence Structure, and punctuation.
Student Writing Analysis Sheet

7. Teaching Expressive Writing
Writing Activities to Find Out about Yourself
Writing Autobiography: "My Earliest Memory"
Early Memory to Full Narrative
Writing Biography: "Description of a Person"

8. Reviewing Prewriting (Invention) Strategies

9. Brainstorming Expressive Writing Topics

10. Creating Writing Lessons following the Instructional Composing Process (ICP)

Workshop Evaluation

Second Workshop

The second workshop dealt mainly with teaching expository and persuasive writing; the topics for the day were as follows:

Teaching Expository and Persuasive Writing

1. Teaching the Expository Essay
   Prewriting (definition of exposition, analysis of models, brainstorming topics, writing topic and lead)
   Drafting (for a particular audience)
   Revising (opening, focus, main points, ending, details)
   Editing (proofreading for mechanical errors)
2. Reviewing revising strategies
3. Brainstorming expository writing topics
4. Teaching the Persuasive/Argumentative Essay
   Definition of Persuasion
   Types of dishonest methods of persuasion
   Elements of persuasive/argumentative essay
   Analysis of model
   Drafting (for a particular audience)
   Revising
   Editing
5. The Rogerian Argument
   (Source: Carl Rogers, "Communication: Its Blocking and Its Facilitation," paper originally presented at Northwestern University's Centennial Conference on Communications, October 11, 1951.)

Third Workshop

My primary concerns in the third workshop were with sentence combining, assessing and evaluating writing, and guidelines for setting up a basic skills writing program; the list of topics for the day is as follows:

Sentence Combining, Assessing and Evaluating Writing, and Setting Up a Basic Skills Writing Program

1. Sentence Combining
   Basis in generative-transformational grammar
   (Sources: Kellogg W. Hunt, *Grammatical Structures Written at Three Grade Levels*. NCTE, 1965.
   John Mellon. *Transformational Sentence-Combining*. NCTE, 1969.
   Frank O'Hare. *Sentence Combining*. NCTE, 1971. Group Activities in Syntactic Structures and Sentence Combining Tentative Scope and Sequence for Student Activities in Stentence Combining, K-12
2. Revising Strategies
3. Assessing and Evaluating Writing
   Differences between Assessing and Evaluating
   Assessing Writing for Diagnosing, Improving Writing, and Giving a Grade Types of Assessment—Analytical and Holistic Scoring
4. Setting Up a Basic Skills Writing Program Assumptions about Teaching Writing Sequence of Student Writing Activities for Curriculum Mapping
   A Model for Improving Basic Writing Skills

Total Workshop Evaluation

Solving the Problem of Basic Writing

The key to the problem is competent teacher-writers, who know what the writing process is firsthand and who are especially trained to teach writing. How do these competent teacher-writers teach basic students to write?

These teacher-writers have their kids write whole compositions, operating under the assumption that writing is a form of discourse in which one person communicates a complete message to another.

Competent teacher-writers have students write various kinds of discourse, including poetry. As the students experience different kinds of writing, become aware of the full range of writing, fill up their minds with all kinds of writing experiences, they become prepared for any writing task with which they are faced. In effect, it doesn't matter whether they are set the task of writing a business letter, an expository report, or a persuasive essay, they will know how to go about completing the assignment.

Competent teacher-writers guide students through the stages of composing process, teaching them prewriting, drafting, revising, and editing strategies. And they teach students to workshop, to have other people on a regular basis—other students as well as teachers—read the various drafts of their papers and give them feedback. The students come to realize that this feedback is necessary if they intend their writing to be responsive to the reactions of those who read it.

Competent teacher-writers teach skills in perspective. If the whole class is having trouble with commas, then the teacher takes the time to drill on conventional comma usage. But if only one student has trouble with periods, they know there is no need to waste the time of the whole class with drill on the use of the period.

Competent teacher-writers have students reading models of writing similar to the kids they are practicing. Where the students once thought that all writing—like the printed matter they are used to—sprang perfect from the mind of the creator, they are no longer intimidated by polished, professional writing but now have a different respect for good writing because they consider themselves authors and enjoy a kinship with all writers.

Competent teacher-writers have students periodically publish their best pieces, knowing the students will come to have a pride in writing which is no longer a drill exercise for a teacher but is a polished, original work.

Only when we have such competent teacher-writers, who are convinced of the worthiness of the job, who write frequently themselves, who keep up to date in the recent research in teaching writing, who are aware of the special problems "basic" writers have and of the unique feelings of inadequacy they suffer from, and who know that the eradication of errors in low-level skills is not the business of writing instruction but that the sharpening of overall writing skills is, will we begin to solve the problem of those students whom we have meanly labelled "basic" writers.

· 2 3 ·

HOW CAN WE HELP OUR TEEN-AGERS?

Robert W. Blake (1966)

What's right with our teen-agers? "Nothing!" say many people. Teen-agers dress outrageously, have no manners, think only of themselves, and waste their time in school, spending all their energy in drag-racing and throwing wild parties. Actually, such descriptions of teen-agers are caricatures, blatant exaggerations, with very little basis in fact. Some teen-agers may fit this description, but in reality only a small, vociferous percentage do.

If these pictures are not right, then, what are teen-agers like? Basically they're people, just people of all shapes, sizes, colors, and abilities who happen to be in one of the most difficult periods of their lives—who are trying to accomplish the almost impossible task of growing up. They need as much help from adults as they can get, but most of them—even if they are left almost entirely on their own—will do a pretty good job of becoming men and women, many times in spite of adults.

Is this process of growing up easy? Of course not. The kids know it isn't, but we adults, who are comparatively secure and comfortable, often forget how hard it was for us. Actually living itself is never easy: conflict is the essence of life. Even as adults, we must continually strive, try new experiences, and meet new people. Just getting up in the morning and going to work sometimes seems impossible. If living itself is so difficult for us, can we have any inkling of how hard this job of growing up is for the teen-ager? And do we realize how well most teen-agers meet this challenge?

What do teen-agers want out of life? Many people feel that they need their "kicks," that they want to shake up the world. Until recently, psychologists thought that the adolescent inevitably *must* go through a period of *Sturm und Drang* in which he is naturally rebellious, cantankerous, and hell-raising. Anthropologists, however, have pretty well disproved this idea; in fact, many primitive tribes bring up their teen-agers without any turbulent period of adjustment like the one that our adolescents face. Not only do the teen-agers in our culture have to adjust to each other, but they have to adjust to our complex, rapidly changing society in which morals, values, and attitudes never seem to remain constant. Our teen-agers, for instance, get almost no help in learning how to be responsible after having been encouraged to be non-responsible for years. Nor do they have assistance in learning how to change from being a dependent child to becoming an independent adult. Furthermore, they are presented with such contradictory attitudes toward sex that they find it particularly difficult to acquire mature, realistic sexual behavior patterns. In almost all of the important ways, we make growing up a frustrating task.

How can we, as parents and teachers, better help teen-agers to become useful, mature people?

First, we must examine our own feelings toward them by asking ourselves such questions as these: Am I confident and secure enough myself so that I can understand this young person? Can I accept his behavior, offensive and contradictory as it may seem at times, and not be offended by it? Can I show him that I am honestly interested in him?

Directly related to our attitudes toward teen-agers are the kinds of actions that we expect from them. Do we want them to depend upon us for everything, or do we want them to learn how to be on their own? Do we want to tell them how to live every minute of their lives, or do we want to encourage them to make their own decisions, even if this involves making some wrong ones? Do we want our teen-agers to feel that the possession and consumption of material goods are the most important goals in our society, or do we want them to believe that performing a useful job in life can be at once satisfying and exhilarating and that the creative use of leisure time helps to make living a valuable process? Until we have formulated some fairly definite answers to these questions, we cannot provide any consistent support for our adolescents.

Second, after we have a fairly good idea of how we would like them to behave, we must try to provide our teen-agers with an atmosphere of stability, order, regularity, even of conformity, if you like. The family is the basic unit of society; we know that it is virtually a psychological law that the child who has grown up without support from a family will have grave difficulties in achieving maturity. Another basic social organization which should give support to our teen-agers is the school. Our boys and girls may complain about teachers, classes, and examinations, but they talk of almost nothing else. Both the family and the school help to give the teen-ager a sense of the structure of society.

Third, we must provide our teen-agers with plenty of opportunities to assume responsibilities in many ways, to take over jobs, and to act on their own with a minimum of adult supervision. When they sometimes fail, however, we must not be too disappointed, because this also is part of their learning. Coupled with this increased awareness of the importance of responsibility should go an emphasis on service, an awareness that we all exist for other members of society as well as for ourselves. Many teen-agers have learned this satisfying feeling by serving in school clubs, in churches, in hospitals, and in organizations of all kinds.

Fourth, at the same time that we are helping to provide stability for our teen-agers and asking them to conform to certain essential standards of conduct, we must be sure that we are urging them to gain new information, to meet many different kinds of people, to travel as much as possible, and to be open to new experiences. This process causes conflict, discomfort, and even pain; but the adolescent must explore if he is ever to find out what he and the world are all about.

Finally, in order to help our teen-agers, we must communicate with them. In this connection, I must stress the importance of mutual communication. If we have seldom listened to our children when they were young, we can't expect them to come to us readily later in life. To regain their confidence we must ask them what their problems are and be prepared to listen. We can't laugh at their problems, though, and we can't preach at them. Whatever we do, we mustn't scold them or yell at them. A person will only tell another about his most important problems, goals, and ambitions if he feels that the other person will listen sincerely. Teen-agers are no different from other human beings, except they are insecure and unsure of themselves and do not have the protective defenses of adults. When the teen-ager feels that no one cares about him, he can only sulk or become rebellious.

The key for starting this mutual communication is the establishing of a warm, helping relationship. How is such a relationship brought about? Initially, we must assume that young people naturally and instinctively want to achieve maturity. We must try not to threaten or to badger but should always strive to support and to encourage.

An outstanding psychologist and teacher once said in class that if we wanted to establish this helping relationship with another person, we should keep these three statements continually in mind:

(1) *I see you.* I recognize the fact that you exist, that you are a person, a human being who has value and inherent dignity.

(2) *I hear you.* I am listening to what you say. I am not laughing at you, because what you say is important to you and therefore to me. I may not agree with your ideas, but I respect your right to speak them.

(3) *I accept you.* I know you are a human being who is capable of being liked. I may not approve of your language or your dress or your manners, but you are a person who can be esteemed and loved. I am convinced that there is nothing more destructive to an individual than the dark feeling, beyond despair, of feeling completely unwanted and unloved.

Because we may take such a position with teen-agers, it does not necessarily follow that we are weak or permissive. Neither does it mean that we expect all teen-agers to respond to this approach. With some young people, the lack of a home, of safety and stability, of affection, and of any communication have already taken their toll. These teen-agers are a terrible sight to see; they are aggressive and rebellious, sure that the world hates them and returning this hate which they feel is all around them. In extreme cases, we simply can't handle such tortured children in normal circumstances; we must refer them to guidance counselors, psychologists, psychiatrists, mental hospitals, and, frequently, prison. These are exceptions, but exceptions that we unfortunately hear a good deal about. We must assume, on the other hand, that most young people want to respond to adult understanding and direction and wish to grow into mature adults.

What happens to these teen-agers who lack communication with one or both of their parents? By way of concluding, I'd like to tell a small part of a story about a girl who, at first glance, seemed like a good candidate for what we so glibly call juvenile delinquency. She'll haunt my memory for the rest of my life, I'm sure.

Although it wasn't her real name, let us call her Valerie. When I first met her, she was in the ninth grade of the high school for which I was the supervising vice principal. Valerie was an attractive girl with tasteful clothes, who wore her long, blonde hair in a stylish manner. She was beginning to make a habit of being absent from individual classes and was even skipping school for several days at a time. Since one of my responsibilities was to check on truancies, I began to see her frequently. Her teachers also reported that she did practically no homework, refused to participate in class when she was present, and was sometimes rude when urged to do her required work. At first she was tense and suspicious when I talked to her, and refused to volunteer any reasons for her behavior. When I asked her what was the matter, she gave the familiar answer.

"I don't know," she said as she shrugged her shoulders.

After she had visited my office several times, I eventually convinced her that I was at least interested enough in her to listen. She finally began to talk more. Her father and mother had been divorced; her mother had remarried. During this second marriage another girl was born, who was five years old at the time.

"When I'm home, my stepfather doesn't even talk to me," she said. "He loves my little sister, but he makes believe I don't exist."

"What do you mean, he acts as if you don't exist?" I asked.

"He won't talk *to* me. He talks *about* me as if I weren't there."

You would have to see this well-dressed and obviously bright girl to realize the complete absurdity of this scene. She lowered her head and began to cry.

"At the dinner table, he says, 'Does *it* want the butter? Does *it* want the salad?' Mr. Blake," she said as she looked up at me, "he calls me *it*. My father calls me *it*."

Just recently, I happened to look at the high school yearbook for Valerie's class. I found her picture. There she was, attractive and sensitive. But under the picture, instead of the typical quotation and record of activities, there appeared the words *Left school.*

I shouldn't wonder.

How can we help our teen-agers? There are some things that we can do, but the most important contribution we can make is to listen and to repeat to ourselves: *I see you. I hear you. I accept you.*

SECTION VIII

TEACHER EDUCATION
AND THE CLASSROOM

In this the final section and final article in this collection, Robert asks us, "Is Teacher Education Governable?" Written in 1973, he lays out a plan that all "good teachers should be able to perform." Rather than focusing on "observable competencies" which essentially reflect "low-level cognitive abilities in a tightly-regimented, monolithic structure," literacy teachers (in fact, all teachers) need to remember that the English Language Arts/English is a field that is, "chiefly humanistic, and ... defies explicit, scientific description."

How refreshing and yet rebellious to read these words today. Teaching literacy certainly is a humanistic enterprise, not one that need be reduced to teaching our children how to write memos for their low-level work in low-paying service or retail jobs. Smacking of the "factory model," Dewey so eloquently wrote about well over 100 years ago, our teaching of literacy, English and the English Language Arts, has been rendered into such a sorry state that parents hold students home on testing days, teachers report feeling overwhelmed by paperwork, and test prep, rather than teaching, and administrators struggle at attempting to recruit good teachers knowing (like in New Jersey at this writing) that 60% of their evaluation as teachers will be tied into how their students do on state-wide and nationally-governed assessments, over which they have little or no control. Brave teachers learn, after they achieve tenure, to close the door and teach what they know is worthwhile. On average, highly sought-after Teaching Fellows in New York City, for example, leave the teaching profession altogether after 5 years. They report inferior working conditions, few resources, little or no autonomy or respect (remember, many of these Fellows leave fields like law, business, engineering, social work, and even medicine to try to "give back.") They become discouraged, disenfranchised, and regretful that they ever felt this need in the first place.

This collection, I believe, therefore offers one powerful perspective; one crucial answer to this strange place we find education today in the U.S. Through tried and true strategies, though the prism of "humanism" and "understanding," we take the journey through both good literacy teaching and good literacy learning. Come along with us on this "road less traveled". Read, close the door, teach, trust and respect yourself and your students.

We, indeed, can put the "human" back into teaching.

· 2 4 ·

IS TEACHER EDUCATION
GOVERNABLE?

Robert W. Blake (1973)

The question for me is not so much who will govern teacher education but rather whether teacher education is governable at all. In New York State, the state education department has decreed that all new programs to prepare teachers must follow the latest Format for Submission of Teacher Education Program Proposals. The Format stipulates that all future teacher education proposals—and revisions of existing ones—shall be in terms of observable competencies and not be based upon college courses.

Problems in Setting Up
Competency-Based Programs

The goal is "to establish a system of certification by which the State can assure the public that professional personnel in the schools possess and maintain *demonstrated* competence to enable children to learn." The convictions "underlying" this goal are that teacher certification should be based on competence rather than on college courses; that the teacher should show competence in general background knowledge, subject matter knowledge, and teaching skill; that teacher preparation should involve many agencies and individuals, such as schools, institutions of higher education, and relevant agencies; and that the training of professionals should integrate theoretical understanding with clinical experience, presumably in a public school setting.

This approach has caused a great deal of consternation among those concerned with teacher education, the chief complaint being that a competency-based teacher education program will be made up of low-level cognitive abilities in a tightly-regimented, monolithic structure. The assurance in the Division's new Format that "more effective preparatory programs can be developed and implemented if wide latitude of freedom is permitted to those who have the responsibility and expertise to do so" hasn't helped to alleviate such unhappiness.

Besides, even though the new Format sounds reasonable enough, in practice the process of developing model competency-based programs has not been without its frustrations.

Let me note some problems. The Division has set up trial projects throughout New York State to develop these teacher education competencies, one of which is located in the county where I live and teach. State officials and others promoting the plan constantly stress the terms "parity" and "cooperative planning." Representatives from area colleges, universities, public schools, and lay groups meet regularly. This is "cooperative planning." All of those who meet, however, are equals, with equal voice and—the implication is very strong—with equal ability, training, and experience. This provides "parity." The members of these committees then prepare lists of competencies of varying degrees of elegance and substance that represent what good teachers should be able to perform.

University Roles in Governance of Teacher Education

According to other rumors, we hear that a good deal of the governance of teacher education will devolve on the public schools, with public school administrators saying when teachers in training have satisfactorily accomplished certain competencies. And we hear that formal graduate preparation for teachers—New York now requires thirty semester hours or a master's degree for permanent certification—will no longer exist. Teachers who have completed provisional certification will become permanently certified by showing they can attain further skills, to a large extent observed and evaluated in the public schools.

In some ways, such events as I have reported them may sound ominous. From another point of view, I find the situation not at all that bleak. At my college, where I am engaged chiefly in the preparation of secondary school English teachers and in their continued graduate study, my academic colleagues often ascribe to me the total responsibility for the poor job that the public schools are doing, presumably because I, and my colleagues in the department of curriculum and instruction, are solely responsible for the preparation of English teachers. I have heard this statement so many times that I now label it the "academic party line."

With increasingly diminished sweet reasonableness, I have explained that, not only do I *not* prepare teachers, but in fact *they* do. And if they wish to complain how teachers are prepared, they must accept most of the responsibility for doing so. My reason for such an outrageous statement: of the 120 semester hours required for a student to earn a baccalaureate degree and provisional certification for teaching in New York State, I am directly responsible for two courses, one three-hour course in methods of secondary English and another in selected problems in secondary education, dealing with guidance, administration, education law, negotiations, and other professional matters. I am only minimally responsible for the student teaching experience, for which students receive nine semester hours, because the bulk of the training is done in the public schools. The undergraduates must complete thirty semester hours for an English major, plus six semester hours in allied areas like "advanced composition," "oral interpretation of literature," and "adolescent literature." These courses are labeled by the prefix ENLE, rather than by ENL, which means that they belong to English education and cannot count for a *bona fide* major in English.

So who governs teacher education? For a long time, as far as I'm concerned, the academic departments did. English departments prepared undergraduates to progress through M.A. and Ph.D. programs in English. And for decades, we never found anything immoral about such a situation because the beginning secondary school English teachers, who were trained as English majors to teach college English, did, in fact, teach college English *in the high schools*—with content and methods transferred directly from college classes—to all high school students, even though only from twenty to thirty percent of the students from a typical comprehensive high school would be going on to any institution of higher learning, including universities, four-year colleges, community colleges, or technical schools. Those kids in the high schools who couldn't hack "college-style" English were called variously "basics," "fourth trackers" in Conant's heinous system of tracking, "non-College preparatory," "non-Regents" in New York state, and "terminals," as well as all kinds of other epithets like "dummies" and "animals."

So I believe that the college and university academic departments have, until very recently, governed teacher education, prepared undergraduates to teach college classes, but have accepted no responsibility for the fact that the majority of secondary school kids had no use for "college" courses in English.

I have seen, however, some signs of change in the English department at my college. Our in-resident Renaissance scholar, an expert on William Beckford, now offers a course for which English education credit is given, called "Dissent in the Classroom," with what he calls "new" books like Carl Rogers' *Freedom to Learn*, Postman and Weingartner's *Teaching As a Subversive Activity*, Kozol's *Death at an Early Age*, and Macrorie's *Uptaught*.

Another English professor whose Ph.D. is in linguistics and whose doctoral dissertation was on Anglo-Saxon metrics teaches his undergraduate course in linguistics with Carl Rogers' *Freedom to Learn* as the basic text, lets the students do "projects" on linguistics, and spends the class time in a variety of sensitivity training sessions. A third English professor supervises an undergraduate program for English majors, who earn from three to six semester hours by tutoring high school students who are having a tough time with their reading and writing. He also teaches a popular graduate course—in the English department—called "Creative Writing for Teachers," in which members of the class mimeograph copies of methods for teaching creative writing.

The Influence of Public School Teachers

So while there is evidence in college English departments that some professors are beginning to see relationships between the courses they teach and what their students do in the public schools, I also see signs that some public school English teachers are no longer dependent upon the materials, content, and methods found exclusively in traditional college English classes. I see high school kids engaged in the study of sports literature, discussion and debate, philosophy and literature, filmmaking, the literature of the occult, mystery fiction, creative writing, film as literature, as well as modern American poetry and modern fiction. Critics may contend that such a variety of electives doesn't necessarily mean that the teaching is any different, and, in some cases, this may be true. But at the same time, I see many teachers treating kids differently than in the past. The teachers talk with the kids, work with them individually or in small groups—as well as in full class situations—listen to what the kids say, request their opinions, and ask how they feel about what they are studying and how they are learning. In a very real sense, high school teachers—at least in English—are becoming a potent force in the governance of teacher education. Many of them are attending graduate college English classes like film study, creative writing, and young adult literature, and are boycotting historical surveys of Renaissance drama, the British novel, and Puritan literature.

Professionalism in English Education

As some professors are beginning to adjust their courses to reflect the needs of all high school students, the public schools are beginning to exert more influence upon the governance of teacher education. At least in New York state, the state education department still grants certificates to teachers and continues with its movement to have teacher education accomplished through competencies. For some professional educators, the use of behavioral objectives for the preparation of English teachers smacks of scientism in a field which is chiefly humanistic and which defies explicit, scientific description. When behavioral objectives define low-level knowledge behaviors, they do reflect a view of education which is simplistic. I think, however, that the insistence on describing competencies for the preparation of teachers will be of benefit to the profession, for when we begin to verbalize, using words which we can all agree upon, about what competent teachers should be able to do, then we have begun to make teaching a profession, and as a result, we shall become responsible and, therefore, accountable for the teaching of English.

I believe that we should welcome the opportunity to justify the profession of teaching. Teaching is at least as complex as medicine or law—the profession with which we are most often compared or contrasted—and a physician or a lawyer has in his possession skills and knowledge which prepare him to perform a valuable social service. Why shouldn't we be able to identify the skills, knowledge, understandings, and attitudes which beginning teachers must have and develop programs so they can learn them? If individuals cannot show the necessary behaviors, why should we let them join the teaching profession? Lawyers and doctors don't practice law or medicine until they have completed a stringent preparation and passed bar examinations or medical board examinations. Why should we then allow anybody off the street to practice our profession—one at least as sophisticated as others, and in many ways, more important to the survival of society?

A Hypothetical Program

Let me offer, for the sake of argument, how I think the preparation of English teachers might proceed. Academic and professional education departments in colleges and universities would work cooperatively with the public schools in setting up and administering teacher education programs, including student teaching internships and prior experience in tutoring. The state education department would issue certificates to all who successfully complete these programs. No one—and there would be no exceptions—teaches in the public schools who has not completed such preparation.

If a prospective teacher completes an undergraduate program successfully, with college faculty and public school people jointly verifying his competence, he is given provisional certification by the state education department and may be hired by the schools as an *assistant-teacher*, earning slightly less than the usual starting teacher's salary. While he performs as a junior member of the public school English department, he continues his professional training in a program, again developed cooperatively by the college and public school. If he is successful during a three-year probationary period and completes his advanced professional training, he is appointed as an *associate teacher* and is given a substantial pay raise. When he has completed seven years of successful teaching, he must be granted tenure. After an unspecified length of time, during which he has demonstrated an extraordinary ability to respond to the individual needs of students, has shown a superior intellectual grasp of his discipline, and has proved to be a leader in his profession, he may be appointed as *master teacher* and receive an appropriate salary.

Such an approach to teacher education would have many benefits. College and university faculty members and public school personnel—who are most likely to know how to prepare competent teachers—develop programs. State education departments—which have the legal right—certify all people who complete such programs and allow none who don't to teach. College students have an early exposure to the profession of teaching and can de-select themselves from the program, if they wish. If they choose, however, to enter teaching, can demonstrate the ability, and are willing to grow in their profession, they know they can eventually earn a salary commensurate with their specialized talents. The public schools benefit because they have the services of free cross-tutoring by college students as tutors and student teaching interns, of relatively inexpensive beginning teachers whom they have helped train, and the continued services of college and university faculty members. Such a plan, I believe, would help to make the governing of teacher education feasible.

INDEX

B

D

E

Studies in Criticality

General Editor
Shirley R. Steinberg

Counterpoints publishes the most compelling and imaginative books being written in education today. Grounded on the theoretical advances in criticalism, feminism, and postmodernism in the last two decades of the twentieth century, Counterpoints engages the meaning of these innovations in various forms of educational expression. Committed to the proposition that theoretical literature should be accessible to a variety of audiences, the series insists that its authors avoid esoteric and jargonistic languages that transform educational scholarship into an elite discourse for the initiated. Scholarly work matters only to the degree it affects consciousness and practice at multiple sites. Counterpoints' editorial policy is based on these principles and the ability of scholars to break new ground, to open new conversations, to go where educators have never gone before.

For additional information about this series or for the submission of manuscripts, please contact:

Shirley R. Steinberg
c/o Peter Lang Publishing, Inc.
29 Broadway, 18th floor
New York, New York 10006

To order other books in this series, please contact our Customer Service Department:

(800) 770-LANG (within the U.S.)
(212) 647-7706 (outside the U.S.)
(212) 647-7707 FAX

Or browse online by series:
www.peterlang.com